ANIMALS AND MODERN CULTURES

For
Lynn

ANIMALS AND MODERN CULTURES

A Sociology of
Human–Animal Relations in Modernity

Adrian Franklin

SAGE Publications
London • Thousand Oaks • New Delhi

First published 1999

SAGE Publications Ltd
6 Bonhill Street
London EC2A 4PU

SAGE Publications Inc
2455 Teller Road
Thousand Oaks, California 91320

SAGE Publications India Pvt Ltd
32, M-Block Market
Greater Kailash – I
New Delhi 110 048

British Library Cataloguing in Publication data

A catalogue record for this book is
available from the British Library

ISBN 0 7619 5622 0
ISBN 0 7619 5623 9 (pbk)

Library of Congress catalog card record available

Typeset by Keystroke, Jacaranda Lodge, Wolverhampton
Printed in Great Britain by Redwood Books, Trowbridge, Wiltshire

CONTENTS

ACKNOWLEDGEMENTS

I am indebted to Chris Rojek for his encouragement and support; to Steve Crook with whom I discussed some critical ideas; to Harriet Ritvo for her stimulating correspondence, books and papers; to Keith Tester for inspiration, kindness and friendship and to Laura Rival for opening my eyes to yet more ways of understanding the relationships between humans and animals.

Thanks are also due to Bridget Berry and Cassy McFarling for their research assistance and to the staff at the University of Tasmania Morris Miller library for their expertise and patience. I would like to thank Robert, Jackie and Vanessa at Sage for their fantastic support and my family for occasionally keeping the noise down.

1 INTRODUCTION

Interest in human–animal relations has expanded considerably over recent years in both intellectual, political and policy terms, but to date there is no text that draws this material together or reflects on its meaning, significance and future. This is partly due to the range of disciplines which have an interest in it and their specificities. Zoology has begun to take a strong interest in human–animal relations (e.g. Kellert and Wilson's 1993 'Biophilia thesis') and joins other life sciences such as sociobiology, psychology and veterinary science. Geographers have also become concerned through engagements in environmental and ecological issues (see *Environment and Planning D: Society and Space* 1995, dedicated to animals and society). The disciplines with a more established track record in understanding human–animal relations are social anthropology, history and philosophy, but there have been few common points of departure or common objectives. Indeed from a sociological point of view these very separate and insular academic projects are among the many types of behaviour and assumptions in modernity that require explication and explanation.

This book takes a broad critical look at the intellectual content of human–animal relations in modernity, as well as a broad ranging survey of the many 'contested' sites of human–animal relations. The main aim is to stimulate a critical means of comprehending the complexities of human–animal relations in modernity and to introduce key topic areas, debates and research. Above all, this is a twentieth-century social change essay. It aims to explain how and why human–animal relations have changed in the twentieth century and to identify the social basis of those changes.

The field of human–animal relations is fast becoming one of the hot areas of debate in the social sciences and is beginning to occupy the centre stage once held by 'the environment'. A mere glance at recent literature shows that this new area is advancing on several fronts. These include, for example: the philosophy and politics of animal rights (Benton 1993; Midgely 1979, 1994); the sociology of animal rights (Tester 1992); histories of human–animal relations (Ritvo 1987, 1994; R.H. Thomas 1983); the social anthropology of human–animal relations (Cartmill 1993; Ingold 1988); animal foods and animals in diets (Bourdieu 1984; Douglas 1975, 1984; Fiddes 1991; Franklin 1996a; Goodman and Redclift 1991; Mennell 1993; Twigg 1983; Vialles 1994); animals, nature and gender (Gaard 1993; Norwood 1993); hunting and fishing sports in modernity (Cartmill 1993; Franklin 1996a, 1996b; Hummel 1994; Ritvo 1987); pets or companion animals (Serpell 1986, 1995; Serpell and Paul 1994); animals, tourism and zoos (Bostock 1993; Mullan and Marvin 1987). Human–animal relations are also an important dimension in recent papers setting the agenda for a sociology of nature (Macnaghten and Urry 1995; Murphy 1995).

While this list establishes a growing diversity of interest in human–animal relations, in recent years much of the literature has been either historical in scope or focused around familiar pro-animal rights positions deriving from moral philosophy. There is, however, much exciting new material emerging in the UK, USA and elsewhere from research projects across a wide range of disciplines (including sociology, anthropology, veterinary science, sociobiology, zoology, nutritional science, medicine, environmental studies, political science) that is more detached and reflective of contemporary issues, but which has yet to be brought together in a coherent framework. There are some edited collections, for example, Manning and Serpell's *Animals and Human Society* (1994) and a collection in *Social Research* (1995) edited by Arien Mack from the high profile New York conference 'In the company of animals'. However, like many collections, they are lightly edited samplers that do not advance a self-conscious narrative structure or argument other than general pro-animal themes. Some of the more theoretically informed and less emotionally charged accounts (e.g. Cartmill 1993; Ritvo 1994; Tester 1992) tend to be historical and deal largely with nineteenth-century social change. Even though Tester's analysis is sociological and a powerful invective against the naive philosophical bases of animal rights, it is mainly a discussion of the social origins of demands for animal rights rather than a 'complete' sociology of human–animal relations. If anything, his analysis points to the need to expand the analysis of human–animal relations beyond grand historical narratives (e.g. R.H. Thomas 1983) and to the essentialism of struc-turalist approaches towards a more precise understanding of global and local cultural milieux.

The scope for a sociology of human–animal relations is therefore much wider than that stimulated by history or philosophy. Some of this scope is estab-lished by the increasingly contentious and conflictual nature of human–animal relations across a number of sites in the twentieth century: from animal husbandry and the food industry, to pet keeping, animals and tourism, animals and sport, and changes in taste for animals and fish as foods. While the claim is often made that animal sentiments or tender-hearted romanticism have extended progressively into the twentieth century, this is difficult to reconcile with twentieth-century demands for meat, modes of meat production, habitat loss, the sustained popularity of hunting and fishing sports and the expansion of animal experimentation.

This is the paradox that lies at the centre of a sociology of modern human–animal relations and it will be used as a central organizing theme for this book. As the book unfolds it will become clear that the possibility of consistency in the realm of human–animal relations is less likely than differentiations. For any one culture the 'animal world' is never seen as an indivisible category, but as an historically constituted and morally loaded field of meanings that derive from the human habit of extending/imposing social logics, complexities and conflicts onto the natural world, and particularly onto animals other than ourselves. In modern nation-states the possibilities for differentiations in meaning and practice in human–animal relations are multiplied by the social differentiations that stem from class, ethnicity, region, gender and religion (among others). The book unpacks this sociological approach, discusses the full range of theories that have been used to understand human–animal relations and provides concrete illustrations and examples. A sociology of human–animal relations would also include how animals are/have been appropriated socially into a range of modern human projects: the use of animals in establishing and manipulating national identity and citizenship; the use of animal categories as signifiers of taste, belonging and distinction; the use made of animals and categories of animals in framing moral and ethical debates (e.g. in popular television documentaries and children's books). However, the main cut and thrust of this book is to identify and explain the changing nature of twentieth-century human–animal relations.

Although animals are caught up in and used by different sociations and social identities in the West, it is also clear that at the end of the twentieth century animals are thought about, used and related to in a very different manner from the beginning of the century. Using modernization and postmodernization theory, this book identifies how these broad social forces of change have brought about a wide range of industrial, ethical, conceptual and emotional changes in our dealing with animals. It will be claimed that:

- an increasing range of animals has been drawn into closer, emotional association with modern cultures;
- the categorical boundary between humans and animals, so fiercely defended as a tenet of modernity, has been seriously challenged, if not dismantled in places;
- the social cause of these changes can be located in at least three processes that frame the postmodern condition: misanthropy, risk and ontological insecurity.

Whereas modernization was predicated on the essential potential goodness of humanity and built upon the twin goals of progress and democracy, in the latter part of the twentieth century these goals have been deemed unaffordable luxuries of a bygone period. In modernity, humanity was closely tied to a series of good works and improvements, bound together in various ways by the centrality of collective will. Animals figured in the modern project principally as a resource for human progress. The destruction of habitat, the enslavement into medical research and the creation of industrial husbandry regimes were perhaps regrettable to those in the know, but they were always justified through their contribution to the greater (human) good. As the modern project collapsed, so also did the sanguine view of humanity.

In the late twentieth century a generalized misanthropy has set in: according to this view humans are a destructive, pestilent species, mad and out of control. By contrast, animals are essentially good, balanced and sane. However, they are also seen as victims of a greedy, uncaring, global economy; a form of suffering with which many humans can closely identify. In identifying with animals as common victims, of course, the socially constructed 'scientific' division between humans and animals is weakened, particularly since the common adversary is an abstract, economistic but nonetheless human cultural formation. Under these conditions, new ideas which isolate animals from exploitation (the animal rights path) or produce the means for peaceful, non-violent coexistence (the 'Greenpeace' path) have appeared and thrived throughout the West. This highly emotional identification with animals, combined with a heightened understanding of them as cultural species (as opposed to merely mechanical beings at the mercy of their instincts), demonstrates that the social constructivist approach is inadequate to the task of a complete understanding of our dealings with animals in late modernity. Yes, humans impose an essentially socially constructed set of meanings and understandings on the animal community (through metaphor and metonymy), but that does not confine the understanding or the relationship to one of social construction.

This problem with social constructivism has been highlighted recently by Kate Soper (1995), Tim Ingold (1988) and Laura Rival (1996). In other words, we are not merely working through what it is to be properly human, using animals as the material for that exercise; we have also broken down some of the necessary conditions whereby animals can be merely metaphor and metonym of the social. Such close identification with animals about the commonalities of existence, material needs and the global–political contexts of risk has weakened the notion of difference.

In a related manner, the modernization of animal resources, particularly as foods, was originally conceived of as providing the basis of a universal healthy diet. Protein had been in short supply at various times and places in nineteenth-century Europe and the regular consumption of meat was a mark of wealth and rank. When meat was made available to all in the twentieth century, its link to strength and vitality and significance to growing children was emphasized. However, as we shall see, over the course of the twentieth century the livestock and meat industries became ever more intensive, large scale and rationalized. New cheap foods made from the excreta and bodies of used animals were recycled into husbandry systems. As a result of these developments and the decline of tight risk management under former welfare state umbrellas, the livestock and meat industries were swamped under serial outbreaks of human diseases resulting from the consumption of meat, eggs and milk products. Some of them were entirely new and related to the new technologies (e.g. BSE). This meddling with nature, together with the collapse of former risk management regimes has created a widespread anxiety about meat and livestock systems and instability for the industry.

But the association of animals with this heightened sense of risk in post-modernity goes further than meat and foods. Like the miners' canaries, animals provide a register of environmental safety. In part, the increased love and care of wild animals has been associated with growing anxieties about pollution of the air, soil, waterways and seas. Again, as common inhabitants of a fragile and threatened planet, the former separation of animals (into wild areas) and humans (into 'habitable' areas) figures less in contemporary thinking. There are no wild areas beyond the control and management of humans (the so-called wilderness areas are highly managed, for example) and, as a result, wild animals join with those other species, pets and livestock that have been drawn into the human world for much longer.

Animals that have shared domestic space with humans have been subject to the third process of postmodernity. Historically, no other category of animal has been drawn so close to humans, but a close look at change in the latter half of the twentieth century reveals an extraordinary humanization of these animals. Eccentric examples are the very stuff of newspapers in late modernity – even the UK *Times* newspaper now boasts a pet column. From gourmet pet foods to pet bereavement counselling, to pet health products such as specially designed cat toothbrushes or pet toilets in parks, it is clear that pets have at least become treated like humans. However, it will be argued that our new behaviour to pets relates to new tensions in relationships between humans, particularly those longer term domestic and community relationships. We are not behaving towards animals in an eccentric manner; we are in fact, substituting pets for a range of close human ties.

An important part of the ontological security of individuals in late modernity is linked to familial, friendship, neighbourhood and community ties. These are the relationships that provide the day-to-day norms and cultural exchanges for most people. However, these are also the relationships at most risk from changes in the post-Fordist, neo-liberal economy and from new flexibilities and freedoms in the creation and dissolution of domestic relations.

[margin handwritten note: increased association w/ pets related to decreased opportunities for human-human socialization]

As we shall see, pet surveys reveal their special significance among those people affected by either the absence or the loss of close ties, or those for whom enduring ties with localities of belonging have been severed. However, while in the 1960s a close relationship with a pet was widely considered dissocial and the cause for some concern, in the 1990s the development of very close, human styled relationships with animals is normative and, indeed, therapeutic. Animals are now considered important for our health, happiness and our recovery from physical and mental illness. Again, the boundary (or the significance of the difference) between humans and animals is challenged by the fluidity and interchangeability of humans and animals in friendships, companionships and love.

This book comprises nine chapters. Chapters 2 and 3 are historical and theoretical while the remaining six are concerned with substantive topics. Chapter 2 is the scene-setting, historical chapter and describes key changes in relations between humans and animals over the main period of modernity up until the twentieth century. A consideration of the Christian 'dominion' view of human–animal relations, specifying their nature and content, is explored. The collapse of dominion thought that is associated with Enlightenment thinkers and the rise of science is outlined. The place of animals in the economy, diet and home are considered alongside intellectual change. As industrialization and urbanization expanded in the eighteenth century, the twin but contradictory development of compassionate sensibilities and a rationalized expansion of industrial meat production began to take shape. These two notions will be later traced into the twentieth century in the form of a series of projects culminating, on the one hand, in the factory production of meats, fish and eggs, genetic manipulation of livestock, global and horizontal integrations of animal production, marketing and fastfoods, and exhaustion of seafood supplies; and, on the other, in the estab-lishment of national parks and conservation areas, protection and rescue of wild animal species, the establishment of global pro-animal organizations and the politics of animal rights.

The idea behind this chapter is to discuss, in broad terms, the main theoretical traditions in this area and to focus particularly on those that promise the means to understand the nature of change and continuity in the twentieth century. In order to do this the book combines a theoretical understanding of the way in which animals are incorporated into human and social projects with accounts of social and cultural change in the twentieth century. This approach will be used as a framework in each of the substantive/topic chapters. The modernizing account by K. Thomas (1983) is contrasted first with an application of Elias's (1986, 1994) civilizing process theory and second with Cartmill's (1993) idealist historical account that identifies neo-romanticism and neo-Darwinian ideas as the principal cause of divisions and conflicts over human–animal relations in the early twentieth century.

The weaknesses of these theories are discussed using, among others, the critical work of the American historian Harriet Ritvo (1987, 1994) and the work of the British historical sociologist Keith Tester (1989, 1992). Ritvo's critique centres on the significance of variations in human–animal relations, about which these theories have little to say. Her critique suggests that the only way we can under-stand change is by looking closely at the local and culturally contingent nature of change. Tester's critique is more penetrating. While acknowledging the critical significance of the historical and cultural variations, he builds on the contributions of social anthropology and Foucault to identify the essentially human and social content of human–animal relations in modernity. By suggesting that all cultural groups use animals to think through human conflicts and problems, Tester's analysis requires us to look closely at those who propose and enact change in human animal relations, and the relationship between their views and social divisions of the day. Tester's approach was never applied rigorously to an analysis of change in the twentieth century, but class and cultural divisions and conflict were identified as the critical social contents of much reform in this area. As we consider more recent change we must add the salience of gender, ethnicity and nation. Tester's framework will be broadened in order to consider the links between changing human–animal relations and theories of postmodernity – in the same way that earlier change was linked to modernizing themes.

Chapter 3 sets out the main analysis of the twentieth century using modern-ization and postmodernization theory as a framework. The application of Fordist production techniques and the expansion of consumption and mass markets, are tied into attitudes to animals as a social, progressive resource. Animal-related leisures also expanded and were shaped by the progressive needs of humanity: animals were therefore entertaining (in zoos and circuses), exciting (as in fishing and hunting), or picturesque (as in tourism). In the second half of the twentieth century, particularly since 1970, this anthropocentric, human progress-orientated view of animals began to change. We start to see the consolidation not only of sentiments, but also of an emotional content and concern not hitherto apparent. As an explanation of these new developments this chapter considers the significance of three postmodern phenomena: misanthropy, risk and ontological insecurity.

Chapter 4 considers the zoological gaze, or the manner in which viewing animals has been organized socially over time. Gazing at animals has been a significant entertainment in modernity, although it has changed in form from the early travelling collections of colonial exotica to whale watching off the Californian coast. This is also an instance of changed relations, reform and regulation and we will consider it in the light of our principal theories of change and recent leisure and tourism theory. This chapter sets out the history of these attractions and practices, including the dramatic growth in the animal gaze over recent years.

Chapter 5 focuses on pets or companion animals. Pets continue to make headlines in a succession of contentious issues: pets and recovery from heart attacks and stress illnesses; dog attacks on humans; pets and transferable diseases; pets and animal rights. But pets are also important sociologically. As animals that have been drawn into the human realm, given human names and qualities, it is tempting to use pets as the best example of recent change in human–animal relations. However, this would be wrong since pets are an enduring and universal cultural manifestation and not the preserve of modernity. However, pet keeping has become an increasingly elaborate cultural activity and is readily explained by the theoretical framework proposed in Chapter 3. This chapter sets out the vital statistics of pet keeping in modern societies (dollar value, demographics, trends and so on), explains why people want to keep pets and investigates the social and cultural content of pet keeping.

Hunting and angling remain among the most popular sports in the Anglophone world, but they occupy a very curious position on the margins of contemporary culture. Chapter 6 aims to explain both its popularity and its ambiguity. It begins with a survey of hunting and angling sports in modern societies (but principally in the USA and UK), documenting the scale of participation, social differentiations in hunting and angling sports, and the nature of changes in codes of practice. The popularity and development of hunting and angling will be evaluated against theories of naturalization processes in modernity – particularly Cartmill, but also Elias, Franklin, Hummel and others.

Chapter 7 surveys the changing position that animals occupy in the meat and livestock industries. The political economy and development of a global meat and livestock industry forms the first half of the chapter, while a description of the new husbandry conditions and regimes forms the second half, and a link into Chapter 8 on meat, particularly its significance to debates on risk and anxiety. One of the most illuminating measures of change in human–animal relations is our willingness to eat them. While almost all mammals, birds, reptiles and fish are edible, human beings everywhere and at all times have designated only a fraction of animals around them as edible, while others have been eaten only on strict ritual occasions and a great many others were designated inedible, taboo or polluting. This chapter begins with a global discussion of animals in the human diet, drawing on ecological, structural and cultural anthropology to set the scene. This forms a useful basis on which to analyse animal eating trends in contemporary Western countries. Using the second body of theory identified in Chapter 3, the following key changes will be examined: the changing balance of meat in diets, the presentation of animal foods; ethnic and gender variations in meat eating; the growth and meaning of vegetarian diets, animal foods, risk and health.

Chapter 9 brings together the theoretical, historical and substantive material in a discussion on the likely progress of change in human–animal relations, with a particular focus on the animal rights argument and movement. The social composition of the movement will be identified, alongside that of its detractors, as a means of socializing the issue. The book concludes that while we may be a long way from legislating animal rights, there is no doubt that the compassionate sensibilities extended to animals in the nineteenth century have extended into new areas of interaction, new groups in society and into new forms of organization. However, this chapter argues that animal rights is not the end point in a series of increasingly civilized attitudes to animals, nor is it the direction in which most of the significant changes in human–animal relations are headed. Indeed, in recent years the animal rights issue has obscured the main changes upon which this book focuses. Whereas the nature of recent change has been to de-differentiate human–animal relations in a spectacular series of challenges to the old enlightenment boundary, animal rights seeks to maintain that division and for animals and humans to live their lives separately. This is not only unlikely but, in a sense, preposterous. It ignores the extent to which animals are involved in modern cultures, the extent to which they are an integral part of that cultural formation, and the new-found sensitivities and reflexivities of those relationships. It is also unrealistic because it presumes that there can be domains into which humans will have no impact or control. While such domains may be contrived, they cannot be politically stable or free from the influence of human economic and industrial activity. Finally, it is unrealistic because it asks humans to relinquish close relationships with their animal companions on the grounds that they are exploitative, just at a point where many are exploring and penetrating the boundaries which for many centuries have divided them.

2 'GOOD TO THINK WITH'

Theories of human–animal relations in modernity

1500s – 1800s

> For human (as distinct from animal) survival every member of society must learn to distinguish his fellow men according to their mutual social status. But the simplest way to do this is to apply transformations of the animal level categories to the social classification of human beings.
>
> The conventions by which primitive peoples use species of plant and animals as symbols for categories of men are not really more eccentric than our own, but in a technologically restricted environment, they became much more noticeable and to scholars of Sir James Frazer's generation they seemed altogether extraordinary. So much so that any social equivalence between human beings and other natural species came to be regarded as a kind of cult (totemism) – a proto-religion appropriate only to people at a very early stage of development.
>
> (Leach 1974: 39–40)

Most sociologists and historians of human–animal relations have been influenced to a greater or lesser extent by an earlier body of anthropological work which found that human conceptualization, classification and theorization of animals signify or encode social thought. First, social structures and morality are routinely extended into the 'animal world' to provide a logical ordering to this parallel metaphorical society. Second, the socially constituted animal world is then used to think through or resolve social tensions, conflicts and contradictions. It is not very hard to understand why animals have been recruited in this manner. Animals are uniquely positioned relative to humans in that they are both like us but not us. Trees and rocks are not like us and not us, but animals are very clearly similar to humans and, taken together as an animal community, have the capacity to represent the differentiations, characters and dispositions of any given society. The universality of this tendency arises, first, because all human societies are surrounded by these metaphoric animal societies and, second, because humans are intimately involved with animal worlds everywhere; so much so in fact, that human and animal societies are often believed to exist on the same plane and to be socially and morally, as well as physically, interactive.

Animals are therefore good to think about what it is to be properly human. When historians and sociologists began their investigations of Western relations with animals, largely from the 1980s onwards, they were already predisposed to extend anthropological theory and findings. Take, for instance, the lead offered by Leach which, like Lévi-Strauss (1966) and Douglas (1966, 1975), provides a clear argument for a universal and modern, application:

It is a fact of empirical observation that human beings everywhere adopt ritual attitudes towards the animals and plants in their vicinity. Consider, for example, the separate, and often bizarre, rules which govern the behaviour of Englishmen towards the creatures which they classify as (i) wild animals, (ii) foxes, (iii) game, (iv) farm animals, (v) pets, (vi) vermin. Notice further that if we take the sequence of words: (ia) strangers, (iia) enemies, (iiia) friends, (iva) neighbours, (va) companions, (via) criminals, the two sets of terms are in some degree homologous. By a metaphorical usage the categories of animals could be (and sometimes are) used as equivalents for the categories of human beings.

(Leach 1974: 40)

While this structuralist conclusion informs the manner by which investigations have commenced, there has not been agreement on precisely how animals have been used to think through social issues. In particular, because later work was interested in social change, the somewhat static universalism of structural analysis has given way to more dynamic accounts. This chapter sets out three of the principal types of investigation and their findings and provides the background necessary to understand how animals figured in modern society at the beginning of the twentieth century – which will be the launching point of the next chapter. First, we will examine the work of Keith Thomas (1983), in particular his investigation of the significance and consequences of the Enlightenment and urbanization in England.

The second section focuses on the implications of the expanded state and increasing divisions of labour, principally through the work of Elias (1986, 1994). Elias's work is important because of its interest in changes in manners and taste, and attitudes to violence. Elias offers an appealing explanation of increasing levels of repugnance at violence and cruelty to animals during the nineteenth century, particularly in relation to sports which involved them. We will also examine the work of Keith Tester (1989, 1992) who uses Foucaultian analysis to fine tune and critique some of the broader brush strokes of Elias. Tester suggests that Western opinion bifurcated into two types of pro-animal discourse during the nineteenth century. One route led to the anti-cruelty legislations of the nineteenth century, while another rights-orientated route emerged briefly at the end of the century and remained dormant until the 1970s. However, while changes in human–animal relations were undoubtedly moving in a more empathetic, pro-animal direction, Tester's work ignores the groundswell of neo-Darwinian opinion which gathered force alongside a softer form of romanticism.

Therefore in the third section we will consider both types of romantic gaze, those of the hunter and those of the animal lover. It was the tension between these two appeals that more than anything characterized the state of play in the first half of the twentieth century.

THE MODERNIZATION OF HUMAN–ANIMAL RELATIONS

Urbanization and the Enlightenment

This first section considers Keith Thomas's (1983) analysis of changing attitudes to animals in the period 1500 to 1800. Thomas argues that major changes did occur gradually over this period, that human attitudes to animals changed from the anthropocentric views of the early modern period to the sentimentalized attitudes of the eighteenth and nineteenth centuries and that the Enlightenment together with urbanization were the principal causes of the new attitudes. The book is important because it seeks to establish the development and causes of modern attitudes to animals in the West.

In Tudor England the Christian theological orthodoxy maintained the view that God had given humans absolute rights to use animals as they saw fit. This included domesticating them, eating them, and sporting with them – fairly or otherwise. According to the Old Testament, man and animals lived in harmony in the Garden of Eden: 'humans were probably not carnivorous and animals were tame' (K. Thomas 1983: 17). However, this was no longer true in early modern England. Most people lived a rural existence in close proximity with animals. During winter it was common throughout Britain for people and beasts to share the same roof. Households were directly involved in their own animal food provisioning. The annual calendar was shaped by the lives and seasons of animals whose bodies were assimilated into every zone of the human economy. Although humans were dominant in this world and had a charter to use animals, it was also true that both humans and animals were seen, in folklore, as common creations of God and, moreover, that their lives and fortunes were causally interlinked. There was a systematic interrelation between humans and the natural world, a landscape that was alive and readable by humans that would come in time to be considered superstition and folklore, but which was occasionally viewed then as witchcraft.

According to K. Thomas (1983), anthropocentricity and dominance was always in danger of being challenged by the contiguity, blurredness and meaningfulness of their lives with animals. As a consequence, some of their actions which we would consider brutal and cruel had some functional purpose: to place distance between animality and humanity. Tester offers an interesting comment on Thomas's material:

> Within this process of establishing animals as a distinctive other, virtually anything could be done to them so long as it did not threaten to undermine the clear and yet fragile boundaries which laid down the truth of human and social life. If anything, early modern attitudes contained an incitement to violence; aggressive behaviour towards animals was an active way for humans to define themselves as the centre of the universe and the zenith of God's work. The spatial blurring of classificatory difference was countered by active domination. The early modern period asserted a unity of systematic difference.
>
> (Tester 1992: 51)

Thomas's account is interspersed with analytical borrowings from social anthropology, in particular from Lévi-Strauss. This structural anthropology ot animals and the natural world is characterized by the claim that humans use animals in order to specify clearly who they are and where the differences lie between themselves and the natural world, particularly between themselves and animals (Douglas 1966, 1975; Willis 1974). All human cultures studied by anthropologists face the problem that they are both animal and not-animal. It is a boundary redolent with meaning, significance and implications for social norms. Typically, humans establish what it is to be properly human in contradistinction to animals, and particularly through the establishment of normative behaviour. In that way disapproved of behaviour within any one culture, or in another culture, may be cast as 'animal' and thereby 'wrong'. While the boundary has to be maintained, the behaviour that truly marks off humans from animals can, of course, change. Changing attitudes to animals are explained by Thomas in these terms: the close classificatory and spatial proximity that threatened human–animal distinction in early modern England changed and permitted a more sentimental attitude to develop.

First, the emergence of natural history and the biological sciences, and later astronomy and geology, undermined the theological anthropocentricism by creating classificatory differences between species and by expanding the human universe. The world and time frames of English society were rendered parochial in comparison with the enormity of evolutionary time that separated humans from animals. In comparison with the newly revealed depth and complexity of the physical universe, knowledgeable humans could no longer delude themselves that they lived at the hub. More importantly, perhaps, they could see that the world was not orientated towards humans and that they were just one small cog in a very large, centreless system. 'The explicit acceptance of the view that the world does not exist for man alone can be fairly regarded as one of the great revolutions in modern Western thought' (K. Thomas 1983: 166).

Second, English society grew less dependent on animal power through industrial–technical development and became an urbanized culture. The English were no longer to feel so close to animals. The metonymic relations with animals based on contiguity gave way to metaphoric relations based on separation and difference. According to Thomas, it was because the separation and difference was now plain that there was no need to entrench the boundary with rituals of separation. Rather, sentiments for animals grew: pet keeping became ubiquitous and passionate; wild animals under environmental threat became the source of regret within a general discourse of discontent at modernity; the old way of treating animals ('badly') became increasingly unacceptable to urban sensibilities; philosophers debated whether animals could be moral subjects; vegetarianism was born. Animals could be viewed from a distance, but that distance created ever-increasing degrees of fascination and curiosity: a new thirst and enthusiasm for understanding animals changed attitudes to them, at least in the educated circles of society.

All these developments grew slowly over the course of the seventeenth and eighteenth centuries, but bloomed in the first half of the nineteenth century. The Enlightenment, the birth and ascendancy of scientific knowledge and the decline of theological based views of the world, began earlier still:

It was only in Tudor times that there began an unbroken succession of active field naturalists, running from William Turner (born 1508) to John Ray (who died in 1705). Members of a wider European scientific fraternity, it was they who, by their cumulative labours, searching for plants, listing and describing wild creatures, and corresponding with continental naturalists, laid the foundation of modern botany, zoology, ornithology, and the other life sciences.

(K. Thomas 1983: 52)

What was so new and important about the scientific method and its classifications? Thomas is very clear:

> For all observation of the natural world involves the use of mental categories with which we, the observers, classify and order the otherwise incomprehensible mass of phenomena around us; and it is notorious that, once these categories have been learned, it is very difficult for us to see the world the other way. The prevailing system of classification takes possession of us, shaping our perception, and thereby our behaviour. What was important about the early modern naturalists was that they developed a novel way of looking at things, a new system of classification and one which was more detached, more objective, less man centred than that of the past ... By 1800 it was possible to regard plants and animals in a light which was very different from the anthropocentric vision of earlier times.

(K. Thomas 1983: 52)

Animal classifications enabled Thomas to trace changing perceptions. The very earliest classifications were based on utility to man: criteria such as their edibility, their tameness or other use values. Later classificatory schemes, including those of John Ray and Linnaeus (Karl von Linne), were based not on human use but their intrinsic structural characteristics: 'More attention was now paid to the creatures internal anatomy, as opposed to its external characteristics; the distinction between tame and wild was abandoned; and utilitarian considerations became distinctly less conspicuous in zoological writing' (K. Thomas 1983: 67). However, such objectivity did not mean that scientists were cold and dispassionate towards their specimens. 'It also became unfashionable to regard any animal species as intrinsically ugly.' The third Earl of Shaftesbury wrote that 'a dunghill or heap of any seeming vile and horrid matter was sufficient to show the beauty of nature' (K. Thomas 1983: 69).

The movement to town was established first by the aristocracy and upper classes when cities were considered centres of civilization. Even then there was a seasonal quality to urban living. The urbanization of the entire population came later, but suddenly, in the first half of the nineteenth century. Thus, the elite in English society were the first to experience the spatial distanciation from metonymic relations with animals, and it was among them that pet keeping became fashionable and passionate. Thomas argues that pets can be defined by three criteria: co-residency with humans (as opposed to external housing); naming (frequently human names); and inedibility. By these terms pets were not new to modern England. Animal companions were also a feature of late medieval society, but from 1500 to 1800 the culture of pet keeping gained refinement. The pampered pooch was in evidence by 1700. 'Pets were often fed better than the servants. They were adorned with rings and ribbons, feathers and bells; and they became an increasingly regular feature of painted family groups, usually as a symbol of fidelity, domesticity and completeness' (K. Thomas 1983: 117). The significance for Thomas is not that they were so drawn into the human world, but that once there they could be observed closely and seen in a different light:

> It encouraged the middle classes to form optimistic conclusions about animal intelligence; it gave rise to innumerable anecdotes about animal sagacity; it stimulated the notion that animals could have character and individual personality; and it created the psychological foundation for the view that some animals at least were entitled to moral consideration. It is no coincidence that many, if not the majority of those who wrote on behalf of animals in the eighteenth century were, like Pope or Cowper, or Bentham, persons who had themselves formed close relations with cats, dogs or other pets.
>
> (K. Thomas 1983: 119)

It was not a major leap from the sentiments of those 'who wrote on behalf of animals' to the actions of the animal reform movement which culminated in the passing of anti-cruelty legislation (from 1824 onwards), the establishment of an organization to monitor and police such legislations, and the establishment of a sentimental, protective popular culture of animal lovers. However, that would not have proved necessary had the changing sentiments spread evenly across all social classes. The years of rapid urbanization of the first half of the nineteenth century were among the darkest in modern English history. For the urban working class these were times of economic depressions, food shortages, appalling living conditions and extreme inequality. Their children starved and went to early graves. Even had they wanted to, they were in no position to offer their animals conditions similar to those offered by the gentry. During most of this time working-class culture was in transition between rural and urban forms. Rural leisures and animal-keeping practices turned up in towns, creating a jarring effect on gentler sensibilities. The unrefined metonymic rural pleasures with animals, including dog fighting, bear-baiting and cockfighting, together with the more exploitative economic relations with animals, as between cabbies and their horses, for example, became a daily reminder of class difference with respect to human–animal relations. Thus, Thomas sees the reforms in terms of one social class imposing its own values onto another. But it is more than that. Once again, attitudes to animals show how one should be human, what it is to be properly human, or humane as it was called. It was a clear demonstration, in Thomas's view, that a rude class culture, which was a potential violent menace to its wealthier human neighbours in addition to its animals, had to be forced to change and tow the line in civil society. Such an idea is clear in the tone of Hogarth's *Four Stages of Cruelty* of the mid-eighteenth century: Thomas cites John Lawrence in 1798 who wrote 'if cruelty be allowable towards brutes it also involved human creatures; the gradation is much easier than imagined, and the

easy jump from mistreating animals to mistreating humans

example is contagious'. The leading mover of anti-cruelty bills in the early nineteenth century, Lord Erskine, emphasized the connection between human violence to animals and violence in society (K. Thomas 1983: 151).

It is important to remember that Thomas's period is 1500 to 1800 and that many of the reforms and changes he seeks to explain took place afterwards. He is constantly moving out of his period into the nineteenth century or the 1980s to show follow-through, connection and consequence. Contemporary readers could well form the impression that *Man and the Natural World* provides an adequate explanation of late twentieth-century attitudes to animals, or at least most of them. However, it is important to consider in more detail theories of social and economic change in the nineteenth and twentieth centuries because human–animal relations have been profoundly altered during this period, even if similar attitudes have persisted. Before we do that we need to consider the adequacy of Thomas's account. On the whole the book is an exemplary work of social history with a strong narrative line of change and process. Human–animal relations are not reduced to changes in the economic, technical, or moral composition of modernity, rather they are the result of a complex interplay between social, spatial and economic change, the unintended consequences of philosophical and scientific discourse, social conflict, distinction and social class. There are some problems, however.

First, the slow, gradual nature of the change process he emphasizes is contradicted by the equal emphasis given to the fact that there were few new attitudes introduced during this period. 'The truth is that one single, coherent and remarkably constant attitude underlay the great bulk of the preaching and pamphleteering against animal cruelty between the fifteenth and eighteenth centuries' (K. Thomas 1983: 153). As Tester remarks, 'Thomas emphasises how the process of urbanisation stimulated a concern with cruelty and kindness, but if it did not stimulate the original ideas where did they come from, and why?' (Tester 1992: 71).

Second, the impact of urbanization itself is made to carry too much causal power. To begin with, human–animal relations and attitudes in towns were never that different from those in the country at any one social level, and at any one time. Further, the elite, whose views inform much of the narrative, were not spatially fixed to one urban home but moved between their own rural and urban residences, as well as those of their friends and relatives. Visits were frequently long, indeed seasonal in length, so it is difficult to imagine the development of a completely separate sensibility in towns. As landlords of rural estates, they were interested in and informed of their farms, their tenants, their workers and the animals on their demesnes. To be sure, their lives were not in such close proximity as farm households, but Thomas has surely exaggerated the difference. Transport was by horse throughout Thomas's period, in town or country, which provided a continuous relation of animal exploitation that no amount of sentiment could diminish.

critique of Thomas

too much emphasis on urbanization

Third, too much emphasis was given to the human–pet relationship in transforming urban sensibilities to animals in general. We are told that pet keeping became fashionable and ubiquitous in urban society, but what is missing from this

overemphasis of human–pet relationship

account is the development of their taste for less kind human–animal relations, namely their enthusiasm for hunting and angling. According to Thomas, hunting is associated with traditional rural culture and the serial round of metonymic relations with animals. However, it is clear from many accounts that it was the urban gentry who were particularly attracted to such rural sports. Itzkowitz (1977) is clear that urbanites made fox hunting the most fashionable sport in England during the eighteenth century. Walton and his companions in *The Compleat Angler* (1653) were from relatively wealthy London backgrounds connected with educated and intellectual circles. One may say, along with Thomas, that a principal objective of reform in human–animal relations was social discipline, but one cannot with confidence say that this was necessarily linked to greater sensibilities learned from pet keeping or living in towns.

Fourth, this account underrepresents the culture of the rural and urban working classes, or for that matter, the intermediate strata of English society. As a result, there are two problems: undue emphasis is given to the educated middle-class elite as a vanguard of change; and the attitude of working-class culture is inferred from secondhand reports of some of the more excessively cruel and unkind practices. We have no way of knowing whether this was typical, representative, or confined to the working class. Routine kindly acts are far less noteworthy or newsworthy and, as Ritvo (1987) demonstrates, the contemporary literature was imbued with sensationalism, moral panic and reform-driven propaganda. Ritvo's empirical approach employs finer class distinctions and enables us to see, for example, that some of the activities associated with working-class culture in Thomas's work were in fact the preserve of a particular fraction of the working class. The very worst cruelties were perhaps the animal fighting and baiting sports which by the early nineteenth century were more or less confined to lumpen culture (Ritvo 1987: 150–1). Cockfighting, however, was known to be a mixed class gambling sport. Itzkowitz (1977) mentions that cockfighting was popular among foxhunters in the late eighteenth century. According to Ritvo:

> Cock fighting was traditionally associated with the aristocratic sport of horse racing
> . . . the Lancashire matches were governed by the rules that were printed in each
> *Racing Calendar* until 1840, several years after cock fighting had become illegal.
> Oxford undergraduates were reputed to buy a great many live rats for their dogs to
> bait.
>
> (Ritvo 1987: 155)

All the evidence appears to support the view that most people, including the rural and working class, were fully the equal of their social betters in terms of animal sentiments and routine kindness by the nineteenth century.

It is not absolutely clear from Thomas, then, how much weight should be given to urbanization, how much to pets, or how much to the role of moral and philosophical discourse. Part of the problem is that urban culture is given more homogeneity than it deserved and the rural–urban or traditional–modern model is too crude. More emphasis should be on cultural and subcultural difference and human–animal relations and uncovering the social base of different groups within the middle classes and in other classes, together with the origins of the social and economic discourses that constituted them. In other words, a more satisfactory account would need a more micro-social cultural focus. There is a general absence of social structural coherence informing and organizing Thomas's historical material and this contributes to the vague nature of causality noted above. The role and influence of the state, church and landowners, for example, are unclear. In addition human–animal relations, which are held to be projections of social relations, were not located within a grounded narrative of changing socialities, dispositions, manners or taste. In the next section we will consider the relevance of Norbert Elias and his process sociology precisely because some of these shortfalls in Thomas may be addressed using his approach. However, it must be emphasized that Thomas's approach is not incommensurate with Elias: Tester has even suggested that *Man and the Natural World* may have been directly influenced by Elias (Tester 1992: 57).

The state, social configurations and self-control

Elias's principal work (1994), *The Civilising Process*, is a theorized history of modernity located over a longer time frame than Thomas's. It is particularly relevant to our discussion because one of its principal concerns is the changing nature of manners and taste over time. Although Elias says very little about human–animal relations, there are clear ways in which such an approach can build on the work of Thomas. If Thomas is correct in his view that new attitudes and behaviours towards animals have a social origin, then we would expect to find their explanation in new forms of social relations and subsequent changes in social conduct. Eliasian analysis offers the possibility of making a tangible link between the growing set of doubts and worries about the violent and cruel treatment of animals by humans and the gradual containment and control of violence among citizens of the modern state.

The historical starting point for Elias was the medieval period where, throughout Europe prior to the formation of stable nation-states, violence between individuals was more common, acceptable and inevitable. Social formations were typified by warring princely kingdoms, critical to which was the maintenance of an armed warrior class. Each small kingdom vied with its neighbours to lay territorial mastery over tracts of land and taxable peasant households; the division of labour was rudimentary and power and control were fluid. According to Elias, such social conditions influenced individual personality and behaviour in distinct ways. Adults were more childlike, they were easily angered, they resorted to violence more easily and were generally less restrained in their dealings with others. This was also reflected in less restraint exercised over the body, particularly over bodily functions, table manners and diet.

As smaller kingdoms were slowly amalgamated into larger states, with more stable land bases and centralized power, so unbridled individual passions and behaviour gave way to more restraint, deferred gratification and delicacy of manner. No longer were resources distributed according to ad hoc grabs by armed war lords. Instead, a more orderly process of state administration organized trade and exchange, taxes and patronage within a more complex social configuration based on lengthening chains of social dependency. As the state became more stable and took over more and more specialized social functions, it required ever more divisions of labour. Under these conditions personality and behaviour had to change. Moreover, the state began to monopolize the use of violence and required arguments between individuals to be settled peaceably. Juridical establishments grew to oversee such tasks. Codes of behaviour outlawing violence became more common and were exercised over increasing areas of inter-personal contact. Over time, violence itself becomes repugnant in a wider range of applications; eventually even those exercised by the state become subject to a process of refinement. Thus, over the past four hundred years executions have been removed from public spectacle to behind prison walls and thence banned altogether or rendered less violent, for example, with the introduction of lethal injections.

Thus the civilization process is a gradual refinement of manners based on the individual self-restraint required by lengthening of chains of dependency. Elias argued that social elites were more open and thus exposed to social discourse with lower strata in modernizing nation-states. As a result the manners by which they distinguished themselves were in a perpetual state of imitation by social inferiors. Through this mode not only did courtly and elite behaviour become established as societal norms (eventually), but new forms of refinement arrived to replace those copied by subordinates.

We can now extend this analysis into the field of human–animal relations by considering its application to the realm of sport, an area opened up by Elias and Dunning. To date the link between sport and animals in modern society has not been developed in explanations of changing attitudes, but it will be argued here that it is of central importance.

Sportization and animals   According to Elias and Dunning (1986) the sociology of sport can be developed as an offshoot to the main civilizing thesis. Contrary to many leisure theorists, sport for Elias and Dunning was not simply about providing relaxation as a relief from the tensions of modern living, but rather it supplied a controlled means of expressing excitement, creating a safe arena of pleasurable tension and offering a resolution through the delivery of a 'result'. Modern life progressively required more and more restraint over the impulses and emotions, but at the same time it produced just as many tensions for individuals to deal with. We can understand modern sports developing out of such a contradiction. Sports set up a planned 'enclave within which a controlled and pleasurable de-controlling of restraints on emotion is permitted' (Mennell 1992: 142). However, as with the civilization thesis, we need to understand the development of modern sports as a process. In order to do that we have to consider the changing nature of sports as related to the social formation of their day.

Elias and Dunning (1986) argued, for example, that the history of sports reveals the gradual elimination of violence. Greek and Roman sports were savage and brutal to modern tastes and sensibilities: blood was freely spilt; injuries were fearful; contests were frequently patently 'unfair'; contestants were killed. The early modern forerunners to the football codes (soccer, rugby, grid-iron, Australian rules, etc.) were also more violent in comparison with today, but they took place in a relatively stable nation-state where violent injury and manslaughter were not only outlawed, but offended public sensibility. In ancient Greece and Rome, by comparison, no such revulsion would have been felt because such degrees of violence were normative and acceptable. Both societies were more or less in a permanent state of armed conflict where physical man-to-man combat was de rigueur and a fatality in combat was not shrouded in the familiar modern emotions aroused by death. What has all this to do with human–animal relations? First, animals were heavily involved in sports over the period in which we are interested. Second, many sports involving animals were violent and became the object of criticism and reform from the nineteenth century onwards.

Contests took place between animals and humans and between animals. In Rome, fierce exotic animals were frequently sent in against gladiators or Christians. Even in modern Spain, bullfighting is a contest between 'a sportsperson and beast' (there are now female bullfighters). Some would argue that bullfighting is not a sport, but it is in the sense that Elias used the term because it is a physical contest, with a build-up of pleasurable excitement and a resolution. The fact that the bull is normally killed is irrelevant: this is balanced by the real danger that a human may be killed or maimed in the process. The stakes are high, which serves to enhance the excitement. Angling is always reported in terms of a contest between angler and fish; often, in the modern context, with the claim that the contest needs to be a fair one or it lacks excitement or enjoyment (Hummell and Foster 1986). In the nineteenth century boxing kangaroos were a regular feature of rural Australian fairs where local men were challenged to fight with them. Contests between animals of the same species include cockfighting, Siamese fighting fish and dog fights. Contests between animals of different species include hare coursing, where dogs pursue a hare until it drops exhausted, and baiting bulls, bears or even rats with dogs. These were extremely popular sports in early modern England:

> The staging of contests between animals was one of their (the English in the sixteenth century) most common forms of recreation. Bulls and bears were 'baited' by being tethered to a stake and then attacked by dogs usually in succession, but sometimes together. The dog would make for the bull's nose, often tearing off its ears or skin, while the bull would endeavour to toss the dog into the spectators . . . Baiting of this kind was customarily regarded as an appropriate entertainment for royalty or foreign ambassadors. Badgers, apes, mules and even horses might all be baited in a similar fashion. Bull baiting, wrote John Houghton in 1694, 'is a sport the English much delight in; and not only the baser sort, but the greatest ladies'.
>
> (K. Thomas 1983:144)

Notice that the word sport was used in this example from the seventeenth century. Its modern use came via such contests and even as late as the mid-nineteenth century it was normatively associated with hunting and angling, as opposed to human game playing. *The Treatise of Fysching with an Angle*, attributed to Dame Juliana Berners, Prioress of Sopworth, tells of a sport where a pike is tethered to a swan and the pair are left to decide which one will be dragged out of its element, presumably to the amusement of the assembled crowd (de Worde 1496). Can these examples really be associated with the antecedents of modern sport? As far as the crowd of human spectators were concerned it mattered very little if the mimetic battle before them was between humans or any other category of 'player'. What mattered was the degree of tension and excitement that the contest delivered, which, of course, depended upon such matters as the predictability of victory, the maintenance of tension and the avoidance of stalemates. One only has to see the spectacle of human excitement at cockfights, for example, to take this point (Geertz 1973: 423). None of these factors would discriminate against animals being used for such purposes. Indeed, the gradual replacement of animals for humans in violent sports contests could be interpreted as a civilizing 'spurt', as Elias did in his analysis of English fox hunting in the eighteenth century. Here he made much of the fact that humans removed themselves from the killing of the fox. The pleasure they took came from watching the hounds keep to a scent, outrunning the quarry and killing the fox as the hunters' proxies (Elias 1986: 163). It might be worth pointing out that foxes are not killed 'humanely' by the hounds; they are usually torn limb from limb by the excited pack and eaten on the spot. The gradual elimination of violence from sports, including violent sports between humans and animals (Elias's essay on fox hunting was entitled 'An essay on sport and violence') is related, in Elias's account, to a particular juncture in the social and political development of the state in English society: in this way sportization was linked to parliamentarization.

In tracing the origin of modern sports, Elias and Dunning took notice of two important facts: that the majority originated in England and that they emerged together between the eighteenth and nineteenth century. Most modern sports developed from previous forms which were less organized, less standardized across the country, less rule bound and policed, and more violent. Sportization refers to the process of civilizing former games and sporting activities and re-organizing them into the bureaucratized, standardized, and globalized modern sports with which we are familiar today. In trying to understand why this took place and why it first took place in England, Elias and Dunning argued that the process was directly related to what they called parliamentarization. This was the seventeenth-century revolution in English politics where, following a civil war, the ruling elite decided in future to compete for power and influence through peaceful democratic means: they decided to carry on their fight in the orderly, rule-bound manner of a parliament. This new form of organization and mode of behaviour was slowly adopted into other areas of civil life. Initially, politics was organized through clubs, an entirely new form of sociality. These became implicated in the formation of modern sports by organizing regular sporting calendars and competitions, and by introducing civilizing new rules. In this way the slow elimination of violence in sport took place; but notice that this was not done in isolation from society, but in line with newly emerging social mores and tastes. During the same formative period, the most cruel animal sports were made illegal. The question is whether it was cruelty, violence or both that were being eliminated from society at this time.

If we reconsider Thomas's (and Tester's) explanation of cruelty to animals, we notice first of all that no emphasis is given to the sporting nature of these activities. That is understandable because we would hardly want to call them sporting. But our views are irrelevant: the English of the seventeenth century thought they were a splendid diversion, containing all the hallmarks of a good sport: excitement and tension, pleasure, resolution. As such we must treat them seriously as sports. Thomas and Tester wish to emphasize that humans project essentially social meanings onto their relationships with animals. Hence cruel sports were rituals that entrenched boundaries between humans and animals during times when the distinction was blurred or unclear. The pleasure aspect of them is left hanging. One must be very suspicious of such symbolic, representational explanations when they are offered in cases such as these without any further evidence. Following Elias, I would argue that a more plausible explanation of cruelty to animals can be found in the conscious social processes involved in the pleasure of sporting occasions. It had less to do with metonymic relation with animals in rural England than with thresholds of tolerance for violence. When this changed, as change it did, animal sports came under greater pressure. Perhaps Tester and Thomas have simply confused cause with effect: cruel sports were about pleasure but they may have unintentionally reinforced the human–animal boundary.

Tester gives Elias a good reception in his book on the sociology of animal rights, but criticizes him on the grounds that there is more to the story of growing sentiments for animals than simply lowering general thresholds of tolerance for violence. This is surely correct. Tester uses the example of cat burning in sixteenth-century Paris to show up the inadequacies of the Eliasian method. Cats were frequently burned alive on certain festive occasions, and the miaowing and screamings of the suffering cats gave the French spectators, including royalty, great fun:

> The populous assembled. Solemn music was played. Under an enormous scaffold a pyre was erected. The sack or basket containing the cats [1–2 dozen] was hung from the scaffold. The sack or basket began to smoulder . The cats fell into the fire and were burned to death, while the crowd revelled in their caterwauling.

> (Elias 1994: 167)

The question is why? According to Elias:

> The cat-burning on Midsummer Day was a social institution, like boxing or horse-racing in present-day society . . . Thus someone who wished to gratify his pleasure in the manner of sixteenth century cat-burning would be seen today as 'abnormal', simply because normal conditioning in our stage of civilisation restrains the expression of pleasure in such actions through anxiety instilled in the form of self control.

> (Elias 1994: 167)

Tester is not happy with this account because further research by Darnton (1985) on European cat burning reveals that cats had a very specific meaning:

[handwritten margin notes: cruel sports reinforced human–animal boundary (Thomas) vs. greater thresholds of tolerance for violence in general]

'Elias fails to recognise that cat burning . . . might, actually, have been redolent with meaning in pre-modern times; might have had a far deeper social meaning than just the relatively free play of aggression' (Tester 1992: 68). Darnton's 1985 work shows that 'the killing of cats had profound ritual value' (Tester 1992: 69). Certainly, Elias is aware that the burning had meaning since he compares it, among other things, with the burning of heretics. However, he also compares the joy of beholding the spectacle to any other pleasurable occasion, 'without any excuse before reason' (Elias 1994: 167). The problem here is that Elias is being dismissed for failing to see that cat burning was a ritual occasion and not simply the free and pleasurable display of aggression. Even if Elias made this error, it has to be admitted that cat burning was a relatively unusual activity: mostly, as we have seen, animals were involved in sporting contests – not pagan ritual. On the other hand, there may well have been other meanings attached to the animals used in early modern English contests.

The manner by which reform was introduced and directed also seems plausible from an Eliasian point of view. In Thomas's account the anti-cruelty legislators were primarily interested in social reform, but the pretext for civilizing the rough working class was to teach them a lesson in civility by first softening their hearts and behaviour towards animals. This is perhaps too convoluted and cryptic to be perfectly plausible. Does it make more sense to see that the reformers were simply and honestly revolted by what some people were doing to animals? After all, animal cruelties were both public and ubiquitous enough to be seen and to give offence where offence could be taken. Of course the anti-cruelty legislation was aimed at the working class and designed to change their behaviour. The issue is: was it enacted in order to prevent unacceptable degrees of violent force (the terms of which were now extending in all directions, including to animals), or to discipline the working class, using their violence to animals as a pretext, in the hope that it would curb violence and cruelty to humans? An Eliasian position would hold that respectable society was revolted because that flagrant use of physical violence had by then become anathema in any civil context or situation. The same idea was changing sport and other areas of civil life. At the same time as anti-cruelty legislation, extremely direct action was taken by English municipal authorities to civilize working-class culture in almost all its public manifestations. The streets were cleared of traders and crowds, new by-laws controlled transport and public comportment and alcohol consumption was regulated. But one of the most pointed objects of their legislation was against working-class forms of leisure, which were deemed too violent and mixed with excessive alcohol consumption (Daunton 1983).

The first police forces were formed to enforce these by-laws. Here the state was clearly taking over the monopoly of yet more areas of violence and its spontaneous 'street' forms were gradually closed down. This action was taken to control and civilize the newly urbanized rural working class, in no uncertain terms. The subtlety of Thomas's argument would have been lost on them. The anti-cruelty acts were also directed against violence, but in their case to specific forms of violence to animals. Ritvo's research on the early years of the RSPCA (founded in 1824) lends some weight to an Eliasian position. Thomas places

(handwritten margin notes:) What was motivation behind anti-cruelty mvmt?

much emphasis on the reformer's rhetorical arguments linking cruelty to animals with cruelty to humans. According to Ritvo, the early campaigners faced a subtle problem: although they had very significant public support for the humane cause and the case for kind treatment of animals, this tended to dwindle when it came to enacting legislation. The idea seemed somewhat eccentric and people asked how far it would be taken once a precedent was established. Ritvo argues that they needed a rhetorical device to give legislation a more tangible, sensible appeal. At a time when the urban middle classes were facing a problem of law and order in the cities, the idea that ill-treatment of animals was the foundation of cruelty generally had very great appeal:

(handwritten margin note: anti-cruelty reformers used concern for human violence to push agenda (sinister concern for the animals))

> The connection between cruelty to animals and bad behaviour to humans proved compelling and durable . . . Crusaders against any particular kind of animal abuse were apt to use this as either their opening volley or their crowning argument.

> (Ritvo 1987: 132)

The RSPCA was genuine in its mission to rescue animals. However, in order to make that possible they had to pass legislation, which required an appeal to the concerns of the governing classes. They had to compromise and the compromise was that working-class cruelties were going to be targeted and policed. As Ritvo shows, their leaflets were clear on who was in the frame:

> Yet the sincere sympathy documented by such statements and corroborated by the energetic prosecutorial and legislative activities of the RSPCA had certain limits, which reflected the analytical function of anti-cruelty rhetoric. By and large these limits corresponded to the line dividing the lower classes, already implicitly defined as cruel and in need of discipline, from the respectable orders of society.

> (Ritvo 1987: 133)

In other words the reformers got their crusade off the ground (after a record of failure) by dressing up their campaign to stop violence to animals as social discipline. Here, the rhetoric they used is as significant as the outcome, but it was clear that while the government used it to appear to be doing something about urban incivilities, the enactors were prompted only in their mission for animals.

What is interesting about the anti-cruelty legislation and its aftermath is the gathering of the lower middle class as champions of the RSPCA and, over time, its growing volunteer support force recruited from the ranks of the respectable working class. Although cruelty and mistreatment of animals continued, it is remarkable how quickly the new legislation, and more importantly the idea of kindliness to animals, gained popularity and support. In other words, it is perhaps remarkable that the anti-cruelty measures against such a supposedly entrenched part of working-class culture were not more resisted. The Eliasian perspective would suggest that the legislators were kicking at a door that was already unlocked. This is evident from their own published data. Ritvo argues that most of their activity was dealing with cruelties 'associated with the most routine economic activities. The horses and other draft animals that filled the streets suffered most frequently' (Ritvo 1987: 137 8). From 1857 to 1860, for example, cruelty to horses accounts for 84 percent of the total convictions and 64 percent of the RSPCA's promotional published case stories. Horse cruelty prosecutions rose to around 8,000 per year prior to their replacement by motorized transports around the turn of the century. In the same years 'canine and feline victims accounted for only 2 percent of the convictions, but they figured in 13 percent of the [RSPCA] reports' (Ritvo 1987: 141). The significance of other animal cruelties was also exaggerated in their annual reports to members. Animal baiting could be prosecuted after 1835:

> The numbers were not enormous – in most years, there were fewer than ten – but the way in which the cases were presented emphasised their significance. In the five years after 1835 they accounted for two-thirds of the cases more than a page long in the reports of prosecutions, and several decades later, when only about 5 percent of the total cases prosecuted were selected for description, every single cock-fighting or dog-fighting case was described.
>
> (Ritvo 1987: 152)

Ritvo's finding are significant and support other evidence. As I have remarked elsewhere, the procession of changes in the humane treatment of coarse fish by anglers in England was implemented, over the past one hundred years, without the need for legislation or strong leadership from outside the ranks of the working class (Franklin 1996a). In the case of angling, which has been civilized to a remarkable degree as we will see in Chapter 7, it is possible to understand why it has remained one of the most popular recreations of the Western world. What is more difficult to appreciate, given our accounts so far, is why over the course of the twentieth century hunting has also grown in popularity. Moreover why was hunting not subject to anti-cruelty legislation? Thomas and Elias do not deal with this issue directly, but it does seem to be at odds with both types of account. It reveals a major blind spot in the discourses on attitudes to animals in modernity: namely, that in their keenness to account for the key changes (anti-cruelty legislation, animal protection, animal rights, the civilizing of manners) they have failed to take stock of continuities or changes that lead in the opposite direction.

To characterize modernity as an increasingly sentimental period of benevolence to animals is to miss the fragmented nature of human–animal relations and the persistence of practices that contradict such a view. Typically this view specifies a somewhat narrow social constitution: the educated middle classes create the vanguard whose writings, tracts, philosophy, speeches and bills constitute the great bulk of the evidence. The uneducated working classes form the group in need of reform: their cruel, depraved acts speak for themselves and require no direct or supplementary testimony. The non-educated, non-literary circles in commerce, trade or the professions are absent from the analyses. Instead there is an implicit polarization between working class and middle class, traditional and modern. This polarization is symptomatic of modern classifications of society, hinging as they do on the centrality of relations of production in modernity. The lesson to be learned here is that a full understanding of animals and modern cultures requires a broader, more inclusive approach based on the premise that most cultures and subcultures negotiate human–animal relations that are specific to their social and economic locations and history.

Hunting introduces new cultural groups into the frame and makes us consider the animal issue as more than a polarized debate about discipline and manners. It introduces the idea that human–animal relations are arranged over many sites of modern societies and among many groups. We will look at hunting in more detail below. Before we can do that we must first turn to consider another site of modernity, and another discourse. In the eighteenth century and increasingly during the nineteenth, the Romantic movement formed very strong views on animal issues. Indeed these views have evolved into the most powerful expression of discontent with human–animal relations, culminating in the animal liberation or rights movement. The Romantics did not favour hunting, meat eating and the destruction of the environment. Here was another middle-class view about nature and animals. Why were their views not also transmuted into new legislation, practice and social change? Here we move into historical questions that cannot be answered using the broader brush approaches of Thomas and Elias. Tester's analysis of changing arguments for the moral treatment of animals is inspired by Foucault whose work has focused on classificatory systems in modernity and the effects of knowledge on social change.

[margin note: Dates of Romantic period?]

In contrast to Thomas or Elias who emphasize long-term continuities in Western thought, Foucault identifies distinct changes or discontinuities which can be used to specify different periods. The anthropocentricism identified by Thomas can be approximately compared to the Renaissance period of knowledge (or *episteme*), which we have looked at. Whereas Thomas sees anthropocentricism disappearing during the eighteenth century to be replaced simply by non-anthropocentricism, Foucault sees a new *episteme* the Classical *episteme* in which knowledge became rooted in observation. Classifications were based on visible similarity and sameness; they were linear and progressive. However, a system based on similarities could fall into confusion and lacked an ordering logic. This is what characterizes the third, modern *episteme*, which begins in the late eighteenth century. The modern *episteme* avoids the confusion of visible similarities by identifying an underlying abstract order that lay behind the visible. Thus the dolphin is nearer to a human than a fish through an analysis of its systemic qualities of body temperature regulation, respiration, and cognitive ability. Life itself rather than just those creatures close to humanity became more highly valued because it created a unity among all living creatures. According to Tester, the rising of compassionate feelings towards animals can be clearly identified with the modern *episteme*:

[margin note: modern episteme; Linne + Darwin]

> People started to worry about the social treatment of animals to the extent that life was identified as the basis of knowledge and made the main principle for the order of things. Classification demanded behaviour which would respect the similitude of all living organic structures regardless of any visible distinctions, whilst also maintaining the privileged status of humanity as the only historical subject able to know life.

(Tester, 1992: 88)

Tester uses a modified Foucaultian approach to explore divergences in modernity, within the modern *episteme*, in order to account for the distinctive nature of animal rights. For analytical purposes he constructs two different types of discourse on the appropriate way for humans to treat animals. Both emerged in or around the beginning of the nineteenth century, but they summarize the positions of quite different groups in society. He calls these discourses the Demand for Difference and the Demand for Similitude. The former led to the set of reforms which we have identified above:

> The Demand for Difference was the first to appear by the space of a few years and, as the label implies, it was an attempt to enhance the privilege of being human through the project of the social extirpation of animality. During the eighteenth and nineteenth centuries, the term 'animal' became a pejorative label which could be applied to humans who seemed to be little more than objects ruled by their natural passions and urges. The Demand for Difference played on an attempt to make humans more subjective and responsive to things which *only humans could know*, primarily the abstract principle of life. Animals were useful because they were a stick to beat social unruliness and 'beastliness'. The Demand involved attempts to create orderly and regulated social relationships through discipline and policing.
>
> (Tester 1992: 88–9)

This is a familiar enough message. The difference between the accounts of events by Tester and Thomas is that Tester sees the influence of knowledge, particularly the arrival of a new knowledge, only as yet in the hands of the elite, shaping their sensibilities and separating them from those of the uneducated classes. In Thomas's account knowledge had played a part, but the main argument hinges on the experiences of the urban elite: they had been separate from animals for longer and they were kind hearted because of exposure to pets.

In specifying the Demand for Similitude as a conflicting discourse, Tester takes us into less familiar territory:

> The Demand for Similitude followed a radically alternative path. It emphasised the extent to which all organic beings, 'regardless of the more obvious signs displayed on the surface of their bodies' (Foucault 1970: 229), were all linked as living things, and therefore of a comparable classificatory status. The Demand for Difference stressed the uniquely human and the properly social. The Demand for Similitude was associated with the idea that humans should live in accordance with the dictates of the natural, organic being. It condemned society and attempted to show how the repudiation of nature had caused a decay of life.
>
> (Tester 1992: 89)

The Demand for Similutude of course derived from the work of writers associated with the Romantic movement. These have left a lasting legacy on human–animal relations in the twentieth century and in the next section we will examine this legacy.

The romantic gaze

In its condemnation of modernity the Romantic movement can be contrasted with [1750 – 1840s] the anti-cruelty reformers who were a quintessential part of the Age of Reason. [industrial revolution] The reformers were not eccentric banner-waving cranks, but men and women drawn from the aristocratic elite and government where their views were largely shared. In all respects they were typical of their class (Ritvo 1987). According to Tester, the reformers comprised a new demand for difference between humans and animals. Science had given people a greater sense of distance from animals but a great respect for life. They were different because they were more evolved and therefore superior, and they were mastering the world through science and rational, abstract thought. Different status required different manners, civilized manners; humans still demonstrating animal inclinations must be reformed. Meat eating was acceptable because this marked the boundary of difference between humans and animals. The cooking of meat was a ritual situated on the human–animal boundary: it emphasized the difference between humans and animals, but also the human claim on animals as food. In Britain meat eating was also associated with social status. Historically, the elite had eaten a great deal of meat, the poor scarcely any. It must be remembered that in Britain meat was an expensive luxury item, even until relatively recent times, and regular eating of meat set the middle class apart from the working class. Providing animals were killed in an appropriately humane manner, there could be no moral objection to farming stock and eating meat.

The Romantics took the opposite view: Rousseau, for example, wandered into forests and discovered the animal in himself, beauty and perfection in nature and nobility in wildness. There are two ways in which such reflections could be taken. The first might allow that humans are indeed animals and must regain and live their animal passions and connections with nature. Since modern man derives from a hunting and gathering past which stretches back millennia, he needs to express this association through re-establishing links with a natural environment and interacting with it by self-provisioning. Such a view would see hunting and perhaps gathering of wild fruit and fungi as a therapeutic palliative to the pathologies associated with modern urban living. The second way would be the opposite: man is an animal but takes from nature only what he needs. Like the animals he is naturally gentle and sensitive to his environment, most of his food needs can be met through fruits and vegetables. Modern man has lost this noble sensitivity and must learn to regain it.

Both views are romantic but they look in opposite directions. The first is [2 romantic perspectives:] directed towards a set of human animal relations that has become extremely common in modernity, a relationship that has been increasingly expressed through sport, leisure and tourism. It points to a sociology of humans–animals in [#1] modernity that centres on a new consumption of animals and the natural world. The second way provides the foundation for a more hard-line revolution in our relations with animals. It calls for an end to animal exploitation, even their passive [#2] consumption as pets, zoo exhibits or wildlife park inmates; it calls for a vegetarian diet without dairy products or eggs. To liberate animals from humans requires a [*] complete separation – no relationship.

The path to animal rights Rousseau is the starting point for Tester's account of a unifying narrative he calls the Demand for Similitude (Tester 1992: 121 31). This forms part, but only part, of the case for animal rights. The narrative can be summarized thus. Humans are animals who have lost their natural connections to nature and other animals. Reason and society removes us from this condition of nature and corrupts us. In particular we invent spurious reasons for supposing ourselves superior and use them to place a barrier between ourselves and nature. If we returned to a state of nature we would be kind to animals because we would identify with them more. We would be vegetarians since that is what our blunt teeth and our single offspring indicate about our nature (carnivores have large litters), and we would be healthier, happier and less violent. The narrative calls on the work of several influential writers: the vegetarian Ritson, who began to blame meat eating for a wide range of human disorders and problems; the poet Shelley, another vegetarian, and Thoreau who put the demand for similitude into practice by withdrawing from society. Tester sees them all as self-made outcasts:

> The Demand for Similitude was originally developed by people who were so unwilling to live the urban social life expected of them that they declared they would rather be like animals. They set themselves up as natural and pure taxonomic legislators, and turned society into a pollution and a taboo.
>
> (Tester 1992: 146)

Clearly, the Demand for Similitude was influential, but it tended to produce misanthropy, reclusivity or art expression, rather than social change through political engagement. Many of the protagonists of the Demand for Similitude were wealthy and independent. An anti-hunting/hunter theme ran through all their work. Byron regularly blasted fox hunting, angling and other field sports because they were cruel, but particularly because they were mindless and completely missing the point of desirable human associations with nature (see, for example, *Don Juan*, cantos X111: 106, XIV: 35).

While the Romantic writers did little of practical political worth, they were extremely influential, as were other poets of their day:

> This was one of the periods in English history when poets, Shelley's 'unacknowledged legislators', had a powerful influence on educated opinion. The poets were regularly cited by the pamphleteers and quoted by speakers in Parliament; and it is impossible to understand the vehemence of the movement unless one takes into account the works of Pope, Thomson, Gay, Cowper, Smart, Dosley, Blake, Burns, Wordsworth, Coleridge, Shelley, Byron, Southey, Crabbe and Clare, to name no more.
>
> (K. Thomas 1983: 149)

Why were hunting and angling not legislated against? Tester and Thomas would no doubt claim that since the object of anti-cruelty legislation was the reform of working-class behaviour, it is not surprising that middle-class animal sports were left untouched. Tester's (1989) paper on fox hunting deals directly with this issue. Although the poets frequently criticized the sport of gentlemen, this critique was filtered through the social–class bias of the pamphleteers and campaigners. Since the poets and the legislators were middle class themselves and required the support of their peers, it was expedient to turn a blind eye to some sports and pastimes. However, it is more complex than that: hunting and angling were actually difficult to condemn at the time. They were hugely popular and gained the somewhat generous reputation of being democratic. Fox hunting was intimately tied up with military training (and thus national security) and pest control. Shooting sports were easily shown to be humane and a rightful food product of the land. Angling was also seen as harmless food provisioning and the extension of such protection to fish risked undermining public support through ridicule. Byron himself showed doubts about his own views on angling by including an additional note, suggested by a friend, which disputes and therefore blurs his own judgement. It is probably true to say that the Romantics preferred their gaze, their place in nature and their solitude – their relations with the natural world – to the humbug of political agitation in the city. Rather than engage, many of them turned away. Anti-hunting and angling as a movement had to wait until the formation of animal rights.

The Romantic legacy was a collection of anti-hunting, anti-development, anti-progress sentiments that were to form a principal plank in the education and mores of modern people. In terms of its impact on human–animal relations, it lay relatively dormant or inactive until 1970 when Peter Singer published for the first time *Animal Liberation* (1990). Although not an entirely new argument this was a potent discourse and ripe for the 1970s. Tester argues that animal rights, which begins with the work of Henry Salt in the 1890s, combines the two narratives of Difference and Similitude. The combination can be specified in the following manner. We must recognize that we are the same as animals; animals are individuals like us and therefore we should not restrict their freedom or harm them. On the other hand, humans are different because they are capable of changing the world and society towards perfection and it is the duty of those so enlightened to do so. Humans are different because they are responsible for their own moral progress. We will have more to say about animal rights in Chapter 10, but for our purposes here we can set out its sociological distinctiveness. Tester (1992:171–9) argues that animal rights involves at least seven new features:

7 features of animal rights

1 Animals should have complete freedom from human interference, with total separation from pets, wild animals, farm animals.
2 It is unequivocal – no possible slippage is possible on any site of human–animal relations.
3 Vegetarianism is essential.
4 It is asserted as a natural right. Animals are individuals with feelings; freedom is a natural need; they can suffer and their ability to suffer stems from their nature.
5 The expression of rights for animals is concerned with what it is to be properly human and implies the moral turpitude of disbelievers.
6 Believers are morally obliged to further the cause of animal rights; it is their responsibility as humans.

7 Animal rights is therefore 'fetishized' ('society is worshipping a thing of its own creation when it falls down before this truth') and is accompanied by the social panoply of ritual including conversion, dietary and clothing restrictions, cult/fraternity, mission.
8 Since Singer combined the morality of animals rights with the radical human liberation movements of the 1970s, 'animal liberation' has had a broader appeal and the social base of the movement is similarly wide.

We will return to consider the global nature of the animal rights argument and movement in Chapter 10. The question that concerns us here is why it should have emerged when it did. Of course, animal rights does not have a mass following, even though it has been extremely successful and has not yet run its full course. It may well win over a significant number of supporters and effect more than the individual reform of its members. For it to do that it will have to challenge dominant and entrenched attitudes to animals in the twentieth century. The difficulty will be great because the argument presented here is that our relations with animals have multiplied as they are consumed at an even greater number of sites. It will be argued that most of these are sites of human consumption and leisure which have expanded and changed over the twentieth century. In order to understand these new relations it becomes necessary to investigate them using leisure and consumption theory. This is the aim of the last section of this chapter but, in addition, it will be suggested that human–animal relations have become or are becoming postmodernized.

Neo-Darwinism and the hunting imperative   The Romantic gaze saw the need for humans to express their animal nature and passions in 'wild' places. It placed great emphasis on action and personal engagements with nature. Byron mocked the angler but admired the tunny or shark fisher and the perilous life of the deep-sea trawler. Placing oneself at the mercy of nature and obtaining food was compatible with romanticism. From the late nineteenth century onwards there emerged a variant of Romanticism, the idea that nature was a beautiful but ruthless system, 'red in tooth and claw'. It became prominent and influential. One of the principal sources of the view came from Darwin, particularly his evolutionary law of natural selection and survival of the fittest. These ideas developed alongside new finds in archaeology and physical anthropology which showed that humanity, or rather the first humanoid apes, made their formative break with other species in becoming weapon-swinging killer apes. The view was formed that humans are naturally or by instinct aggressive, competitive killers. Moreover, by killing animals and gradually subduing nature humans elevated themselves above animality. Hunting was more than just food collecting, it was a ritual celebration of difference and superiority over animals.

Both Cartmill and Ritvo relate the popularity of this view to the period when European powers were carving up the world into imperial domains over which they would be masters of both humans and animals. It was an ideology that flattered the sensibilities of Europeans and their colonies at the height of global domination. Big game hunting thrived during this period and continued into the twentieth century. Occasionally, the boundary dissolved between non-European animals and non-European humans and hunting turned to acts of murder and genocide. It was the sport of kings, military officers and colonial administrators, and later capitalists, tycoons and movie stars and for a long while the ultimate expression of social power. For Europeans, escape into wild environments meant the colonial environments of Africa, India or Australia – most of Europe was tamed. For Americans, however, the wilderness was an aspect of their nature that distinguished them from Europeans. Modern America was in part formed through its struggle with the wild and a close association with the wilderness is deeply embedded in North American popular culture. In some of the conservative Darwinian American writings there is the clear link between the spiritually uplifting and invigorating hunting trip and health. Modern living, city life and *urban life* affluence are regarded as debilitating, emasculating and unhealthy. President *but* Theodore Roosevelt was the quintessential hero of such a view:

> He was a devout conservationist but his view of man's relationship to nature was thoroughly hierarchical and Darwinian. An enthusiastic imperialist and a staunch believer in the superiority of the Anglo-Saxon race, he was also a renowned Great White Hunter who devoted much of his life to killing large animals throughout the world and writing books recounting his adventures. He favoured the preservation of America's wildlands because he thought that wilderness adventures inculcated 'fighting, masterful virtues' and 'that vigorous manliness for the lack of which in a nation, as in an individual, the possession of no other qualities can possibly atone'.
>
> (Cartmill 1993: 153–4)

However, since America also had its fair share of anti-hunting or, as Cartmill calls them, 'tender-minded' Romantics – writers such as Mark Twain, Charles Dudley Warner and their following – it meant that the great wilderness areas soon became the source of philosophical and political conflict:

> From the very beginning, the American conservation movement has encompassed two rather different sorts of nature lovers: tender-minded Romantics who want to preserve nature because it is holy, and tough-minded Darwinian types who want to preserve it because it is healthy. For the Romantics, nature is an open-air chapel in which one can commune with the Infinite and make friends with the forest creatures; for the Darwinians, nature is a kind of vast exercise salon, in which one can get rid of bodily flabbiness and spiritual malaise, work up a glorious appetite and polish off a couple of those forest creatures for supper. These views are not mutually exclusive, and most nature lovers hold both to varying degrees; but there is a tension between the two attitudes, which sometimes breaks out into fights over such matters as hunting.
>
> (Cartmill 1993: 149–50)

The most famous and extreme exponent of the neo-Darwinian view was Nietzsche, whose ideas were taken rather too literally with devastating results. However, in a less extreme form it comprises a very common attitude in modern societies, certainly in the USA, Australia, Scandinavia and Britain, and also extends into the motives given by anglers. We will be examining this in more detail in Chapter 7, particularly which groups in society make up the modern neo-Darwinians and why they are almost always men.

CONCLUSION

In this chapter we have traced the development of human–animal relations from the very earliest period of recorded history until the end of the twentieth century. We have concentrated on key patterns of change, the causes of these changes and competing theoretical perspectives. To keep things as clear as possible, and to get the longest coherent stretch of history, English material has formed the main focus. That many modern societies in the West share an English inheritance provides some justification for this choice. In the chapters that follow the emphasis will be more international.

We have confined our attention to historical developments up until the twentieth century and the approach has been predominantly ideational, that is to say it has been a history of the ideas and knowledge that have influenced patterns of behaviour and the structuration of attitudes. Partly this is because so many of the theoretical debates have taken this approach. This is not simply a matter of preference: to a great extent the changing shape of human–animal relations and the principal shifts in attitude over this period have been the subject of theological, scientific, philosophical and ethical thought. Another reason is because historical data cannot permit the interrogation of human–animal relations in the manner which we might want. It has been noted that the lower income–status groups in society are relatively absent from the historical record in comparison with the wealthy; and we may suppose a degree of bias to be present in the over-represented views of the educated classes. This is almost certainly true for the anti-cruelty debates of the early nineteenth century. But we simply cannot know how ordinary rural workers felt about animals, what their beliefs were or how much they varied.

One aim has been to reconstruct the development of three dominant ideal type attitudes to animals which describe the full range. The most central and perhaps most common attitude has been summarized under Tester's somewhat inelegant phrase 'the Demand for Difference', but it might be better described as the 'sentimental' attitude. Those subscribing to this view today are animal lovers to some extent and may at some time have had a companion animal or pet. They believe in the fair and humane treatment of all animals. They enjoy watching TV programmes about animals, visiting zoos, safari parks and national parks, and they believe that a sympathetic knowledge of animals is an important part of their children's education. They are most likely to eat meat, support a limited application of animals in scientific experimentation, be concerned about endangered species and have ambivalent feelings about hunting. At one extreme of the spectrum are those who support the notion of animals rights. They feel that animal love is patronizing and demeaning. They do not keep pets because that involves relations of control and denial of freedom. They care a great deal about the plight of animals in the modern world and support some sort of action towards achieving animal liberation from humans. They are vegetarians and avoid all animal products, including media products and leisure attractions. At the other end of the spectrum are the neo-Darwinians, many of whom would be active hunters. These people are not sentimental but are nature lovers and feel they have a natural, real relation with animals. They are also concerned about animal conservation and see it as a duty to maintain animal habitats. They frequently keep pets, often dogs which are enlisted in hunting activities. They prefer outdoor hunting trips to the simulated nature of contemporary animal parks and, although most of them profess a keen interest in natural history, they prefer the application of knowledge to knowledge for its own sake. They are most likely to be men and seek to recruit sons and grandsons into hunting as part of their up bringing.

Most people will tend to the middle view or to one side of it, but the range will cover the majority of the population of the West. The indicators we have used to describe these attitudes will be the subject of a separate chapter. It will also become clear that the distribution of people across the range of attitudes is far from random or simply a matter of personal choice or conscience. We will be arguing that different groups in society have quite specific relationships with animals, the principal lines of differentiation being gender, class, occupation, ethnicity, nationality and region.

In Chapter 3 we examine in more detail how social and economic changes in the twentieth century extended the sorts of relationships people had with animals. Animals became especially important as the objects of leisure in the first half of the century and, while retaining their legal rights to fair treatment, they were still consumed for human pleasure in a relatively anthropocentric manner. However, as we shall see, the modernist project based on the key objective of human progress began to break down in a number of ways. As it did so a new series of equally bizarre relations with animals came into being.

3 FROM MODERNITY TO POSTMODERNITY

20th Century

Chapter 2 examined the historical transformations in human–animal relations which resulted in the establishment of many attitudes and values that are familiar to people today. Four key themes were already well formed by the beginning of the twentieth century: the sentimentalization of animals; the role of the modern state in regulating appropriate, civilized behaviour to animals (the anti-cruelty laws, for example); the demand for animal rights; and the growing significance of animals in human leisure. While these attitudes persisted into the twentieth century, much more has occurred in the field of human–animal relations. The twentieth century has transformed the nature of sentiments towards animals, added considerably more legal and institutionalized apparatus concerned with animal welfare, advanced the idea of animal rights to a mainstream debate and decentred the form in which humans engage with animals in leisure. In addition, the twentieth century has substantially changed the economic, political and cultural face of human associations with animals. This chapter will establish the pattern of such changes and suggest a framework for their understanding. In turn this will provide a more systematic guide for the analysis of particular sites of human–animal relations, five of which form the subject for the remaining chapters.

The most appropriate general framework for understanding twentieth-century changes in human–animal relations is a specifically adapted version of familiar theorizations of modernity and postmodernity. The work of Beck (1992), Giddens (1990, 1991), Harvey (1989), Lash and Urry (1987, 1994), Rojek (1995) and Urry (1996) will be drawn on. Although these theorists provide general accounts of social change in the twentieth century, saying almost nothing about human–animal relations, their work is still useful because it is to be expected that our relationships with animals are closely tied to historically specific social and cultural conditions. As we will see, it is possible to account for the new ways in which humans have related to animals in the twentieth century, and their growing significance in our lives, through an analysis of key economic and cultural changes.

The chapter is organized into three sections. The first outlines the main economic and cultural composition of the first half of the twentieth century. The economic manifestations of this period are often referred to as Fordism, but since Fordism and modernity are such closely linked ideas, our discussion will be made under the heading of 'Modernity, Fordism and Animals'. The second section considers the later period of the twentieth century, after which the modernizing project and Fordism began to break down, but not disappear completely – hence the rather tentative terms, 'postmodernity' and 'post-Fordism'. There is no sudden switch from one to another and so no date can describe the point of transformation, although most agree that radical change took place in the 1970s. The second heading then, following the style of the first, is 'Post-modernity, Post-Fordism and Animals'. The concluding section takes a closer look at the ways in which more recent social change has affected the nature of our sentimental attachments with animals.

The impact of Fordism and post-Fordism on human–animal relations in the twentieth century provides a useful analytical tool, particularly in identifying important discontinuities and changes. A key difference to emerge from this analysis is the transformation of sympathetic but instrumental, anthropocentric relations under Fordism to increasingly empathetic, decentred relationships in postmodernity. Postmodern relations with animals are characterized by a stronger emotional and moral content, a greater zoological range of involvement and a demand for more regulation and order. During the early part of the century animal sentiments were widely established but modernization privileged human progress: animal exploitation, extinction and experimentation were the prices to pay for the greater (human) good. After the 1960s, this compromise began to fall apart. As the modernization project was abandoned, unparalleled development was accompanied by deregulation and the scaling down of social programmes. As the essentially moral dimension to modernity evaporated, the compromise with animals was revised (particularly by sections of the new service class), in a series of pro-animal developments and movements, combined with changes in the ways humans involved animals in their lives. It will be argued that the development of strong emotional attachments to animals can be accounted for in terms of the moral crisis and disorder of postmodernity. In particular, this chapter identifies three features of postmodernity which have been important in the organization of this response: misanthropy, ontological insecurity and risk/reflexivity.

In the early to mid-nineteenth century, paternalistic capitalists and their middle-class urban managers imposed anti-cruelty legislations in order to regulate the recently urbanized rural working classes and restore a productive social order to the city. The changed human–animal relation had a clear social foundation. Similarly, over the past twenty-five years or so, a fraction of the educated middle classes has worked hard to revise the human–animal relation, but the sorts of values they have mobilized were precisely those associated with a more regulated social order in line with new social and economic conditions. It was a reassertion of older collectivist values which promoted the notion of social responsibility, social planning, justice and equality, combined with the more recent promotion of decentred sensibilities, multiculturalisms and planned sustainabilities (e.g. sustainable environments, sustainable economies and preventative human medicine). In a variety of ways, which this book aims to illustrate, animals grounded these ideas in a number of new projects and practices.

The morally worthy project of modernity, with its concern for human progress and emancipation, gave way after the 1970s to a culture dominated by economic rationalism, selfish individualism, ethnic conflict, consumerism and new right politics focused specifically on destroying the jewel of modernity: welfarism.

post - 1960

Society became essentially disorganized, confused and morally ambiguous; individuals were less bound to one another by the moral ties of family, neighbourhood community and class. In short, it became increasingly difficult to identify clear, morally imperative relationships and regimes. In all sorts of ways, the care and love of dependent animals, whether as companions in our homes, managed wild populations, or animals involved in food production, have enabled people in late modernity to engage in morally good acts. Animals provide a clear, unambiguous feel-good factor in people's lives and an object for human responsibility. In part then, change in the twentieth century can be understood as the normative extension of moral debates onto the parallel community of animals, but there is also a keen sense that the boundary separating the human from the animal was finally being eroded. This book suggests that humans began to build social and emotional ties with animals because it had became increasingly difficult for them to establish and maintain such ties among themselves.

MODERNITY, FORDISM AND ANIMALS

In this section we concentrate on social change as it affected human–animal relations in the first seventy years of the twentieth century. Before we commence this examination, it will be useful to situate this period within the overall history of modernity.

Modernity can be divided into four periods or phases and, while never completely distinct, the division does help to clarify the development of key modernist ideas. In the first phase, which we can call the *Enlightenment*, modernity was little more than a small number of scientists, mathematicians, philosophers and writers who hoped and believed that the world was controllable through scientific discovery and rational organization. In this period the idea that 'there was only one answer to any question' (Harvey 1989: 27) was widely shared and the search was on, in disciplines such as economics, sociology, and the natural sciences, for universal laws and singular paths to progress.

The second phase (*classical modernism*) commences just before the second half of the nineteenth century, a period during which there was much political turbulence. People were beginning to question their faith in capitalist development as a blueprint and panacea for all human ills. Criticism, debate and experimentation characterized this period, leading to a total breakdown in the orthodoxy of the Enlightenment. Throughout Europe and the USA, modernism broadened and bloomed in every field. Divergence and difference characterized development and this common spirit led to an efflorescence of innovation in the arts, sciences and productive capacity in the first two decades of the twentieth century. During this period the first large corporations were formed from the proliferation of smaller companies. These were to play a vital role in developing mass production and consumption and transforming the cultural composition of the working class. While Western society benefited in all sorts of ways from the relativism and freedoms of this period, it lacked a clear sense of purpose: on the one hand a set of discontents manifested themselves in the despair, anomie and restlessness in the ever-growing metropolis; and on the other, a set of discontents based on perceived injustices, anarchy, inequality and disorder threatened to undermine its social and economic foundations.

The period of *heroic modernism,* between the wars, saw the search for aesthetic visions to provide a sense of purpose. Europe was war torn, economic crises deepened and through the perceived need for visionary solutions, destructive aesthetic visionaries were elevated to positions of power and influence.

Whereas this period was dangerously unstable, the period after 1945 (*high modernism*) was extremely stable. This stability was built on the political and economic hegemony of the USA, a long period of economic growth and full employment, city and suburban development, material plenty if not surplus, successful welfare programmes, the modernization of the Third World and the development of a global political economy.

Modernity is often described in terms of three principal themes or objectives: enlightenment, progress and emancipation (Crook et al. 1992; Harvey 1989: 12–15). From the Enlightenment onwards, the comforts of religion and the limits on human control of nature were rejected in favour of human progress. Although modernity was neither orchestrated nor directed, it makes more sense to see it as a 'project' (Habermas) or a 'trajectory' (Crook et al.):

> The idea was to use the accumulation of knowledge generated by many individuals working freely and creatively for the pursuit of human emancipation and the enrichment of daily life. The scientific domination of nature promised freedom from scarcity, want, and the arbitrariness of natural calamity.
>
> (Harvey 1989: 12)

Modernism is therefore selfishly human in orientation, self-absorbed in its clear sense of human materiality and interest. As an idea of the wealthier, educated classes, modernism was always aimed in part to improve the lot of the poorer classes. Until all humans were elevated from want and domination, the idea of radical reform of human–animal relations was impossible. Thus, Salt's *Animals' Rights Considered in Relation to Social Progress* (1892) was bound to fail when it was first published, despite its rhetorical title and ethical appeal. At that time, workers were frequently on the breadline, most children lacked adequate healthcare, women were not enfranchised, and blacks and indigenous peoples had no civil rights. Apart from the sorts of growing sentiments documented by Thomas in the English case and by Cartmill in the American, it was undoubtedly the case that animals must, in the last instance, take second place to humans.

Fordism is a particularly apt marker of change in the modernization of human–animal relations. The arrival of cheap motorized transport did away with horsedrawn carriages and, in a single stroke, removed the last animals to be in close, visible, daily relations of service to mainstream modern culture. This was the last instrumental relationship with animals that most people accepted as a necessary part of their lives and which served as a link to other instrumental relations, particularly with meat animals. The working horse, with its technical apparatus of harness, bit, reins and whip, was a powerful symbol of subjugation.

Because it was so centrally placed in metropolitan life, it maintained a strong link with pre-modern, traditional rural and instrumental relations with animals. By the time of its demise it was already, of course, enjoyed with a sense of nostalgia. With the city finally cleansed of all pre-modern relations with animals, it became very nearly devoid of animals altogether, with the exception of pets and a subset of tolerated species: city flocks of pigeons, waterfowl collections on ornamental lakes and ornamental rodents such as squirrels ('rats with good PR') and chipmunks. Fordism ushered in this final separation, but it made possible an entirely new set of relations.

Fordism centres on the cultural vision of Henry Ford rather more than on the arrival of cheap motor transport. Ford's vision went beyond the mechanics of production line manufacturing, control over the labour process through time and motion techniques and direction from corporate structures. His was a vision of capitalism in the round, but particularly of improvement and progress of the life style and conditions of his workers. His vision of modern capitalism involved morally upstanding workers relinquishing their autonomy in mass-production factories and benefiting from both higher wages and cheaper, mass-produced goods. Ford believed that in this way it was possible to achieve an even, stable capitalism; affluent workers with good homes served by technical innovations; and economic growth and stability maintained by strong demand. The vision was only partly realized by Ford, corporate USA and large manufacturers elsewhere during the inter-war years, but it succeeded after 1945 for almost thirty years. Thus during the first part of the twentieth century the Western economy was erratic and the labour market highly segmented. In the USA and the UK wages in the corporate manufacturing sector rose steadily in real terms over this period although the spatial distribution of affluence was uneven. From the late 1930s, affluence grew and became more even and sustained.

In contrast to most of the nineteenth century, the twentieth century was driven by a more progressive, corporate and powerful capitalism in which the maintenance of high levels of consumption was achieved in most social classes. Fordism was the equilibrium of mass production and mass consumption. However, it tended to flourish in conditions which were regulated and planned by an expanded state and bureaucracy, such that the economy was attached to strong national goals and objectives (Lash and Urry 1987: 3). At the same time these national formations were dependent on favourable if not exploitative trade terms with less developed nations, formerly dependent parts of larger empires. Nations such as Canada, the USA and Australia had vast stores of cheap resources which were gradually developed into large-scale primary and manufacturing industries in the twentieth century. Although the economic and industrial bases of Fordism had profound effects on our relations with animals, the formation of mass markets, generalized affluence and mass popular culture had the greatest impact. However, affluence did not simply produce consumers and consumer cultures: combined with more free time it created the conditions for modern leisure and leisure cultures. Fordism was therefore a powerful ethos which had far-reaching consequences for human–animal relations in the twentieth century. These can be summarized in the following interconnected features:

1 The extension of extensive grazing and pasture creation in the new world resulting in a spectacular growth potential for the global livestock herd.

2 Technical and scientific development resulting in reliable long-term freezing of meat, the possibility of long-distance exportation and substantial growth in Old World meat consumption.

3 Technical and scientific development resulting in new, rationalized intensive livestock industries, exploiting cheaper grain prices and proximity to major markets.

4 The rationalization and concentration of the slaughtering, butchery and meat packing industries, resulting in new, fully integrated, production line systems, typically removed from former urban locations.

5 Industrial fishing changed continuously in response to growing markets, resulting in overfishing and depleted home water stocks.

6 The growth of a motoring and touring market eventually assumed mass market proportions. This stimulated demand for parklands, national parks, the establishment of parks and wildlife bureaucracies with a remit to provide trails for walking and riding, organized and regulated angling and hunting, and educational information and activities for visitors. Status-confirming leisure activities were established by the wealthy and quickly copied by middle and working classes as incomes rose and costs decreased.

7 As the amount of annual paid leave grew, so more opportunities arose for trips to outdoor locations and activities involving animals; walking in wild areas became the most popular leisure activity; hunting become a mass masculine culture in the USA, New Zealand and Australia; angling becomes a mass (male) popular culture throughout Western society; birdwatching, nature study, zoological gardens and wildlife reserves became major popular leisure activities.

8 Higher wages supported the massification of pet keeping and pet populations expanded; zoological range of pets widened; pets and animal leisure organizations provided basis for social identity.

9 Increased interest in animals arising from hobbies and outdoor leisure stimulated the demand for mass media representations of animals; animals became principal characters in cartoons and children's stories; animals were given moral identity in media representations; films, cartoons and novels used by reformers to broaden the popular support for sentimental attitudes, anti-hunting, conservation and protection.

10 Animals, particularly indigenous animals, were adopted by nation-states as part of nation building, establishing national identity and distinction. The association of indigenous animals with nationalism led to further symbolic animal adoptions by national companies and corporations; animals were used in the mass media, especially children's media, to inculcate patriotism, and nature study (particularly national nature) was widely recommended for school curricula. This established for the first time a mass, standardized knowledge of national fauna and flora upon which citizens could assert a national pride, interest and, later, concern and responsibility. Designated organizations and appellations such as the National Trust in Britain and,

later, World Heritage Areas demonstrate the link between animals and citizenship.

11 The foundation of international charitable organizations extended regulation, protection and Western notions of animal sentiments, especially to the Third World. Global interest was elevated and maintained through popular animal documentary genre and Third World states imposed restrictions on indigenous peoples' use of wild animal hunting in favour of managed international big game hunting tourists and safari parks.

12 Science laid a claim to expert knowledge and control over significant domains of animal regulation and policy (e.g. zoology, veterinary science, conservation, ecology, food and nutritional science). Science served to differentiate expert from popular knowledge and to distance laypersons from informed, significant or relevant opinion. The priority and status given to scientists in this period and their central relation to the project of modernity weakened and separated popular sentimental attitudes to animals from the scientists' use of them in pure or applied fields of science. Again, in this period the prior needs of social progress were expressed over and above the moral interests of animals, and the morality of the experimenters.

Animal luxuries

The emergence of mass consumption rendered formerly luxurious commodities more commonplace. Two luxuries that were formerly the preserve of the wealthy were of particular importance to the development of human–animal relations: meat and leisure.

Throughout the Western world, meat eating was a key register of social progress (Burnett 1966). Meat eating grew dramatically from the last quarter of the nineteenth century as a result of the further extension of grazing in North America, South America and Australia; intensive animal rearing developments; improvements in freezing technologies that permitted long distance exports; and the growth in effective mass demand. The production of meat became subject to the same process of rationalization as any other commodity production under Fordist conditions. Factory production concentrated meat production in smaller spaces; controlled feed, water and temperature efficiently; enabled the health of animals to be monitored easily; and cut down on inefficiencies resulting from 'unnecessary' animal movement. This particularly affected the rearing of pigs, chickens, turkeys and ducks, but egg and veal production and some beef and dairy techniques were rationalized along similar principles. The slaughtering, butchery and packing of meat was also rationalized and spatially concentrated: the Chicago stockyards being the exemplar case. Meat was a food strongly recommended by governments and health authorities in all Western countries. It featured in all pictures of ideal diets and was recommended in ever-growing amounts. However, the newly affluent workers required very little inducements to eat meat: it was a preferred food and the sine qua non centrepiece of all Western meals (Douglas 1975: 250–73). While meat was eaten unambiguously and vegetarianism considered eccentric for most of this period, the animals from which it came were surrounded in ambiguity.

Livestock, reared for their meat, were a highly ambiguous animal category throughout this period of modernity. On the one hand, as sentient feeling creatures and the object of human management, they were protected against cruel treatment. On the other hand, through genetic selection, husbandry and rearing they were also increasingly perceived as human products, the result of considerable human effort and therefore rightfully consumable like any other product. The ambiguity of domesticated livestock has been noted by others. Clutton-Brock (1995), for example, argues that through the domestication process, livestock animals are deemed by scientists to have lost their nature and are considered unsuitable objects for scientific study. Ingold (1994) notes how the truly natural was increasingly defined as untainted by contact with humans; that human contact and association denatures animals. Lévi-Strauss's analysis of food is also useful in understanding our ambiguity to these animals. In structural terms they are neither true nature nor truly humanized (as are pets), but nature worked on by humans. Lévi-Strauss shows that the category of edibility in Western society is, in part, defined in the same way. Pets, by contrast, are humanized to a considerable degree and are therefore inedible.

The paradox of livestock was marked by their spatial separation from humans. Livestock were completely removed from the British city in the first half of the nineteenth century. Until the passing of by-laws that prevented the keeping of animals within cities, pigs, chickens, rabbits and even milking cows were a part of city life. The new regulations marked a significant separation between humans and animals that was finally completed with the replacement of horses by motor vehicles. The slaughter and butchery of animals was an inner city and visible phenomenon until relatively late into the nineteenth century. In several stages, however, these industries were removed to outer areas and thence to greenfield sites in rural areas. The entire process of production, slaughter, butchery and packing was an entirely rural activity by the early twentieth century. The fragmentation of the production process was another new development of this period. Specialists emerged to cart animals to the slaughterhouse and thus separate the farmer from complicity in the killing. Husbandry was a wholesome, caring, nurturing industry, to be insulated from the stain of death and slaughter.

The entire farming enterprise was slowly reworked in the popular imagination along romantic lines: the obscurity and backwardness which attached to farming and rural life from the Enlightenment onwards was forgotten in favour of the nostalgic and pastoral. Farms were no longer sites of ignorant vulgarity: they were splendid survivals of a simpler, moral and natural living. The slaughterhouse itself was revamped and given the obscure euphemism *abattoir* (from the French 'to fell'). It was subjected to a process of rationalization and production line systems were employed. Most workers were separated from contact with whole animals and the act of killing was divided between two separate tasks (stunning and bleeding) so that no person was completely responsible for deaths (Vialles 1994).

While meat consumption has a long history in Western society, meat has only relatively recently been eaten with such regularity, on such a scale, and by so many. In Europe meat was relatively scarce until the latter part of the nineteenth century. Before then it was a high status food and many ate it only occasionally, rarely, or on special occasions (Franklin 1997). As meat was understood to have superior nourishment qualities, as well as being a marker of status, its merits as a food were compelling. Cheaper and more abundant supplies of meat, following the expansion of the industry in the USA, Australia and South America, were a clear marker of social progress, particularly because, even as late as 1870, the possibility of food scarcity was still a major political concern (Bartrip 1988). Moreover, livestock were not covered by the logic used to protect and senti- mentalize wild animals. Sentiments that accrued to wild animals were initiated by the acknowledgement of widespread destruction of habitat, diminishing populations and species loss. By contrast, in the nineteenth century livestock farming had prospered and spread and livestock were superabundant. However, better supplies arrived at a time when attitudes to animal abuse had reached generalized levels of repugnance. The superabundance and desirability for meat, combined with repugnance for killing, resulted in the ambiguity and reticence surrounding livestock animals. One resolution was spatially to separate the livestock industry from urban populations; another was to differentiate the animal from the meat. Such differentiation became increasingly more elaborate. In the earlier period butchers' shops displayed meat in a form where the animals were recognizable as hung carcasses and part-carcasses or semi-plucked birds. At the end of this period, however, the animal was no longer recognizable from the displayed pieces in the butchers' shops and supermarkets; the pieces were smaller, typically boned, skinned, plucked and filleted.

The second form of animal consumption to expand from its former elite status was in the sphere of leisure. Over the course of this period the growth of mass leisure significantly increased both the range and scale of human–animal relations. These can be summarized under three broad types or relation: pets, interest in and activities to do with 'wild animals', and hunting/angling. All three were first developed in their particular modern leisure form by the wealthy.

Pets were a narrow range of animals in the early twentieth century and more the preserve of the wealthier classes (Ritvo 1987: 177–9), but they became socially ubiquitous and zoologically more diverse as the century proceeded. Pet keeping became subject to differentiation: specialty societies or 'fancies' burgeoned first for animal species and then for the 'breeds' within any one species. Shades of distinction and class went as far as colour on occasions. As a major field of consumption and leisure, social identity was easily transferred to the fancy or to the species or breed in a quasi-totemic fashion. In this period, however, the social identity invested in pets mirrored social class: the wealthy kept pet ponies, the larger and more exotic pedigree breeds of dogs as well as the toy breeds and the Asiatic breeds of cats. Working-class pets were more likely to be crossbreeds of cats and dogs, the more 'vulgar' pigeons, 'fancy' rabbits, mice and caged birds. Pedigree animals, especially dogs, were the outcome of a nineteenth-century innovation which clearly marked the established and emerging distinctions, rankings and hierarchies among their owners (Ritvo 1987: 82–93).

Wild animals attracted enormous curiosity during this period, although interest varied considerably. Britain had eradicated most large and dangerous species in its own home territory and most people rarely saw its indigenous wild species except in books or in zoos. The surviving species lived in marginal areas, were nocturnal or semi-nocturnal or simply rare. However, they featured in many metaphorical stories which carried a variety of morally loaded messages on humanism, inequality, class conflict and nationalism. Indeed, indigenous animals were widely used as symbols of nation and citizenship. Also at this time, anthropomorphized, misanthropic and anti-hunting tales proliferated in Britain, as elsewhere. Misanthropic tales of the hunting of indigenous animals coincided rather awkwardly with other animal bestsellers: the colonial big game hunter stories, again ostensibly for children and teenagers. These contained several themes: the naturalization and dominance of Europeans in places such as Africa and India; the aggressiveness and danger of wild animals; the heroism of the hunter. Contemporary zoos housed these animals as dangerous captives (cages emphasized prison bars); like prisoners of war, they were put on public display for the entertainment of the victorious. The exotic wild animal became a source of exciting entertainment spanning all popular media: in children's adventure and pictorial books, cinema features and films and later in the very popular television documentary. In the USA and Australia a similar pattern evolved with the exception that one class of exciting wild animals was indigenous and 'at large'. As more familiar and acceptable symbols of nationhood, sensationalization gave way to sanctification. Indeed, the use of indigenous animals for national symbols and nation building shows how culturally specific and differentiated animal classifications became in modernity, in opposition to the flat uniformity of scientific classifications. Over this period wild animals began as a source of excitement/sensation/entertainment, often quite removed or distant from the animals themselves. But gradually, exciting entertainment gave way to new forms based upon study, education and tourism in which humans moved closer to their objects of interest. Natural history burgeoned. New natural history clubs and other societies such as birdwatching associations were founded early in the twentieth century. Walking, rambling and bushwalking clubs put natural history among their interests and concerns. Natural history was sold to children and adults in an ever-widening range of commodities: pictorial publications, equipment to support collection hobbies (butterfly nets, mounting equipment, birds egg identification books, for example), animal identification manuals, microscopes, aquatic study equipment, bird feeding stations and equipment, and so on. The interest was reflected in cinema features, typical of which were the animal drama documentaries made by Walt Disney. Television was launched at precisely the time when this form of interaction with and interest in animals was highly developed as a set of active pastimes. Building on this, television provided an increasing range of applications and rapidly realized the potential of animal programming to boost and maintain critical ratings at peak times of family viewing.

While the passive consumption of animals in leisure became a popular object of interest, other less passive activities thrived at the same time without any keenly expressed contradiction. Angling became extremely popular – the single most popular participation sport in England, the USA and Australia – even though it was essentially male. In these countries there is an undoubtedly masculine cult aspect to angling. This evokes the mysteries of ritual fishing trips between buddies, the essentially masculine father-to-son line of initiation and the ubiquity of local men's fishing clubs. In all three locations, the study of fish and their habitats and surrounds became part of the mysteries of fishing if not one of the most explicit reasons given for the pleasure gained. Only a few species were regularly eaten and, as we will see in Chapter 7, food-gathering motives gave way, albeit unevenly, to conservation and protection over the course of the twentieth century. Angling was very visibly class differentiated. Categories of fish and the valorization of different fisheries fractured along class lines and provided a rich source of cultural imagery for angling class cultures to develop. Hunting in Western societies has also become extremely popular, cultish and generalized as a masculine leisure pursuit. Over this period it was less confined to rural cultures (especially in the USA and Australia) and the social elite (especially in the UK and Europe). Increasingly, men from the city, beginning with a middle-class elite, began to take up hunting and to seek a place in the biotic order in the wilder parts of their country (naturalization). In the USA, Australia and New Zealand, for example, hunting became a mass male activity, affordable by all, and gained particular recognition as a significant ritual of male bonding between friends and fathers and sons. Educational, military, recreational and civilizing qualities were emphasized by the organized hunting fraternities, alongside semi-mystical references to Darwinian themes: the naturalness of killing, the need to express aggression, the need to hunt and so on. Summarizing we can offer the following characterization of human–animal relations in the first seventy years of the twentieth century.

First, the volume of interaction with animals has increased enormously. More animals were drawn into human contact either as pets, the object of nature study or in the hunting field. In addition to physical contacts, animals were principal subjects of media growth (entertainment and education) in the twentieth century.

Second, most of the interactions were explicitly anthropocentric: animals were clearly there for the pleasure and entertainment of humans and read explicitly for their leisure use value. Hence animals were a useful and popular educational stepping stone to the sciences. Conservation efforts were explicitly couched in terms of human consumption and needs for a nature in which to play and roam. Modern hunting and angling were physical extensions of the same idea. Meat was plentiful, guaranteed in supply and an essential food. It lost its status connotations and acquired a popular image reflecting the triumph of science and social progress.

Third, animals became central to the reconfiguration of leisure and identity in consumer society. At various levels of society animals became the signs and symbols of modern identities, including national identity, social class iden-tification and individual identity through the formation of new societies (e.g. angling clubs, birdwatching groups, natural history associations, pet fancies).

Fourth, sentiments were generally distributed evenly. Human control and domination of animals and the caring manner in which it was to be conducted reached an agreed upon consensus or hegemony. Science, the state, the media and the leisure industries were four powerful authors in this hegemony.

Fifth, despite the relatively peaceful terms of this hegemony, it was unstable and contained contradictory logics, ambiguities and, ultimately, self-destructing tendencies. Meat, hunting and animal experimentation were not completely benign issues, but because they were so spatially separated from urban centres and so confined to class cultures, it took time for them to become widely known. The media could not continuously recycle the same animal programme formats. When the market for general knowledge of animals in their pictorial and geo-graphical sense became saturated, they searched for new themes. In the 1960s, for example, the BBC turned to such issues as extinctions, animals facing danger from developers and principles drawn from ecology that challenged the possibility of separating human from animal interests in the global big picture. New program-ming such as *Survival, Horizon* and *Disappearing World* featured the plights of animals alongside those of indigenous peoples. The new sociations based upon specific leisure relations with animals began to reflect critically on the recreational and entertainment orientations of their leisure and to construct new fields of vision: the ecological, moral and ethical. Social identities formed from leisure and entertainment shifted to place the animal or the animal community as their object. Indeed, different leisure societies with such opposed interests as, say, bird-watchers and duck hunters, began to compete over the use of particular habitats and to lobby for new legislations. By the late 1960s the post-war cultural consensus was beginning to be challenged and to break down. In a period characterized by the arrival of liberation groups, it was not surprising that Singer chose the term liberation for the title of his book advocating animal rights. *Animal Liberation* (1990) was extremely successful and this alone demonstrated that views on human–animal relations were reaching beyond the consensus of modernity.

POSTMODERNITY, POST-FORDISM AND ANIMALS

Around the 1970s the fundamental pillars of Fordism and modernity began to look extremely shaky. The stable post-war economy collapsed and went into decline. The welfare state, built on the proceeds of economic growth and sup-ported by both sides of politics, came under attack from the political right. The large manufacturing base of the West went into decline and liquidation. The economic and political relations of modernity were rigid and unable to adapt to the difficulties they faced. In the 1970s the countercultures and social movements of the 1960s grew in strength and entirely new issues, socialities and values, often explicitly opposed to the consensus of modernity, came into being and thrived. In the vanguard, of course, were artists and intellectuals, musicians and political activists. It was a very young, university-educated vanguard. At the same time, another group of young people began to see an alternative means of achieving economic and political success. Grouped together, these new values and practices established something radically new which was given the label, very hesitantly (since everything now lacked strong definition), of postmodernity. As with the formation of modernity and Fordism, the implications for human–animal relations were going to be profound.

Postmodernity and post Fordism are potentially very confusing concepts. In both cases they may be taken to mean something entirely new and different from modernism and Fordism, or merely new extensions of modernism and Fordism, containing much that continues unchanged. The confusion arises not only because these two propositions are opposed but because they are both true to some extent. It is important to remember that these concepts are being used to trace change in key patterns of economic and cultural life in the twentieth century. There are no seams to this historic change, there are no dramatic events that usher in a new age, there are no particular people whose dramatic contributions have recast social relations. Rather, there were limits to the social conditions and growth of Fordism and modernity; there were internal contradictions that rubbed and worked free towards new resolutions; there were developments in Fordism and modernity that undermined the foundations of both. The history and theory of this transition are well-worked themes in the literature (see, for example, Harvey 1989: Chaps 9, 10; Lash and Urry 1987: Chap. 9) and need not detain us much further here. What is important for our purposes is to get a clear understanding of the origins and nature of the key changes that affected human–animal relations.

The love of animals in the late twentieth century

The scene is set first by a brief consideration of three key changes in human–animal relations in the period since 1970: first, an extraordinary further growth in the range of activities associated with animals; second, the politicization of human–animal relations; and third the decline of meat eating in the West. This is followed by a consideration of the reasons for these trends. It is argued that we can only make sense of this bewildering set of changes by relating them to the general social conditions and sentiments of postmodernity.

If the massification and extension of leisure relations with animals occurred in the first half of the twentieth century, this trend continued with a new vigour after the 1970s. Whereas it was possible to identify human entertainment and progress (through education, for example) as the characteristic object of relations with animals in the first half of the century, after the 1970s it is possible to discern a more differentiated and decentred set of objects, chief among which was a desire for a closer relation with animals and nature, a concern for the animals themselves and their well being, a search for new ways of accommodating animals in the global economy, involving difficult choices between human and animal interests, and an increasingly therapeutic role for animals in a more privatized, individualized culture.

Getting closer to animals　In the first half of the twentieth century it became increasingly easy to travel from the city to the countryside in order to see and interact with animals, while the city itself became nearly devoid of animal life. Most of this interaction was in organized leisure: weekend trips and holidays. After the 1960s, city dwellers extended their more enduring and close experiences with pets to include new urban interactions. For a start, urban nature was discovered in the parks, waste grounds, buildings, railway sidings, canals, and so on. Birds of prey, including kestrels and peregrine falcons, were discovered in major cities feasting on flocks of pigeons and starlings. Study groups were set up, minders protected their sites and schools and other parties came to visit. Schools and other institutions set up urban nature reserves on unused ground or redeployed former recreational areas. Suburbs were planned and built to include nature areas, complete with ponds, wooded areas, banks and other habitats. Populations of amphibians, birds and small mammals were encouraged. During the 1980s in Britain the fox, hedgehog and badger, which were all under threat in many rural areas, became established and secure in the city as animal lovers gave them breeding sites and food in their gardens. Grey squirrels and a wide variety of birds were given city tree nesting sites that were in decline in the country. According to *The Times* newspaper:

> London is emerging as one of the richest places in Britain for wildlife, as intensive agriculture, development and neglect push many species in the countryside to the brink. Experts who yesterday launched a conservation strategy for the capital backed by the Government, councils and charities, said that the range of plants and animals in London was proving remarkable. Surveys indicated that many rare species on the decline elsewhere, including the water vole, dormouse, marsh warbler and green-winged orchid, were surviving in London. Some sites in the capital deserve as much protection as the Sussex Downs or the Fens it was said.
>
> (*The Times*, 20 September 1996: 5)

In Australia at this time, suburban gardens underwent an extraordinary transformation: formal gardens of exclusively exotic European plantings gave way to a new fashion for Australian natives. Part of this Australianization of the suburb included finding space for animals. Possums, for example, formerly considered pests and removed from the city, were given nesting boxes and became the focus of much love and attention from their hosts. The Australian capital city, Canberra, built in the twentieth century, included in its plan the planting of thousands of trees to encourage parrots and other birds to live in the heart of the city. The emphatic message from all of this activity was that people wanted more animals and nature around them. Action days when local people are encouraged to gather along a river course or other site to clear it up, remove garbage, plant trees, install bird nesting boxes and so on have proved extremely popular. In addition, therapeutic motives were now as strong as the educational motives. This is evident in another 1980s development, city farms. Placed in inner city positions their purpose was to fulfil a number of therapeutic aims. Contact with animals was held to have beneficial effects on underprivileged urban children, many of whom, it was discovered, had never seen animals such as sheep, cows and chickens. Small groups were encouraged to take responsibility for feeding, cleaning and so on, and to benefit from cheap eggs, milk, yogurt and cheese. The elderly and infirm were brought in for an afternoon tea among the animals as a break from their isolated and housebound lives. The physically and mentally impaired, the depressed and mentally ill were encouraged to spend therapeutic time in the city farmyard.

The number of urban zoos and wildlife parks situated a short distance from large urban centres proliferated in this period. Again, the focus was quite new. The small, barred cages disappeared; the former emphasis on collections changed to one of specialism and breeding programmes, especially of endangered species. The mood of entertainment and spectacle shifted to one of empathy and moral support; the visitors paid large entry money in order to support worthy causes such as breeding and restocking programmes. An aura of dignified moral imperative prevailed. Increasingly, animals were kept in larger, micro habitats with an emphasis on their welfare and interests. Monotonous food regimes gave way to simulations of real diets; food was hidden and had to be found by the animals, encouraging 'natural' activity and preventing boredom. Humans comported themselves with solemn righteousness; they observed behaviour and animal cultures rather than antics.

Television and video brought animals into the living room in greater quantities and in changing formats. As interest in animals broadened and became more significant than mere entertainment and general knowledge, so new TV formats emerged. Children's TV continued to be dominated by animal characters and themes, but there was innovation such as the BBC's magazine *The Really Wild Show* in which punk-dressed presenters revealed the politicized terrain of human–animal relations in addition to a more hands on, interactive, custodial approach. The presenters were lay enthusiasts and activists rather than scientific experts (in contrast with, for example, Desmond Morris who presented *Zoo Time* in the 1960s, in his capacity as Curator of Mammals at London Zoo). This removed the barriers preventing much more than passive gazing and consumption, as had occurred in the 1960s. *The Really Wild Show* had a live, interactive audience of children who asked questions, handled reptiles and insects with care rather than with repugnance, and joined in a dazzling series of quasi-scientific activities with a strong moral basis. Scientific barriers also came down in new pet shows, where much emphasis was on do-it-yourself pet care, preventative medicine and advice on how to make informed choices of pets. The experts were more often than not representatives from pet societies. Animal documentary formats grew in terms of air time (culminating with their centrality on special documentary channels) and their emphasis changed. Again, the stress was as much on endangerment from humans as it was on animals themselves; documentary makers moved away from the pre-1970s accent on mammals and towards all genera, including micro, nocturnal and subterranean fauna. Attenborough's *Life On Earth* was the quintessential expression and apotheosis of this trend. Documentaries could be on any aspect of human engagement: from the anti-McDonald's theme in farming and rainforest, restocking schemes and in-depth anthropologically styled approaches to the study of animals, through to documentaries shot in urban settings and back gardens or the home. Moreover documentary makers employed the fly-on-the-wall approach to bring the intimate lives of animals closer to humans, decentring humanity by further reducing the perceived distance between humans and animals.

Companion animals From the 1960s onwards, pet keeping grew very significantly. For example, in Britain the numbers of pet dogs grew from 4.4 million in

1963 to 6.3 million in 1987; over the same period, cat numbers grew from 4 million to 6.2 million (Council for Science and Society 1988: 11–12). The morally questionable habit of keeping caged birds, popular enough until the 1960s, decreased considerably. The British budgerigar population dropped from 4 million in 1963 to 1.8 million in 1987; the importation of wild parrots halved during the early 1980s (Council for Science and Society 1988: 13–15). The keeping of mini-menageries grew in relation to affluence but also because the zoological range increased: stick insects, terrapins, tropical fish, ant colonies, snakes and lizards. Beehives, goats, chickens and other backyard farm animals all grew in popularity. Even where this new desire to be surrounded by animals did not run to menagerie keeping, there has been a trend since the 1970s of keeping dogs or cats in pairs. There are reversals in trends: the rat, loathed throughout modernity, is making steady progress as a pet, admired for its gentility and intelligence. The fighting dogs of the nineteenth century, which almost vanished in the twentieth, are currently voguish in some quarters. Indeed, the Staffordshire bull terrier was the tenth most popular dog breed in Britain in 1987, but relatively rare in the 1960s.

At some point over the past twenty years the term companion animal was coined and is rapidly becoming the politically correct term, while 'pet' carries negative connotations of plaything, and entertainment value. Recent fashions in dog breeds confirm this trend: toy breeds were the most popular in the 1960s but in the late 1980s they were not even making the 'top 10 breeds sold' (Council for Science and Society 1988: 12). However, this transformation is not cosmetic: in recent years the friendship and therapeutic value of pets has been vaunted as a significant discovery. The Council for Science and Society demonstrates a wide variety of applications from children's socialization and substitute friends during difficult periods, to assisting the recovery from heart disease, bereavement, isolation and loneliness, and maintaining mobility. Pets are used in the treatment of depression and schizophrenia, the care of the elderly, the terminally ill, seriously handicapped, and prisoners (Council for Science and Society 1988: 25–37).

There is also much evidence to show that pets have been drawn even closer into human society. New foods arrived in the 1980s featuring gourmet ingredients and recipes. Pet graveyards appeared, together with other (human) mortuary rituals such as obituary columns, church services and bereavement counselling. Pet psychologists, trainers and astrologers also became popular. In the 1990s the UK *Times* inaugurated a pet page, presumably because of new levels of public interest. We will argue in Chapter 5 that many of these changes in pet keeping suggest a movement from being regarded as mere companions and friends to becoming quasi or pseudo family.

Wildlife leisures Other leisure spheres involving animals demonstrate similar types of change. The rural leisure scene, which the new service class have made its own, has undergone profound change since the 1970s (Urry 1996). The consensus of the 1960s has given way to conflict and competition between rival groups. Bush walkers and nature lovers in the USA, Britain and Australia have maintained a spirited protest against hunters. Radical animal rights groups have taken direct action against organized hunters and shooters in addition to actions against fur farms, battery farms and animal experimentation establishments. In the 1990s their activity extended to disrupting anglers in Britain. But it is not simply extreme minority groups who are active in the protection of animals against hunters and others. Mainstream organizations with royal patronage, such as the Royal Society for the Protection of Birds (RSPB), are major players in animal politics. The *Electronic Telegraph* summed up the RSPB in the following terms:

> How is it that a charity that was founded by amateur birdlovers to cherish and protect a defenceless part of the animal kingdom has become in certain quarters one of the most hated organisations in the country, as reviled, if not more so, than the taxman, the traffic warden, and the VAT inspector? A vast and august organisation that exudes authority and patriotism, the RSPB couldn't be anything but British. It is the ornithological Church of England, only much more successful. Founded in 1904, it is today not just the biggest conservation charity in Britain, it is the biggest and most powerful in Europe, with an army of 925,000 members. If anyone thought for a moment that the organisation was happy to let that figure rest, a large coloured board in the entrance to the RSPB's headquarters in a vast Victorian mansion, near Sandy in Bedfordshire, puts you right. 'Let's Make it a Million', the board urges in coloured print. The RSPB doesn't put it so crudely, of course, but the million members will help attract the millions. The society's income last year came to just under £35 million, a vast inflow by anyone's standards, and in addition it owns or controls more than 240,000 acres of land throughout Britain.

> (*Electronic Telegraph* 570: 14 December 1996)

Animal rights organizations also find themselves opposed to environmentalists and the green movement which, in places such as New Zealand and Australia, advocate the eradication of introduced, non-indigenous animals in favour of a preferred type of landscape and biotic community.

The anglers and hunters have not remained unchanged over this period, however. Some English foxhunters have switched to hunting an artificial trail. Hunters in Australia avoid popular censure, deeply affected by a nationalistic environmentalist discourse, by concentrating their efforts on introduced 'pest' species. In the USA hunting ranches provide short-break, trophy-hunting experiences that involve killing 'stocked' animals in fenced-off areas, rather than the socially more valued 'wild' animals (Franklin 1996b; Hummell 1994). In some parts of the USA, the whitetailed deer, of Bambi fame, have been so protected from hunting that they have become an urban pest (*New York Times* 1996, reprinted in *The Age* 30 April 1996: 6). Clay pigeon shooting has grown relative to the shooting of real wild birds and less efficient methods, such as bow hunting, which keep the hunter in a low-impact, 'natural' relation to 'prey' animals, have grown in popularity, especially in the USA. In the Netherlands, hunters have to pass 'wildlife' exams before being granted a licence, and afterwards they are required to carry out certain wildlife conservation activities as well as pest control. Anglers in all Western nations have significantly modified the aesthetics of their sport. Beginning with British 'coarse' angling, the emphasis is more custodial and protective, with seemingly eccentric methods invented to reduce pain, harm and depletion. Fish are now routinely returned and rules to ensure safe treatment of captives have become increasingly refined. Great emphasis is now placed on the angler in the landscape as a knowledgeable, reflexive custodian, effecting positive outcomes in freshwater environments. Since these cannot be isolated from the wider landscape, anglers and their powerful associations are regularly involved in actions against rural and industrial polluters and are frequently the first to alert the public to the pollution of human water supplies. Again, what was once a sphere of idle, contemplative pleasure and entertainment has become politicized and, to borrow from Elias, civilized. Trout fishing, which involves a more sophisticated dovetailing of anglers with the aquatic biotic order, has grown rapidly at the expense of bait fishing; catch and release waters have increased in number and barbless hooks are now widely preferred.

The increase in contact with animals since the 1970s is nowhere more evident than in tourism and rural recreation. Making animal habitats visible and visitable, while at the same time ensuring a sustainable impact on the environment, is now widely preferred and in many ways cheaper than the staged entertainments and caged collections of modernity. Whale watching is a good example of this. Whales were scarcely a consideration up until the 1970s, but their rise in popularity and symbolic presence in the environmental movement testify to the zoological extension of sentiments in postmodernity and the enormous rise in energy given over to animal care. Whale watching began in vanguard sites along the Californian coast, but has now become a major tourist attraction around the world. All manner of aquatic animals that can be reached by unobtrusive boat parties are visited by caring tourists. Indeed many marine parks and heritage areas have been established in this period and national parks with a strong animal theme have thrived: photo safaris in Africa, diving holidays on the Great Barrier Reef and the Caribbean, Antarctic tourism. Other animal-based holidays have emerged: pony and camel trekking, ranching holidays, family holidays on sanitized 'working farms', rodeo workshops.

The demise of meat Meat eating has declined since the 1970s. First, the quantities of meat eaten have declined in response to health scares and raised thresholds of repugnance. Meat is no longer required to centrepiece meals or as a symbol of social progress; high consumption can indicate vulgarity. Meat is increasingly sold in marinades, stir fries or sauces as a pre-prepared meal with exotic origins, thus further disguising its animal beginnings; new boutique meats and game have appeared with 'wild', 'free range', 'stress free' or 'organic' labels. Farmers facing declining prices for standard modern carcasses have diversified to accommodate new tastes and stimulate fresh demand. Emus are now raised in Britain and wild gannet culls fetch premium boutique prices. Fordist mass-production, factory meat systems have attracted substantial criticism and sections of the service class avoid their products. A substantial minority have become semi-vegetarian. The Maclibel case in which McDonald's was involved in a potentially self-damaging civil case against two London critics attracted enormous public attention and highlights the contentious as opposed to the celebratory status of modern meat-based fast food.

Second, vegetarianism has grown substantially in this period. Because of the reflexive nature of postmodern culture, the causes of this are multiple, varied and often highly individualistic and quirky. These include health and safety reasons, disgust at farming methods, moral, ethical, sentimental, ecological and religious reasons. Lupton (1996) is inclined to view vegetarianism as eccentric but, as a reflection of postmodern anxieties among the service classes, it is quite consistent with other trends in human–animal relations. For those not bothered about the new ethical arguments, the avoidance of meat eating altogether on health grounds may be seen as unnecessary, but they are left with increasing anxieties about the risks involved, and have continued surreptitiously to reduce their meat intake. Meat scares now seem a routine occurrence: cholesterol, salmonella, bovine spongiform encephalopathy (BSE), Creutzfeldt-Jacob disease (CJD), and a variety of bacterial dangers: bST, *E. coli* and vanomycin-resistant entrecocci (VRE). The celebration of meat eating in modernity marked the triumph of mass production of sufficient animal protein. However, since the 1960s the industry produced the less-celebrated spectre of a meat glut. Fatty meat byproducts which had been introduced to raise profits from working-class consumption were tied unambiguously to heart disease, the treatment of which was very costly. New healthier forms of protein that were more efficient in terms of energy and land inputs, such as soya beans, soya bean products, other pulses, and nuts became widely available. Fish and sea foods that had declined relative to meat in the earlier part of the century were embraced with renewed vigour (Franklin 1996a).

The mood of increased concern coupled with the establishment of mass tender-hearted sentiments, the politicization of such concerns and increase in social movement type activities, the increasing desire to decorate the city with micro-habitats and contented animals, the perceived need to interact meaningfully with animals and to feel their benefits therapeutically are all postmodern trends, but how can they be understood socially? Is there a common meta-narrative in postmodernity that sheds light on these developments?

The first attempt to produce an explanation for this explosion of positive human–animal relations came not from sociology but from biology, in Kellert and Wilson's *Biophilia Hypothesis*:

> Which sought to provide some understanding of how the human tendency to relate with life and natural process might be the expression of a biological need, one that is integral to the human species' developmental process and essential in physical and mental growth . . . The biophilia hypothesis proclaims a human dependence on nature that extends far beyond the simple issues of material and physical sustenance to encompass as well the human craving for aesthetic, intellectual, cognitive and even spiritual meaning and satisfaction.

> (Kellert and Wilson 1993: 20)

Clearly, the biophilia hypothesis was a product of its own time, inasmuch as it embarks from the multiplication of pro-animal and environmental issues since the

1960s and draws upon many New Age themes, including the reverence given to indigenous peoples' cosmological relations with the biotic world. However, because the authors wish to create links between indigenous cosmology and the efflorescence of biophilia in the postmodern West, they do not dwell on the conditions producing each, but seek to impose an overarching, scientific narrative that renders history as merely the unfolding of natural propensities:

> The biophilia hypothesis . . suggests that when human beings remove themselves from the natural environment, the biophilic learning rules are not replaced by modern versions equally well adapted to artefacts. Instead they persist from generation to generation, atrophied and fitfully manifested in the artificial new environments into which technology has catapulted humanity. For the indefinite future more children and adults will continue, as they do now, to visit zoos than attend all major professional sports combined (at least this is so in the United States and Canada), the wealthy will continue to seek dwellings on prominences above water amidst parkland, and urban dwellers will go on dreaming of snakes for reasons they cannot explain.
>
> (Wilson 1993: 31–2)

Indeed, the origins of biophilia were formed in the somewhat mystical 'deep history' of evolutionary time (Wilson 1993: 32). The notion of 'deep history' is an inadequate device to place analysis beyond empirical–historical investigation and reduce history to genetics. Kellert and Wilson describe the biophilia thesis as 'daring', 'challenging', involving 'daunting assertions'. '[The] human inclination to affiliate with life and lifelike process is:

- Inherent (that is biologically based)
- Part of our species' evolutionary heritage
- Associated with human competitive advantage and genetic fitness
- Likely to increase the possibility for achieving individual meaning and personal fulfilment
- The self-interested basis for a human ethic of care and conservation of nature, most especially the diversity of life.

(Kellert and Wilson 1993: 21)

This thesis is fanciful and empirically flawed. If we can be clear about anything, it is that human sentiments to animals have altered in response to economic and cultural change.

People may always have liked animals but history teaches us that they like them in profoundly different ways under different historical conditions. Indeed, we can situate the appearance of the biophilia thesis during the 1980s into clear currents of contemporary change in human–animal relations. Since it was written by scientists, it can perhaps be taken as a knowledge claim stimulated by the increasingly marginal and criticized place of science in a number of animal-related and environmental issues. Scientists have been held at least partly responsible for modern environmental destruction, rationalization of animal husbandry, genetic engineering and animal experimentation. The biophilia hypothesis

restructures the relation between science and nature in a more positive light, and
enables scientists to transcend a dangerously critical popular discourse by
reducing it to core scientific principles such as genetics and evolutionary theory.
It legitimizes contemporary sentiments through a genetically driven functionalist
argument. While this may satisfy or even gratify some in the environmental
movement, it is nevertheless an attempt to replace the reflexive morality of late
modernity with a more fixed notion of human–animal relations that only science
can properly reveal.

However, the biophilia thesis contains a clue to a more fruitful line of inquiry.
The love of nature and by extension animals clearly references human emotion, or
rather the transference of human emotion onto nature. Under what conditions, we
must ask, would nature and animals become objects for the transference of human
emotions such as love, care, and protection? It is suggested here that three features
of postmodern culture provide these conditions: misanthropy, ontological
insecurity and risk-reflexivity.

Misanthropy. Misanthropy as it is used here refers to a general antipathy to
humanity as a species, rather than an individual dislike or hatred of people or
others. Specifically, it refers to those who see humanity as disordered: a species
which is out of control, deranged, sick or insane. This form of misanthropy was
evident in the early part of the nineteenth century if not earlier, and reached a
developed form among Romantics and social Darwinians. However, it remained
an eccentric position for most of the nineteenth century and the first half of the
twentieth. This is clearly because the modernity project cast human society in a
very favourable light. Modernity was about providing adequate nourishment,
clothing and medicine; people were to be educated, enfranchised and liberated;
working hours were to be reduced, wages were to rise and luxury goods to be
within the grasp of everyone. Modernity was a series of good works, and it was
possible for most people to sense this directly through their own lives and in the
lives of others. In the first half of the twentieth century the despoliation of nature,
ethical uncertainties in dealing with animals, pollution and so on were evidently
of great concern, but they were seen as the inevitable, regrettable compromise
– the price to pay for the greater (human) good.

A series of anthropomorphized anti-hunting books written in the first three
decades of the twentieth century were influential in their own right but did not
achieve Walt Disney's vast audiences for his pro-animal genre of cartoons
and films, beginning with *Bambi* in 1944. These genres stirred mass public
sympathies but did little to raise consciousness beyond generalized and fleeting
feelings of regret and guilt. As urban dwellers most could claim a benign or
indirect responsibility for the suffering of animals which occurred in distant, rural
places. The Nazi holocaust and World War II were directly responsible for the
eventual form in which humans were represented in *Bambi*. According to Cartmill
(1993), Disney was also personally disturbed by a hunting incident during his
childhood and remained firmly against it all his life. Disney's films always
conveyed the essential goodness of animals and the unpredictable treachery of
humanity. In comparison with humans, animals were good, peaceful, healthy and

sane. Misanthropy derived from a critique of modernity and saw not progress but regression: humans were bad, sick, dangerous and deranged. Cartmill has shown that influential intellectuals such as Freud and poets such as W.H. Auden subscribed to and promoted such a view (Cartmill 1993: 158). Humans frequently played the villains or spoilers, although it was more evident in the war-weary, post-1945 period. This relatively benign, sweet view of animals as better sorts of people than people themselves influenced every generation of the twentieth century, although, again, the mass appeal of this literature spread more widely after 1945.

When the modernity project crashed in the early 1970s and the political economy of post-Fordism became established in the 1980s, it was no longer possible to detect the greater good, while the human capacity to destroy the environment became more apparent. In place of full employment under the Keynsian economics of Fordism, there was mass unemployment, the long-term unemployed and the suggestion of an underclass. Entire regions were rendered idle and poor, while greedy new businesses made quick profits from asset stripping, takeovers and liquidation. 'New right' politics ushered in greater levels of overt competition, less secure employment, lower pay, less industrial bargaining and worker control. Their principal political target was to reduce public spending associated with the welfare state. The era was characterized by greed, loss, instability, disorder and change. These conditions favoured the extension of misanthropy Human destructiveness and ascendancy over animals was less easily condoned. The speed with which habitats were being destroyed, species were becoming extinct and populations endangered by pollution were identified with similar social processes. It became possible therefore to identify with animals under conditions of common adversity. The Green philosophy that human interests were directly tied up with those of animals became only too apparent. The essential goodness, sanity, and healthiness of animals stood in direct opposition to the values of postmodernity and provided a source of nostalgic longing. Thus, by bringing animals closer to human worlds, invoking a caring and loving relation towards them in which clear, morally good acts are identified and conducted, a philanthropic moral counterbalance is achieved in day-to-day life. Humans can be good and engage themselves in worthy acts.

In Giddens's discussion of life politics and the growth of environmental concern and action, he argues a similar line: that there are both institutional and individual implications for action; consumers must change their habits and practices as well as supporting organizations to promote change. But there is an emotional and moral content that is missing in Giddens's account which is essential to recognize in understanding postmodern human–animal relations. The difference between animals and environments is that the latter are perceived as abstract objects (e.g. the ozone layer, desertification), while the former are perceived as (anthropomorphized) subjects with many needs identical to those of humans.

However, the cultural centrality of animals in postmodernity is more complex than simply one of moral counterbalance. Animals can also provide emotional compensation for the loss of ontological security.

Ontological insecurity The churning nature of postmodernity, its lack of direction and plan and its distaste for government and bureaucracy creates, on the one hand, freedom, liberation and a perpetual state of change but, on the other, a sense of confusion, loss, unpredictability and anxiety. Giddens defines ontological security as 'a sense of continuity and order in events, including those not directly within the perceptual environment of the individual' (Giddens 1991: 243). This sense of continuity and order is achieved for people everywhere not only through their ability to interpret and account for the actions and events around them ('discursive consciousness'), but also because they possess a practical consciousness or a non-conscious, taken for granted set of assumptions that enables them to detect such things as normal behaviour and the expected responses and social compositions of everyday life: 'The notion of ontological security ties in closely to the tacit character of practical consciousness – or, in phenomenological terms, to the bracketings presumed by the "natural attitude" in everyday life. On the other side of what might appear to be quite trivial aspects of day-to-day action and discourse, chaos lurks. And this chaos is not just disorganisation but the loss of a sense of the very reality of things and of persons' (Giddens 1991: 36). Saunders (1984), Marshal et al. (1985, 1987), Newby et al. (1985) have all used the notion of ontological insecurity to describe the essential state of privatism and social isolation of modern individuals and cultures in the West. Some transformations took place such as the decline of local community and the stretching of social networks over greater spaces. During the past twenty years, a wide variety of social ties have weakened or broken in response to new economic and social reorganization. Family and domestic organization have fragmented into more fragile, smaller and ephemeral units; strength of ties and permanence of relationship are often impaired. In a rapidly changing social environment, it is unlikely that strong, enduring interpersonal commitments will be made to substitute for the strong, morally binding ties that formerly held the family together in the earlier part of the century, or the worker to the company or union. Rather, friendship circles and the new socialities – clubs, associations, networks and groups – involve forms of sociability that are more shallow, short lived, voluntaristic and tied to specific sites and activities. The postmodern social identity is potentially more fragmented across a number of sites, never achieving the solidity and continuity of the early twentieth century.

Giddens begins his book (1991) on social identity in late modernity with an illustration drawn from a recent study of divorce and remarriage. It is a good example of the double-edged nature of postmodern social change:

> The sphere of what we today have come to term 'personal relationships' offers opportunities for intimacy and self expression lacking in many more traditional contexts. At the same time, such relationships have become risky and dangerous, in certain senses of these terms. Modes of behaviour and feeling associated with sexual and marital life have become mobile, unsettled and 'open'.
>
> (Giddens 1991: 12)

One can extend the list of risks and dangers to all stages of the life cycle: the elderly can no longer rely upon familial support or company from their children and are more likely to be socially isolated; careers and housing markets can combine to make individuals put off having children altogether or until an income reduction is viable; few young adults can expect to secure a good job in their home town, among friends and relatives, and in a predictable and known local culture.

Under these conditions, individuals do not simply wallow in self-pity or suffer in isolation. Social identity becomes recomposed around new objects, and insecurities and anxieties find new forms of resolution. The self is no longer fashioned into a culturally specific and fixed set of contents, but becomes a reflexive 'project' with 'trajectory' and choice. Giddens and others understand the recent expansion of therapy as the result of these processes. We have already seen how animals have been used in a number of recent therapeutic applications, but the love of animals and the desire to have them closer to us can, in part, be related to ontological insecurities and new problems in establishing and maintaining enduring human relationships. Animals become substitute love objects and companions precisely because they can be involved in enduring relations of mutual dependency. Single person householders and childless partnerships frequently purchase an animal to love and keep them company and, as animals have been more routinely substituted for family, so attitudes towards them have changed.

In Chapter 5 it will be argued that recent trends in pet keeping can be understood as the extension of familial relations to non-humans. However, this relation is not confined to pets alone. One only has to think of the popularity of wild bird feeding during the depths of a cold winter to understand how this relation can be extended. Groups of Britons spend cold early spring nights assisting frogs and toads across perilous roads en route to spawning ponds (see Figure 3.1). Hunt saboteurs save their shorthorn, deer, fox and otter friends. Groups of Australian women across the country nurse and foster animals injured in bush fires. Birdwatchers everywhere get to know their birds. As a result of this increased familiarity, intimacy and interaction, the scientific principles by which we distinguish ourselves from animals have come under greater scrutiny and criticism. Jossica Newby's (1997) recent claim, for example, is that humans and their companion animals should be understood as a cultural unity – a view which privileges the shared communications between humans and other animals rather than differences in the medium of their separate modes of communication (Newby 1997).

Risk-reflexivity During the earlier part of the twentieth century, there were three types of space relevant to the consideration of animals: urban areas, intermediate development areas and marginal, wild areas. It was assumed that urban areas had been cleared of animals; that animals were in difficulty or under threat in development areas; and that they were relatively safe, if not protected by statute, in wild areas. There were vast, undisturbed tracts of land and ocean that were reservoirs of wild nature, and their existence provided a comforting buffer zone against the depredations of humanity, rendering the development zone a morally defensible compromise. From the 1970s onwards, this spatial trinity dissolved as encroachment into the wild areas grew apace. The Amazon was a benchmark of

VOLUNTEERS NEEDED FOR THE

- - - - - - - - - - - - - - - -

TOAD CROSSING

People of all ages are needed to help out on one or more evenings between 1st March and 30th April.

Contact _____

on telephone number _____

Bring warm and waterproof clothing, a good torch and a clean bucket. Those under 16 years of age must be supervised.

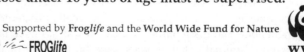

Supported by **Frog***life* and the **World Wide Fund for Nature**

FROG*life*

WWF UK

FIGURE 3.1   *In the UK volunteers assist frogs and toads across roads to spawning ponds (Froglife and World Wide Fund for Nature)*

global change and over the past twenty years the decline of its rain forest areas has been a regular news update item. The pollution, overfishing and whaling of the oceans is another instance. The status of the whales changed from relative obscurity to huge popularity as their numbers dropped to the endangered mark. Perhaps even more significant is the way in which all wild areas have been brought under human control so that there simply are no areas beyond man. Put another way, there is no wilderness or perhaps no nature since everything everywhere is subject to human control. No animals are safe and their only hope of survival lies with the willingness of humans to take moral responsibility for their protection. This can also be put in a different way: animals have become a human moral responsibility. National parks and wilderness areas are not secure, guaranteed habitats: they contain much valuable timber and minerals which may be 'cashed in' during times of rural recession, simply in order to secure the support of rural electorates. Increasingly then, the world's animals have been brought closer to humans and the relationship has changed. Now they are just like all other categories of animals and humans have to make decisions about their future; the world's animals are all dependent upon humans. So animals are cast as a permanent political fixture, and their consideration the duty of all citizens. An increasing number of people keenly feel the weight of this responsibility, and it is expressed in a variety of active ways.

CONCLUSION

In the West there were areas everywhere under threat. These drew widespread public support and governments could enact tough new protective measures to maintain electoral popularity, particularly from the cities. Outside Western nation-states, new organizations like Greenpeace were active and drew massive support of every kind, simply because individuals everywhere were persuaded that they had an individual moral responsibility to act. Although frequently obscured by the 'environment or ecology' blanket, there is no doubt that animals were the trump cards. Denuded, eroded and wasted landscapes, such as the Lake District in England with its dying trees, can unfortunately still look beautiful. This is because the Romantic movement developed an aesthetic taste for bare (essentially 'logged'), rugged and open hills. However, a starving or dying animal or a struggling population can invoke much more sympathy than an unhealthy ecosystem, particularly when the development creating the risk is done for so little material return or long-term benefit. This is typically the case for woodchip or beef pasturage. However, in a broader sense, animals were also the litmus paper of environmental risk: for example, the rapid decline of the North Sea seal population in the 1980s was taken as symptomatic of the condition of the waters. In this way the moral responsibility for animals precipitated by the globalized human control of nature was tied in with environmental risk factors. As individuals and institutions acted reflexively on improving sources of global information, creating anxiety about and responsibility for areas further and further afield, they extended the love and care of animals on a global scale.

Risk-reflexivity is also triggered by the sense of natural imbalances and distortions wrought by science and technology and the modernist 'project'. A key factor in decisions to eat less meat or become vegetarian is associated, in part, with the risks attached to the modernist mythology of a correlation between meat and health. Normative levels of meat and animal fat consumption were clearly a major cause of heart disease. Further risks have been found: the spread of salmonella in intensive production systems; BSE in cows reared on feed containing diseased animals; the entry of hormonal additives into human foods through meat and milk; the development of antibiotic resistant bacteria as a result of adding strong antibiotics to animal feeds. All of these incidents combine to reduce confidence and trust in scientific interventions in the food chain, and to create the growing demand for safer, more natural foods and diets.

Misanthropy, ontological insecurity and risk-reflexivity have been separated here for the purpose of exposition, but they are clearly related and coterminous in practice and they vary in salience among different groups and in different places. Certain groups of the service class, such as Savage et al.'s (1992) *ascetic-aesthetics* will be influenced by all three, but the argument being advanced here is that these are now so generalized in Western society that few will remain completely unaffected. The postmoderns identified by Savage et al., for example, tend to follow trends set by the ascetic-aesthetics, but the ubiquity of these three characteristics is not dependent simply on the influence of taste and lifestyle, but also on central organizing institutions such as labour markets, health, education and the mass media. The general state of reflexivity in the postmodern society, or what Giddens calls 'institutional reflexivity', represents a dynamism that replaced the fixed areas of knowledge and practice in traditional society. It is driven by a continuous flow of new information and knowledge of changing conditions and there are very few areas of social life that can remain quarantined from it. You do not need to have studied health or biology to understand the risk of animal fats: it is referenced in product packaging, advertising and restaurants; it is regularly featured in popular magazines and newspapers and TV; medical practitioners take cholesterol readings and advise against high animal fat intake as part of routine healthcare. Not everyone will become a vegetarian on the basis of animal food scares, but the majority appear to have reduced their intake. Similarly, the processes creating ontological insecurity are not confined to a minority in society. Restructured labour markets, high house prices in high employment regions, geographical mobility to employment centres, rural depopulation and so on are systemic changes with very wide ramifications for human–animal relations.

Strict social constructionists, such as Hannigan (1995) and Tester (1992), might want to go further in their interpretation of this material. They would want to show that human action and morality towards animals is a projection of ideal relations between humans. No doubt a compelling argument could be made to show that the warm, companionate, caring relationships expressed towards animals by humans in postmodernity relate to a longing for such relations to be re-established between humans. Although this view deserves serious consideration, and is certainly true at one level, critics would be correct to point out that such a conclusion seems to deny the integrity and morality of the human–animal relation, as if it were merely symbolic gesturing. Tester, for example, scoffs at the notion of human–animal relations on the grounds that animals are subjugated and incapable of rendering their understanding of the relationship in a manner that would be at all meaningful to humans. This has to be conceded, but the interesting point is that the literature is replete with examples of humans claiming the exact opposite: that a deep and meaningful relationship based on communication is possible between animals and humans (see Newby 1997). Such a view is well established in the lay literature and is beginning to find a respectable place in the scientific community. The launch of two new journals, *Anthrozoos* and *Society and Animals*, provides a forum for the development of these arguments. Although social anthropology is the discipline from which much of the symbolic analysis of human–animal relations derives (Douglas 1975; Leach 1964; Lévi-Strauss 1962; Willis 1974), setting the scene for a social constructivist orthadoxy, this is now under attack from a new generation of scholars. Recent debates in anthropology have questioned this orthodoxy with some powerful new theoretical reinterpretations of older material and new approaches in methodology (Descola and Palsson 1996; Ingold 1988; Rival 1993, 1996). Rival, for example, argues that the social constructivist position was based on interview material where the anthropologist searched only for the social logic of relations with animals. She argues that they rarely accompanied hunters on their expeditions or travels between camps, but it is in those situations that a more balanced view of their relations and understandings of animals can be made (Rival 1993).

It is not crucial to come down on one side of this argument or the other because it is possible for them both to be true: that is, relations with animals are indeed historically and culturally sensitive and, frequently, socially constructed. However, this is not to deny the moral and affective ties that exist between humans and animals at any one time. The latter seems to be worthy of more thorough empirical examination in contemporary Western societies, perhaps using anthropological methods of fieldwork which were designed to explore culture rather than behaviour.

The argument presented here makes a connection between some general conditions of postmodern sensibility and the general direction of change in human–animal relations since the early 1970s. But the historical transition from Fordism and modernity has also been analysed. This general framework will now be used to look at key areas of human–animal relations in more detail. Each of the following chapters considers a key area and examines it comparatively using the USA, UK and Australia as the main comparators.

4   THE ZOOLOGICAL GAZE

With the exception of a small number of species which have been drawn into companionate, domestic relationships, most people in the modern West live in relative isolation from animals. However, in most Western nations the demand to see and gaze at them has grown significantly over the past two hundred years, and particularly since the advent of mass leisures, mass transport, publishing and the visual media. In pausing to consider the zoological gaze, we seek to explain not only the desirability of looking at animals, but also why it has become so pleasurable and important in our lives. In the previous chapter we have suggested a framework for understanding the burgeoning of contact and interest in animals in modernity. In this chapter we focus on the historical transformations of the zoological gaze using that framework as a guide.

Looking at animals is considered desirable and pleasurable in all Western societies, but this attitude is neither confined to the West nor to the present. However, while the fascination and pleasure from looking at animals may be universal, it is not identical everywhere. People from different cultures and times look at animals in different ways. Animals convey meanings and values that are culturally specific; in viewing animals we cannot escape the cultural context in which that observation takes place. There can be no deep, primordial relationship underlying the zoological gaze since it must always be mediated by culture. Because animals are like us and different, they can be incorporated into discourses of similarity (of me, us, we, etc.) and difference (of they, other, etc.) within the social. Moreover, it is argued that although many might want to understand animals, we tend to understand them in terms of our own experiences, language and emotions. They are seen differently but understood socially. When zoos consisted mainly of animals in small cages, separated from the viewing public by iron bars, people were frequently reminded of prisons, the sadness of separation and punishment, and the high value placed on freedom, liberation and openness. Conversely, the recent popularity of whale watching from ocean-going boats is not merely the pleasurable sight of large marine mammals (difference): to see pods of whales or dolphins swimming freely in open oceans, frolicking and diving, evokes not only freedom, space and autonomy, but also family togetherness, nurturing and even leisure. We will go to some lengths to see large marine mammals in the wild but when we see them we are just as likely to say they are just like us. As Berger (1980: 2–4) reminds us, animals are silent, they have secrets and cannot reveal their thoughts. We have always to interpret, to provide the meaning for what we see, and for that we can only draw upon human values, emotions and interpretations. When we gaze at animals we hold up a mirror to ourselves.

Although this chapter will be concerned to examine how the zoological gaze has changed in the twentieth century and how we have organized and reorganized that gaze through changing institutions and social practices, all along the aim is to show its relation to important changes in society. To understand those changes only in relation to ethical debates is to miss the most important point. Shifts in ethics and new modes of interaction have a social origin and dimension. To understand these changes we must go deeper and delve into the social discourses that give rise to them.

This chapter is concerned specifically with those human–animal sites where the gaze is the principal if not the only objective. Considerable time will be devoted to the quintessential site of the zoological gaze, the zoo. To some people this may seem unjustified. Surely zoos have been superseded; they are outmoded and barbaric institutions, survivals of nineteenth-century values and culture. However, zoos have moved with the times and these changes offer us a good opportunity to analyse the shifting social constructions of the zoological gaze. In altering their format, content, aim and design, zoos have diversified into many new forms: thematic leisure centres such as the rising number of Sea World centres; wildlife parks such as San Diego Wildlife Park where the public views African and Indian animals in realistic landscapes from the vantage of a slow-moving monorail; safari parks where the visitor simulates the experience of close animal encounters; endangered animal breeding centres such as Howletts Zoo in southern England, which pioneered new techniques for breeding gorillas and Siberian tigers and where the visitor both learns about and contributes to the conservation movement. Indeed some private zoos became commercialized and opened their gates to the public, not because they wanted to sell leisure and entertainment, but because entrance fees would enable breeding and conservation programmes to proceed (Masters 1988: 212).

If zoos are outmoded they are certainly not less popular. The number of zoos around the world has grown dramatically during the twentieth century from 120 in 1920, to 309 by 1959, to 883 by 1978 (Mullan and Marvin 1987: 113). By the 1980s zoos still rivalled most other leisure attractions: San Diego and Washington zoos were both visited by over 3 million people annually; London Zoo by over 1.3 million; Berlin Zoo by 2.5 million; Ueno Zoological Gardens in Tokyo by 7.2 million; and Beijing Zoo by 8 million (Mullan and Marvin 1987: 131).

Although zoos continue to attract large numbers and have an especially strong position in the market for children's outings, they have become the subject of much criticism over the past thirty years and have lost some of their middle-class patronage. While the original purpose of zoos was to bring wild animals to urban populations who were unlikely to see them otherwise, transport innovations in the twentieth century have made it possible for more urbanites to visit wild places and see wild animals for themselves. A large number of public sector, voluntary, self-help and charitable organizations have promoted and organized this form of zoological gaze, notable among which are the field naturalists, birdwatchers and animal photographers. As a result of a robust growth in these organizations, the taste for merely seeing and knowing animals (an educational, scientific and behavioural knowledge) which characterized the first half of the twentieth century, has evolved into an aesthetic of their habitats and their character, particularly their struggle against a growing number of human impediments. As with pet keeping, a leisure interest has developed into a more emotional attachment. From the 1960s onwards the notion of an animal lover became acceptable, approved and indicative of a civilized attitude. Rural and wilderness spaces became politicized as they acquired 'habitat' and recreational status. The zoological gaze created a new rural interest group and lobby and some of its organizations, such as the Royal Society for the Protection of Birds in Britain, have gained enormous power and influence. These activities will be examined in later sections of the chapter, alongside one of their later elaborations, the discovery and development of an urban zoological gaze. These national organizations were the forerunners of later international animal organizations such as the World Wildlife Fund, Friends of the Earth and Greenpeace. Their members and subscribers were less interested in organizing the zoological gaze and consuming the sight of animals than in species and habitat preservation. By the 1970s this became a general feature: the recreational and entertainment content of the zoological gaze, both of which were anthropocentric in focus, gave way to a more empathetic and decentred content and a 'zoocentric' focus. It is possible to discern not only an increasing demand for contact with animals, supported by a rhetoric of therapeutic gain, 'naturalness' and natural benefit, but also the demand that passive consumption of animals should be replaced by active support, protection and communication.

THE CHANGING ZOOLOGICAL GAZE

Books about zoo history normally begin with the argument that zoos are neither modern nor Western in their origins. This is easily supported by evidence of collections of animals in ancient Egypt, Mesopotamia, Greece, Rome, China and Aztec Mexico (Bostock 1993; Mullan and Marvin 1987). Typically these collections were princely or stately, used as part of the lavish adornment of palaces, and a marker of status and power. They might have entertained and impressed court society and guests, but they were not always open for public display or entertainment. Wild animals, especially large or rare ones, have been significant in the content of gifts exchanged between princes and states: in the fifteenth century the Chinese emperor Yung-lo received the present of a giraffe from the East African kingdom of Melinda; in the twentieth century this tradition continued. The Chinese government has given pandas to the USA; Australia has given koalas to Japan (Mullan and Marvin 1987: 92, 149). The earliest modern zoos such as London Zoo and the Paris Zoo acquired much of their first collections from royal menageries, but it would be a mistake to infer a long continuous tradition in the organization of animal displays. Mullan and Marvin's *Zoo Culture*, for example, tends to overemphasize the continuity of institutionalized collections, from ancient to modern princely menageries and from these to the more public and scientifically based zoos. This ignores the significance of small, travelling, commercial animal displays which, until the opening of the larger metropolitan zoos in the late nineteenth century, were how most people in the West viewed exotic animals.

From the sixteenth century onwards Europe expanded in all directions after having been more or less confined to its old borders. New explorations and discoveries encouraged interest in all manner of natural and cultural phenomena. A market for exotic animals emerged by the seventeenth century and although some were bought for private collections, others were bought for public display. Up until the mid-nineteenth century, the pattern of leisure in Europe was quite different. The most significant feature or highlight of the leisure calendar were local festivals, or revels – survivals or remainders from the medieval carnivals. These were annual, often week-long events, at Easter or Whitsun. The various activities which comprise such events were carnivalesque, a series of inversions of normal day-to-day life, including much inebriation, sexual activity, dancing, play acting, sports, music and entertainments. While much of the content was specifically local, professional travelling entertainers introduced exotic novelties. Building on an already popular diversion, the baiting of an exotic animal was probably one of the first means by which most British saw non-indigenous wild animals. Many of these travelling entertainments, however, were based on the brief gaze: customers paid for a fleeting glimpse of such exhibits as human freak shows, historical or religious artefacts and exotic animals. Only in London were menageries open to the public for most of the year. The royal menagerie was located at the Tower of London and from 1770 there was an infamous commercial menagerie known as the Exeter Change which featured a large collection including a 'unicorn' (rhinoceros), zebra, wolf, tiger, jaguars, an orang-utang, python, bison and monkeys (Bostock 1993: 26).

It was a characteristic of these menageries that a large number of animals were crammed into a very small space. This was partly to do with the logistics of a travelling show, but also the concentrated nature of the exhibit was related to its purpose as spectacle. The public could get quite close to the animals and were guaranteed a good view. Cages were made of iron bars, were very small and of uniform rectangular shape which gave the animal no respite from the public gaze. As with other exhibitions of this kind, the object of their gaze was spectacle. The public were to be roused into a pleasurable delight based on strangeness, grotesqueness, dangerousness and otherworldliness. The gaze was frightful, exciting, hideous. Because the animals were little more than monsters, the idea that they should have restricted movement in prison-like accommodation was perfectly consistent, sensible. To lavish homely comforts on them would diminish the effect. In any case, the audience had no idea whatsoever about the animals' natural habitat, other than that perhaps this too was dangerous and probably unpleasant. The idea that they had a home which might be simulated as a condition of their captivity was not and could not be considered. Instead they were aware in a heightened manner of the conjuring of the animal, especially its body, from an unknown place to the here and now. But the voyeur was also moved, momentarily. Animal menageries were typical of the carnivalesque: they created a liminal zone into which people stepped from their normative day-to-day world and were suspended in a halfway space. Crudely speaking this space might be described as between culture and nature, or this worldly and other worldly, Britain and darkest Africa, or 'home' and the 'frontier'. Nothing distracted the gazer from this dark, sensory pleasure. The brevity of the glimpse prevented, perhaps, the opposite realization, of familiarity, sameness. The structure of the menageries as buildings or frames for the gaze were plain, purely functional and non-distracting. There were no extraneous, decorative embellishments to detract from the full impact of otherness, or to domesticate it, to render it more acceptable, normative. Indeed, it is characteristic of the carnivalesque, rooted as it was in the social permanency of the feudal regime, that social inversions and the return from liminal experiences were functional to the reproduction of social order.

The experience of the menagerie reinforced, through a look into the terrible spectre of the other side, a sense of belonging to a superior, civilized and ordered society. It positively confirmed the civilizing influence and European ordering of the New World. It maintained a sense of superiority which was based on an inflexible, ordered social hierarchy. This was the zoological gaze before social progress and egalitarianism became a powerful driving force of modernity. Up until the late eighteenth century and into the nineteenth, this was how the majority of people experienced exotic wild animals. It must be remembered that the menageries travelled to the provinces and to rural communities, reaching ordinary, uneducated people. Their view of animals, arguably underrepresented in Thomas's (1983) *Man and the Natural World*, has left few documentary traces, but the singular archaeology of the animal menagerie which has survived from some earlier memoirs also show traces that among the better educated the menageries were considered brutal. In the immediate post-revolution years, Thomas Hood's poem based on the Exeter Change menagerie is a satire in which the animals liberate themselves; an event not without French parallels because the revolutionaries also insisted on liberating the French royal menagerie at Versailles. The intended humanity of the poem is reinforced by the satire:

> To look around upon this brute-bastilles,
> And see the king of creatures in – a safe!
> The desert's denizen in one small den,
> Swallowing slavery's most bitter pill –
> A bear in bars unbearable. And then
> The fretful porcupine, with all its quills
> Imprison'd in a pen!
> A tiger limited to four feet ten.
>
> (Thomas Hood 1965: 206, cited in Bostock 1993: 26)

The widespread liberation of captive animals did not result from the French Revolution or the work of late eighteenth century poets. However, the transformation from menageries to recognizably modern zoos did involve major changes in the zoological gaze. The royal menageries in France, for example, had been opened up to the scientific as well as the public gaze before the Revolution and clearly, from then on, the zoological gaze could be not merely spectacular but also educational. Moreover, the world was smaller and the colonial discoveries became less the object of wonder and spectacle and more routinized in the content of education and scientific investigation. Widespread familiarization was achieved in the French royal menageries, and the inclusion of exotic animals in highly stylized, extensive decorative gardens, complete with picturesque oriental architecture, highlights how they also became ornate and domesticated. These spacious, decorative, domesticated and familiar spaces in which to view animals encouraged a leisurely, relaxed form of gaze, with the emphasis on recreation. Animals became additions to gardens and the zoological gaze became influenced by the habit of walking, strolling in formalized gardens and parklands. Although the building of private parklands and gardens and an interest in the educational benefits of zoology were more or less confined to the social elite in the eighteenth and nineteenth centuries, both were to feature in the approved leisure pursuits recommended to the working class in the nineteenth-century city. Modern zoos were going to be different because they were orientated to a popular market. In order to understand the emergence of modern zoos, it is critical to understand how popular leisure was transformed in the nineteenth century.

Working-class leisure was reshaped by nineteenth-century bourgeois reforms in two main ways: first, particularly in the first half of the century, through the passing of new urban regulations which effectively outlawed many of their previous leisure pursuits; second, particularly in the second half of the century, by recommending and promoting through voluntary associations and religious organizations a series of rational recreations. 'Through it the bourgeoisie sought to bring about moral improvement, not by physical repression but by example and persuasion' (Rojek 1993: 32). We have already seen how rapid urbanization in the first three decades of the nineteenth century resulted in the introduction of regulations or urban bye-laws designed to change working-class comportment and behaviour (Daunton 1983: 12–15). A considerable number of bye-laws in English cities targeted rural sports and leisure which had been imported by the migrants. In particular, gambling, racing animals (greyhounds and horses), animal baiting, cock and dog fighting were outlawed. Daunton shows how the redesign of nineteenth-century city planning and housing from a system of closed courts with semi-communal courtyards into a grid system of open terraces gave working-class communities fewer opportunities to control their own immediate leisure space. They were more exposed to public scrutiny and the newly formed police forces. However, the cities were not simply repressive: mixed with their intolerance of certain behaviours was a strong sense of paternalism, leadership and improvement. The working class lost their courts but in most areas they gained from the new municipal sense of responsibility to provide adequate recreation of an approved type. City parks, gardens and playgrounds, modelled on the parks and gardens of the wealthy, were included in all Victorian city developments. They were laid out in lavish style with elegant plantings, shelters and lawns, often with sporting facilities. The earliest zoos were inextricably linked into these municipal reforms of leisure.

The first prospectus for the Zoological Society of London (opened 1827) was perhaps the first formal statement of how the zoological gaze was to change in modern zoos. The words of its author, Sir Humphrey Davis are worth repeating:

high aims for zoos

It has long been a matter of deep regret to the cultivators of Natural History that we possess no great scientific establishments either for teaching or elucidating zoology, and no public menageries or collections of living animals where their nature, properties and habits may be studied . . . Should the Society flourish and succeed, it will not only be useful in common life, but likewise promote the best and most extensive objects of the scientific History of Animated Nature, and offer a collection of living animals such as never yet existed in ancient or modern times . . . animals to be brought from every part of the globe to be applied either to some useful purpose, or as objects of scientific research, not of vulgar admiration.

(Cited in Mullan and Marvin 1987: 109)

Although the scientific foundation of the zoo was emphasized, developing a zoological science and exploring 'useful purposes' to which animals may be put was only part of the project. Apart from training zoologists, a general knowledge of animals was to be encouraged in the general public. The object of the popular zoological gaze was instruction or improvement, an activity entirely consistent with rational recreation. The model or medium for this instruction was clearly the museum. The museum or art gallery belongs to high culture, which includes not only the institution, its discipline and staff, but also its objects, their finders, creators or performers. In museums and galleries the public is reverential or solemn before such high culture; they are quiet and orderly and children are kept strictly under control. Although mainly superfluous, attendants stand guard over the collections and keep watch over the visitors' discipline.

When London Zoo first opened it was reserved for the Society's members only. Only later did members of the public have access to it. The entry fee was designed to keep the vulgar classes away, but whether it achieved its stated aim of reducing vulgar admiration is a mute point. From its very inception until the 1960s the recreational qualities of London's zoological gardens, and others of its type, have not achieved the serious high aims of its early prospectus writer. The significance of the animals appeared to lie in their entertainment value and it is easy to see why. Unlike the objects of high culture which were venerated, precious, even sacred, animals at that time were clearly subjects of humanity, useful for their service and value to society. Exotic animals with some commercial value were constantly sought and London Zoo brokered such animals for colonial acclimatization programmes. Zoos also provided animals such as monkeys with which to conduct experiments that would benefit humans. Exotic colonial animals were held in the same low esteem and standing as other colonial cultures; they could be odd, funny and stupid as well as treacherous and dangerous. Zoos were about social progress; they were safe diversions, rational recreation, approved leisure. Being amused by the 'antics' of animals was harmless, clean fun. The educational gloss was not completely bogus. People could become aware of zoological diversity and minimal other data about exhibits, but zoos were more like gardens than museums, more artifice than nature, and the information about animals was scarcely more than the labels on plants or trees. Mullan and Marvin argue that this lack of respect or regard for animals as high culture had to do with the gaze itself:

Zoo visitors tend to respond to living animals not simply as creatures which have a separate existence and separate identity from human beings but as reflections of themselves (or at least of something human). In the zoo the activity of the animal stimulates a response in the viewer which is not that of desire to understand something about animal behaviour per se. Behaviour is certainly interpreted, but it is interpreted as though it were motivated by human-like emotions or needs: 'It is sitting like that because it is sad.' 'It is splashing about in the water because it is happy.' . . . In a natural history museum animals cannot . . . elicit this response – they are merely objects. The fact that they are dead and arranged in terms of some zoological schema in a glass case is a proclamation of their scientific status. Viewers cannot so easily fantasise about them or imagine mental states for them; they are specimens. They are representations of real animals and in their fixity they are in some real senses equivalent to any other museum object.

(Mullan and Marvin 1987: 123)

Arguably this is simplistic, ahistorical and confusing. By ignoring the cultural status of animals at that time, as well as the centrality of human interests in the institutional zoo, which in this case was first rational leisure and second education, they appear to suggest that human responses to captive animals are timeless, inevitable. To say that people will always interpret animal behaviour in human terms is not to account for the peculiarly condescending manner in which animals in the late nineteenth century and the first half of the twentieth were viewed. It is not merely that people 'see themselves in animals' but that they read animals socially. Perhaps this is what the authors meant by their somewhat cryptic and unhelpful addition, 'or at least something human'. This is a very different proposition because the particularly infantile reading of animals in zoos of this period reflects not how viewers viewed themselves but how they tended to view others, particularly non-Europeans. Until fairly recently it was quite usual for non-Europeans to be represented as infantile and, worse, animal-like. Because zoos mainly contained exotic, non-European animals, this form of colonial condescension was clearly extended to them. The zoological gaze is not merely social and cultural, it is also historically specific.

Mullan and Marvin also ignore the way in which zoo animals were set up to be infantile, amusing and entertaining. There was certainly nothing inevitable about the chimpanzees' tea party, which was the main attraction at London Zoo from the 1920s until the 1970s. The willingness to reduce the zoological gaze to human entertainment value is clearly demonstrated here. The tea party was a set piece of comic theatre. As the former curator of mammals at London Zoo explained, the chimps had to learn this role, 'they had to learn to misbehave' (Morris and Morris 1968: 68, cited in Bostock 1993: 34). Moreover, they wore human clothes and acted out a human social meal. This was not a one-off: zoos during this period gave plenty of cues as to the appropriate manner in which humans, especially children their main clientele, were to relate to their animals. The animals were there to provide fun and games; elephants and camels were made to give rides; cheetahs were made to go on walks; llamas were made to pull carts. According to Bostock 'the "wolf man" in London zoo . . . used to take wolves for walks and wrestle with them' (Bostock 1993: 34).

Natural history museum exhibits are not acceptable high culture merely because they are dead or arranged scientifically; it is because museums themselves are a vehicle for the operation of high culture. High cultures are an epiphenomenon of nation building and of nationalism. Museums can be seen both as the way in which a nation choses to see itself constituted historically, and as triumphs of national culture, the treasure chests of the nation. The British claim to expertise in natural history belongs to a narrative of imperial dominance, in which its scientists and naturalists could make pathbreaking discoveries through scientific expeditions to any part of the world. But its collections were also the envy of the world.

From their inception then, modern zoos differed from the earlier commercial menageries in their middle-class institutional approval and educational, scientific gloss. The object of the gaze was also different. Zoos were less about spectacle and more about entertainment. There was nothing particularly liminal in the setting and archaeology of the zoo; it recreated an ideal (affluent) domestic background and animals were in various ways either ornamental or domesticated. No attempt was made, for example, to simulate natural habitat gardens in zoos, despite the considerable knowledge and ability of the Victorian gardener. Instead, the lavish, eye-catching gardens were formal and concentrated on shows of blooms, merely superior versions of most people's domestic gardens. The plantings were not in groves, clumps or dells to simulate natural forest, scrub or forest edges, but in the serried ranks of a formal 'border' or shrubbery. In some early twentieth century American zoos the animals' cages were framed in ritzy art deco furniture and furnishings, and so came to resemble more the International Arts and Craft Exhibitions, forerunners of ideal home exhibitions. The animals merely provided a decorative interest to a design piece or architecture which was worth seeing in its own right.

For the most part, zoological gardens of the nineteenth century used cages with iron bars or wire and some animals, such as the big cats, were no better off than they had been in the travelling menageries. Their average life expectancy in the early years of London Zoo was two years (Bostock 1993: 29). There was also an emphasis on having a large collection rather than a healthy, happy collection. Short-lived, single, sulking specimens in small cages were the norm in the nineteenth century. These cages obscured a perfect view of the animal and their prison-like form detracted from the high jinks entertainment atmosphere that the paying public grew to want. In many European zoos therefore the architecture of the animal houses also came to vie for attention, in a bizarre way, with the animals themselves. London's elephant and giraffe houses were visual puns: based on an elementary, children's toy house design, they were respectively 'giant' and 'tall'. As accommodation for these animals they were completely inappropriate. Elsewhere the humour was lacking but was more than made up for by exotic architectural grandeur: Berlin built Chinese pagodas and Indian temples; Antwerp built an Egyptian temple; Budapest built African huts, Arabian temples and mosques. Setting animals alongside entertaining human architecture was one innovation; more open *trompe l'oeil* designed enclosures were another. When Carl Hagenbeck opened his zoo in Hamburg in 1907 several things were new. First, animals from warmer climates were no longer kept in heated indoor accommodation. Second, enclosures were designed to separate animals from the public and each other using concealed moats. Third, mini-panoramic scenes were created in which animals appeared to be free and together in a sort of naturalistic collage. Hagenbeck designs caught on and were reproduced widely. They were cheaper to maintain in the long run and because the main material was concrete they were durable. By this method some animals had more space and many were healthier outdoors, but essentially this was an innovation in entertaining design; the animals were still confined, even more exposed and just as bored. However, perhaps one should not expect a major challenge to the zoological gaze from someone who also displayed (and introduced for the first time) non-European humans: 'whole groups of Lapps, Nubians, Eskimos and many many more' (Bostock 1993: 31). Coming from a background as a wild animal catcher and trader and with noted skills as an animal trainer, it is not surprising that Hagenbeck progressed into the zoo business and improved on its showbiz appeal.

Under Hagenbeck's influence, zoos of the first half of the twentieth century drifted away from lofty ideals about instruction and improvement. Zoos were in the children's entertainment business and as the century progressed they faced stiffer competition from new sources, particularly the cinema. The new 'sets' and theatrical routines performed by the animals made zoos closer to circuses than museums. Like theatres and circuses, the zoos had to generate new attractions, new acts. Under the secretaryship of Chalmers-Mitchell in the 1930s, London Zoo introduced a long sequence of new attractions. First, in 1931 they introduced the concept of larger scale enclosures and wider open spaces on a par with deer parks in stately homes or parkland farms. Whipsnade Zoo in Bedfordshire was set in 500 acres in an attractive rolling landscape, with buildings designed by Berthold Lubetkin. Ungulates could eat real grass and run for the first time and viable breeding groups could be established. It was a major attraction and part of its success can be put down to its similarity, in terms of the zoological gaze it offered, to other countryside-based 'serious' leisure pursuits of the 1930s which also had a natural history content. Second, in 1938 London Zoo introduced a penguin pool into the main zoological gardens. The pool, another Lubetkin design, has been vaunted as a twentieth-century classic, even significant in 'widening the acceptability of modern design'. According to Pearce (1991: 88), 'the coincidental link between the penguin's black and white plumage and man's formal evening dress brings to the London Zoo's Penguin Pool the atmosphere of a 1930s film musical', clear evidence that the zoo was competing with the movies. This set was indeed stylish but there was perhaps for the first time a sense that human entertainment must be consistent with the needs of the penguins. The project had a strong sense of humanism, which was evident in the brief and choice of architect:

> That the pool has an air of being a set is, however, no coincidence, for its designers, Lubetkin and the Tetron Group, had been briefed by Sir Peter Chalmers-Mitchell . . . that it should be a showcase for the penguins, giving maximum scope for their natural tendency to congregate in groups, as well as providing surfaces to dive from and a large swimming area. Without becoming embroiled in the issues of the moral rightness of

zoos in general, it is notable that this represented a new humane attitude to the zoo's exhibits, an attitude which was reflected in the choice of Lubetkin, who . . . is chiefly known for his strong social commitment, exemplified in the Finsbury Health Centre and his proposed, but never realised *Project for Working Class Flats.*

(Pearce 1991: 88)

This design attended to both the aquatic and land needs of the penguin, and the rendering of high-modern materials into an abstract arctic landscape signalled good accommodation and natural setting. It may well have set a new course in the development of the zoological gaze, because the penguins responded to their accommodation by acting and interacting almost naturally, apparently oblivious to their human onlookers, whose view was restricted to a relatively narrow viewing aperture. It was as if they were peering into a pool of penguins from within the landscape itself. However, although new and delightful, it was still very much in the old genre: to all intents and purposes here was an artificial 'set' of performing penguins. The pool had the look of an expensive human swimming pool; the penguins splashed and played as if on a seaside holiday and were thrown fish to dive for at special feeding times. This lavish set was obviously also seen as lavish accommodation. Rather than merely laughing at their childish antics, the gaze shifted occasionally to awe (their swimming skills were impressive relative to humans) and envy (they lived in apparent luxury). As *Mother and Child* magazine noted in November 1938: 'How many citizens of London have brooded over the railings of that pool, envying the penguins as they streak through the blue water or plod up the exquisite incline of the ramp – and have wondered sadly why human beings cannot be provided, like the penguins, with an environment so well adapted to their needs' (Pearce 1991: 89). However, the luxury was only an illusion. The pool was not really deep enough to allow the penguins to swim properly; the lighting and temperatures were not realistic and their lives were entirely artificial. These animals were merely actors on an expensive stage.

Chalmers-Mitchell had further plans for showbiz-style attractions at London Zoo in the 1930s, a cinema and nocturnal house. World War II intervened before the latter could be built, but the Society objected to the cinema out of concern for 'the prestige of the Zoo as a learned society' (Huxley 1970: 237–40, cited in Bostock 1993: 34). Given the degree to which the zoo had already become a circus this may seem strange, but it reflects more on the moral doubt about cinema as appropriate leisure than the principle that zoos should offer entertainment (Durant 1938).

One can really only understand the changing zoological gaze in its social context. After 1945 the Western nation-states were modernized and the modernization project was heavily influenced by welfarism and the building of a mass affluent society. Reacting strongly to the socially disastrous depression years of the 1930s, this period was dominated by a series of state-led reforms of key areas of consumption, namely housing, health, education and urban infrastructure. In addition, governments maintained policies of full employment. These represented major benefits to the working class and the spirit of the period was of social gain. A popular working-class majority dominated the main discourse of need and reform, and the universal provision and guarantee of basic needs represented a massive boost to the booming Western economy. In a relatively short period of time Western nations went from austerity to affluence and as they did so zoos had to compete with a growing range of mass leisure industries. Increasingly in the post-war period, the working class increased as a proportion of all zoo visitors. Everyone could expect to participate as consumers in the mass leisure industry. Thus the zoological gaze was dominated by the need to provide fun and amusement, under conditions of considerable competition. In other words it was an anthropocentric gaze, focused on the maximization of human pleasure. This mood of consumerism began to break down slowly from the mid-1960s and gained pace during the 1970s. It did so in a manner which questioned many of the moral and ethical dimensions of progressive modernization. Zoos were changed absolutely and fundamentally as a result of the postmodernizing trends of the last thirty years of the twentieth century.

Several changes in this period can be highlighted. The investment in a mass higher education system in the West produced the first generations of college graduates. These liberal, progressive institutions encouraged a decentred and critical view of modernity; blind consumerism, the effect of unchecked economic growth and the distributional system were all in question. Hitherto silent groups in society emerged with new claims to voice, rights and liberation. The list includes the women's movement, civil rights and black power, groups based on sexual orientation, the mentally and physically disabled and indigenous peoples. Moreover, although these were interest groups they were arranged within a discourse of change, democracy, mutual self-help and cooperation. It was a coalition of issues gathered around principles of rights. New issues flowed logically from the rights and liberation principle, as did sympathy, support and new organizations. Tester (1992) has shown how the animal rights movement, beginning with Singers' (1990) *Animal Liberation*, was just such an extension of human principles.

It might seem odd for an essentially humanitarian movement to cross the species boundary, but in many ways animals were a perfect issue or platform for the expression of these values. First, animals were a silent majority. In the global community of species, animals outnumbered humans. Second, they suffered manifold forms of exploitation and oppression by man and a crisis could be pointed to – the destruction of complete ecosystems and the extinction of species. Third, animals were defenceless against development and habitat destruction, pollution and commercial exploitation. As with the early years of black civil rights and the indigenous rights movement, such a silent, helpless and deserving cause generated strong paternalistic sentiments among the white, educated middle classes. The animal rights movement, however, was modelled on a protocol of political correctness which emerged in liberational politics at this time, namely that liberational groups should be autonomous and self-determining. For this reason, practically all contact with animals by humans was considered inappropriate: the pet–human relationship was one-sided and condescending; with the best intentions zoos were prisons and ghettos. As a result of this view, animal rights activists marginalized themselves, as we shall see in Chapter 9. However, perhaps the more significant protocol to emerge in this period was one of mutual support and cooperation. To this end difference became something which was to be both 'celebrated' and supported, but also examined: it was incumbent on people to learn about other cultures, other environments and by extension habitats and 'beings'. Arguably, animals were the ultimate challenge in this new ontology, and the species boundary became one of a long series of boundary walls which were challenged, crossed and bridged at this time. It was no coincidence that a new branch of zoology claimed that, like humans, animals also had culture and that anthropological methods were an appropriate research instrument.

As multiculturalism became embedded in complex national formations (particularly those such as the USA and Australia with significant migrant populations) and across nation-states (such as the European Community and United Nations), it was perhaps consistent with the manner in which animals were arranged socially that the natural world should be seen increasingly as an important community. This ecologistic vision maintained a rhetoric of human self-advantage, that it was in human interests to maintain a viable and rich ecosystem, but arguably it was profoundly influenced by the decentredness of postmodern sensibilities and by the exercise of individual and corporate restraint in favour of common interests. In this climate of change the principles of zoo keeping, management and design were radically altered. The zoological gaze was re-examined and refocused.

DECENTRING ZOOS

From the 1970s onwards it is possible to detect a decline in the anthropocentric content of zoo presentation, an orientation that had long been focused on the priority of human entertainment and advantage. Where entertainment was maintained it was organized under very different conditions which increasingly placed the interests of the animals first. Animals could of course be delightful and engaging but sentiments were also expressed in narratives of concern and empathy. Young children might well point and laugh at difference but they could be familiarized and taught tolerance (see Figure 4.1). However, it was not just a rescripting and emphasis that changed the zoological gaze, two major types of innovation occurred in this period.

The first might be called endangered animal zoos or modern arks. These tended to be newly constructed in this period rather than redesigns of older zoos. They were typically small and based on lower and more specialized numbers of animals. The word collection was avoided because, while the older zoos were predicated on building up large collections for public display, these had a completely different *raison d'être*. Their main purpose was to breed endangered or rare species in the hope that they might assist in repopulating wild habitats, providing that these become more secure in the meantime. John Aspinall's zoos at Howletts and Port Lympne in England are good examples, but others include Jersey and Marwell. Aspinall was a high profile, high society gambler and owner of a successful casino in Belgravia, London. His zoo at Howletts began in the

FIGURE 4.1 *Wombat cuddling used to be a regular attraction at Bonorong Wildlife Park, Tasmania. Now the entertainment of humans takes second place to the rehabilitation needs of these orphaned animals (Adrian Franklin)*

1950s as a private collection of animals, not unlike the collections of exotica in other wealthy English country houses. By 1960 he had a growing number, including bears, gorillas, tigers and cheetahs, and local objections to a spate of escapes resulted in a more rigorous approach, including the hiring of keepers. Aspinall was one of the earliest radical pro-animal activists in Britain. He refused to sell veal or pâté de foie gras at his club; he appeared on a prime time TV debate before a live audience in which he argued that wildlife should take precedence over people (Masters 1988: 139); and he organized a 'Save the Tiger' rally at the Royal Albert Hall.

Aspinall's methods of keeping animals were also radical, new and influenced by different values. Conventional zoos discouraged the formation of close relationships between keeper and kept, but at Howletts he and his keepers went into wolf, tiger and gorilla enclosures, spent time with the animals and played with them (see Figure 4.2). Whereas conventional zoos maintained very sanitary if not sterile conditions for the animals, Aspinall and his keepers considered their comfort and preferences. In the gorilla enclosure, for example, 100 bales of oat straw formed a thick soft bed, far more like the floor of tropical rainforest than washable concrete. Because Aspinall maintained a personal relationship with the animals he was sensitive to their moods and overall happiness. Gorillas especially were prone to boredom, even when kept in an extended family or band structure. For this reason they were encouraged to forage for their food by having it scattered into the litter. The 200 or so items of natural food available to wild

FIGURE 4.2   *John Aspinall with his tiger Zemo*
(From the private collection of John Aspinall)

gorillas was mimicked at Howletts with over 90 different items, including treats such as chocolate, beer and treacle. By comparison, gorilla diets in conventional zoos were limited, bulky and required vitamins and trace element supplements (Aspinall 1976: 28). Also at Howletts clean bedding was spread out at night to encourage nest building.

Despite initial criticism of Aspinall's methods by conventional zoos, his methods paid off and spectacular success was achieved in breeding Siberian tigers, gorillas, clouded leopards, snow leopards and elephants. 'He had offspring from no less than thirteen different species of cat, many reputedly impossible to breed . . . Out of a total of 147 individual animals at Howletts, no fewer than 79 (i.e. over half) had been born on the estate (Masters 1988: 160). Not only did he win the approval of top zoos such as Lincoln Park in Chicago, which initiated many transatlantic exchanges, but his methods were adopted elsewhere.

Aspinall's successes and growing reputation as a more humanitarian animal keeper and saviour of endangered species ensured that when the scale of operation grew too large to finance personally a paying public would be affected or at least made aware of his view. Apart from knowing that the zoo existed only to breed animals endangered by humans, visitors were aware that they were being 'allowed' in to see a very special operation that existed only for the benefit of the animals. Unlike urban zoos where the animals have been brought into human space, at Howletts the classy rural setting of the park, together with the functional nature of the enclosures and personal, private 'breeding' space, reversed the sense of belonging and ease. Enclosures were not designed to guarantee a view of the animal:

> The visitor to Howletts and Port Lympne may on occasion be disappointed. What is listed as an animal enclosure appears to contain no living creature at all. This is simply because Aspinall understands the need that some animals have for severe privacy and will not compromise with their requirements. Enclosures which seem empty hide an animal in a far corner which is keeping itself from the common gaze.
>
> (Masters 1988: 264)

The second innovation in this period was very different to Howletts but shared in a radical reorganization of the zoological gaze. These were lavishly expensive additions to existing zoos or entirely new developments. They were based on the simulation of complete ecosystems from which the animals came. They therefore mimicked the climate, vegetation and terrain of these environments and tried to display not individual animals but communities of species that had evolved together. The exemplar of this style is Jungle World which opened at the Bronx Zoo in New York in 1985. In contrast to previous zoo architecture which competed with the animals for the public gaze, here architecture has been suppressed to simply containing the exhibit. 'The real architecture, the design and construction of space, is to be found inside, and what is inside is a representation of the rainforest, the mangrove swamp and the scrub forest of Asia' (Mullan and Marvin 1987: 53). The zoological gaze is no longer outsiders looking in. Here the public join the animals in their world and experience that world. It is consistent with a more decentred attitude to animals and was designed to be so. According to its director, William Conway:

> Could we find ways to separate visitors and the Jungle World animals unobtrusively? Could we keep leaf-eating primates (capable of eating ten leaves a minute) in a lush leaf environment? Could we establish uncommon animals in common Jungle World spaces in ways compatible with the requirements of other species and the need for the zoo-goer to see them? Could we convey hard information to visitors without damaging the affecting message of the habitat's naturalness and soft beauty?
>
> Not all the answers are yet in hand but if the power to affect visitors, to arouse concern and admiration for tropical forest is a proper criterion, the experiment has been a success.
>
> (Conway 1985, cited in Mullan and Marvin 1987: 54)

Another example of this 'theme-zoo' is the Penguin Encounter at Sea World in San Diego. Here the set designers have gone way beyond Lubetkin's modern abstract Arctic at London Zoo and provided a 5,000 square foot section of simulated Antarctic. Kept at freezing point and supplied with 10,000 pounds of fresh ice daily, the penguins not only have a pool to swim in, it is deep enough, cold enough and icy enough for an exact replication of the natural habitat. The new zoological gaze has been wholeheartedly embraced by a new generation of specialist zoo designers. According to Jones and Jones, creators of Woodland

Park, Seattle, 'a new approach to zoo design begins with the presentation of animals in such a way that their right to exist is self-evident'. In their design for a zoo in Kansas City they specify the educational emphasis:

> The educational message accompanying this presentation should be clear and persuasive. Whole habitats should be exhibited, with rock and soil substrates and vegetation supporting communities of species typical of the environment and logically associated. Visitors should feel they are passing through a natural environment, with a feeling of intense involvement. The point should be made that animals live in habitats, and that it is the destruction of these habitats that is the principal cause of wildlife extinction today.
>
> (Jones and Jones 1985: iv, cited in Mullan and Marvin 1987: 60)

The Jones and Jones philosophy is clearly a dominant influence in American zoos, and it follows its own credo with almost puritanical zeal: 'In order to emphasise the ecological aspects of the zoo site, all recreational activities which are not related to the zoo experience, or are of an energetically active nature would be excluded' (Mullan and Marvin 1987: 63). However, other reconstructed zoological gazes were more fun, interactive and multilayered, but no less expressive of the same values. Sea World, at San Diego, at various other locations in the USA and in Queensland, Australia, is a theme park idea based on marine animals and marine environments.

Aquaria were arguably one of the first popular means of keeping animals in a manner that simulated their natural environment and community. Marine animals and seascapes were popular design motifs for domestic decorative arts throughout the 1950s and 1960s and the keeping of tropical and coldwater aquaria grew in popularity over this period. Without doubt, this marine/aquatic aesthetic grew from the mass base of the post-war seaside holiday. Marine life became associated with leisure and fun. The most exotic locations promised the most exotic marine life, the most luxurious holiday experiences promised the closest encounters (rock pools on coral reefs, scuba diving, glass-bottom boat trips). The American TV show *Flipper* is a narrative about a perfect childhood at this time: growing up in a top marine holiday location; having one's own powered watercraft; parented by someone with an exciting job (a marine park ranger); best friend is a real wild dolphin; regular crime-fighting adventures. The progression from seaside leisures to *Flipper*, home aquaria and Sea World theme parks is clear enough but it follows a pattern which we observed elsewhere: the shift from a human centred interest to a more decentred, ecologistic and zoocentric gaze.

The idea that marine animals were decorative additions to the home and other human pleasure sites featured in the consumerism of the 1950s and 1960s. For instance, the original idea for Sea World was a decorative background for eating. According to the San Diego Sea World web site (June 1997):

> In the early 1960s, four UCLA fraternity brothers dreamed of building an aquatic-themed restaurant. While the restaurant concept never materialised, it sparked the idea

for Sea World. In March 1964, on 22 acres of land leased from the city of San Diego, Sea World became a reality. Featuring a few shows and a saltwater aquarium, the park drew 400,000 visitors in its first year.

These early shows were circus acts designed to amuse humans by displaying how marine mammals could be taught neat tricks. The education content was low and the degree of empathy and support required from the audience was minimal. Such shows were copied elsewhere.

Mullan and Marvin are able to trace the gradual elimination of the circus content at Sea World by comparing Cherfas's (1984) account of the 'Shamu – Take a Bow' show with the 1986 show they saw called 'Celebration Shamu'. In the earlier show Shamu the killer whale is exhibited as a sensation which the audience are invited to experience. The killer whale is not juvenilized but admired as an animal. According to the show commentary: 'We may never really understand, but we can experience all of his strength and agility . . . Combined with an intelligence . . . And in it there is a beauty, like the finest gymnast or ballet dancer . . . And there is a spectacle . . . Focus your attention on the centre of the pool . . . In one fleet moment – diving, leaping , spinning . . . Natural grace, beauty, power' (Cherfas 1984: 48). In the 1986 show less attention was drawn to these physical and mental attributes. 'The emphasis was still on experience but now much more so in terms of a changed understanding and a concern to establish a relationship with the whales' (Mullan and Marvin 1987: 21). Here the commentary specifies how that relationship should be: 'We mustn't forget that at one time so little was known about these magnificent creatures that killer whales were hunted and shot for the sheer pleasure of it and in some parts of the world it still occurs. We like to believe that because of marine zoological parks such as Sea World the public has turned fear into fascination and is going to respect the killer whales *and even love one* like Shamu or Kandu' (Mullan and Marvin's emphasis: 1987: 21).

Mullan and Marvin (1987: 22) argue that the notion of friendship changed from one where the trainers are able to cross the species barrier in order to act alongside the animals in 'Shamu – Take a Bow' to one of mutual understanding in 'Celebration Shamu':

> To the accompaniment of soft and mellow music the trainer drifts gently around the pool with the whale and a prerecording of his voice drifts with him. 'At times it's a quiet moment that Shamu and I enjoy together when we are just lying still and not doing anything at all. I'll touch him and he'll look up at me and I'll know that he's thinking just as much about me as I am about him.'

There are parallels here with the work of Aspinall at Howletts. In order to keep his animals happy he encouraged them to develop a relationship with him and the keepers. Although this involves some tension with the longer term aim of helping wild animals to survive, he rejects the idea that human companionship robs them of their species being and suggests that both sides of the relationship have much to learn and gain. However, these shifting notions of friendship with animals have to be understood in their historical–social context.

The whales have been anthropomorphised   not in the crass way of a circus animal whose behaviour is interpreted in human terms, but rather as a creature that shares and exhibits the same deep emotions, feelings and desires of the human trainers and by implication with the rest of the human observers. Such a concern could well be understood in terms of the general concern in this society with interpersonal relationships, but it is more complex than that, for the whale has become a special symbol of being in contact with nature.

(Mullan and Marvin 1987: 23)

This shift towards familiarity, love, mutual understanding and empathy has been extended even further in the intervening period. In a manner which seeks to deny any crass touristic front-staging, the new Shamu for 1996 is called 'Shamu Backstage'. Here the killer whales are no longer a 'show' and visitors are no longer an audience. The promotion material refers to them now as 'guests', suggesting a warmer, closer relationship. Indeed this is precisely what Sea World want them to experience. Instead of watching the trainers' relationship with Shamu, they are to have one themselves backstage. Instead of a pool there is a 'naturalistic habitat':

Shamu Backstage, a 1.7-million-gallon naturalistic habitat, debuts in 1996. Eight different interactive areas provide guests with the opportunity to give visual, audible and tactile signals that whales associate with specific behaviours. Guests are able to help with feedings and interact during play and training sessions. Guests may also view killer whales underwater through a 70-foot-long acrylic wall.

(Sea World, San Diego, web site, June 1997)

As potential paying visitors to Sea World, visitors to the web site are treated to much more than a list of attractions and indeed the message is that this is not merely another theme park. Sea World has an educational, conservational and scientific mission and would-be tourists are encouraged to think of their involvement as more than as just visitors. Indeed they are invited to participate in the spirit of the mission. Children can hook into this prior to a visit: 'More than 275,000 people participate in Sea World of California's in-park and outreach programs annually. Millions more children are reached via "Shamu TV," a groundbreaking satellite learning program. Programs allow students to learn about the ocean's wonders and an increasingly threatened marine environment.'

GAZING AT NATURE

While the zoological societies offer a useful record of change in the zoological gaze, we cannot ignore the significance or importance of animal watching in uncontrived (or less contrived) natural settings. Zoos provided objects for the curiosity of the nineteenth-century urban centres, but during the twentieth century the reduction in rail and bus fares and extension of car ownership meant that increasingly more people were able to see animals in the wild. The opening of the national parks in the USA, together with a national enthusiasm for wildlife, assured the attractiveness of wild animals in these places. The 'natural zoological gaze' was consumed in three main ways. The first, was by an essentially middle-class, educated group of amateur field naturalists and bird watchers. These were relatively few in number but were frequently organized and recruitment orientated. Field naturalists have a long history as an improving leisure pursuit in the UK, USA and Australia and membership was not confined to middle-class circles. A second group of middle-class Americans, influenced by writers such as Henry Thoreau, John Muir, Aldo Leopold, Negley Farson and John Maclean, was orientated less to field study than to country or wilderness living: rural sojourns combining hunting and fishing with walking, painting, writing and so forth. Third, the natural zoological gaze was consumed by a mixed group of urbanites who took vacations and other breaks in national parks or equivalent locations and whose contacts with animals were ad hoc, poorly informed and the subject of some anticipation as in meeting campground bears, raccoons, possums and so forth.

Since the 1960s the degree of ad hoc encounters with the national park regulars has declined in favour of guided and planned trips to see more unusual sights: the spawn runs of salmon, nestings, nocturnal trips. The amount of information available to visitors has increased together with information trails, guidebooks, safety equipment and equipment for wildlife watching and photography. While the UK lacks many of the larger and more exotic mammals of North America, it still offers a large range of bird habitats and for this reason perhaps bird-watching has become a major specialist zoological gaze. What began in 1904 as a small group of middle-class ladies in London protesting about feathers in the hat trade has grown into the largest conservation organization in Europe. The Royal Society for the Protection of Birds (RSPB) has increased, particularly in the last quarter of the twentieth century, to almost one million members, with an income of just under £35 million and land assets of more than 240,000 acres throughout Britain (Rocco 1996). With such an interest in birds, the number of bird conservation areas, protected bird sights and wildfowl centres, such as the RSPB's Slimbridge, have increased dramatically, as have the numbers of active birdwatchers and 'birding' clubs.

While it is not possible to account in precise terms for this burgeoning of birdwatching activity in Britain, in the USA the Bureau of Census in conjunction with the Fish and Wildlife Service publish a survey of fishing, hunting and wildlife associated activities. From this it is possible to gauge, roughly speaking, the contemporary significance of the natural zoological gaze. In the category 'nonconsumptive activities' they include observing, feeding and photographing wildlife. These data are divided into residential activities defined as those taking place within one mile of the respondent's home and non-residential activities which take place at least one mile from home. In 1991 76.1 million US residents (39 per cent of the population over the age of 16) enjoyed a variety of non-consumption wildlife activities. Seventy-three million Americans participated in one or more of these activities near their residence and 30 million engaged in non-residential activities and trips where the primary purpose was wildlife related. Feeding wildlife was the most popular residential activity (65 million participants), followed by observation (55 million), and photography (17 million). Observing wildlife was the most popular non-residential activity (29 million), followed by photography (14 million), and feeding (13 million). These data show a very significant interest in observing and being involved with wildlife. This significance is highlighted by the amount of money spent on such activities: altogether $18 billion was spent in 1991. Of this $7.5 billion was spent on trip-related expenses; $10 billion on equipment; and $1 billion on magazines and memberships.

These data also support the claim made in Chapter 3 that contemporary interest in wildlife ranges beyond those creatures most like ourselves. Of the 55 million residential wildlife observers, 94 per cent observed birds, 68 per cent observed mammals, 29 per cent observed insects and spiders, 22 per cent reptiles and amphibians and 21 per cent fish and other wildlife. Of the 30 million non-residential participants, 82 per cent fed, observed or photographed birds, 75 per cent land mammals, 34 per cent fish, 10 per cent marine mammals and 49 per cent others such as turtles, butterflies, etc.

Participation rates varied in proportion to both income and education, though the variation was more significant for non-residential activities. For example, while 28 per cent of those with five or more years of college participated in non-residential activities, this proportion fell to 20 per cent among those with one to three years of college and 11 per cent among those with only nine to eleven years of school. In terms of residential participation, 51 per cent of those with five years or more of college participated as compared with 42 per cent of those with one to three years of college and 33 per cent of those with nine to eleven years of school. Slightly more men than women participated in both residential and non-residential activity. In terms of age, a different age distribution characterized each type of activity. Among residential participants, there was an even amount of participation among all groups over the age of 25 (39–44 per cent), whereas for those under 25 there was much less (26–30 per cent). However, non-residential activity peaked at approximately 20 per cent among those in the middle age bands (aged 35–44) and fell off evenly on each side, to 12 per cent in the 55–64 band, and 14 per cent in the 18–24 band. There is likely to be a generation effect in these participation rates, reflecting changes in the emphasis on wildlife in schools and colleges in recent years, but these data suggest that this will be minor at most.

What is very clear is the extent to which gazing at wildlife and zoos has become part of mass leisure culture. While these data demonstrate the intensity and variety of interest in animals, it is possible that they reflect merely a net increase in leisure of all types. However, the zoological gaze is very significant relative to other types of leisure and travel activities, especially those that dominate recent leisure literature. In Rojek's (1993) *Ways of Escape*, he concentrates on a variety of postmodern tourist attractions ranging from heritage sites to theme parks: the zoological gaze is ignored. But all around the Western world animals are a major draw card. In Australia, for example, where there is a typical range of leisure activities available in recent years, bush activities, visiting a national park or fishing attracted 62 per cent of the Australian population as compared with only

13 per cent who visited a heritage site and 8 per cent who visited a theme park. Among international tourists to Australia, 51 per cent visit a zoo, animal park or marine park and 44 per cent visit a national or state park, while only 22 per cent visit amusement or theme parks (ABS 1995: 160).

In this chapter we have seen how the universal human interest in looking at animals took particular forms in the modern West through travelling animal shows, commercial menageries, modern zoological gardens and thematized animal parks and centres. The zoological gaze was shaped by specific social and political processes. First, we discerned a series of changes that suggest that the early twentieth-century zoological gaze was highly anthropocentric, reflecting perhaps the centrality of human progress in Europe and the USA. Zoos were influenced by colonialism and familiarisation with the exotic 'other'; the modernization of leisure and the promotion of rational recreation in the late nineteenth century; from the 1930s onwards, the elaboration of mass leisure and hedonistic pleasure seeking and entertainment. Second, dating from the late 1960s, it is possible to see a more decentred, empathetic, ecologistic zoological gaze which reflects postmodern sensibilities. Here is an example of how good animals are to think with: the babyboomer generation developed a postmaterialist culture, resulting in a powerful critique of modernization; a corresponding concern with the environment and a new call for global organization and cooperation; emancipatory and liberation social movements, particularly those affecting disadvantaged minorities; an exploration and reexamination of personal relationships. By the 1970s animals were a perfect terrain for the exercise of these new values: they were becoming super-exploited in industry and in industrial farming systems; they were being exterminated and annihilated at a growing rate; society was losing touch with the natural world. As we have just seen the postmodern zoological gaze has reversed most of the principles and objects of the nineteenth-century zoo. Of particular interest perhaps is how far the species barrier will continue to be questioned and breached by innovators such as John Aspinall and Sea World. The development of empathy, friendship with and love of animals has already reached an advanced stage in the West which is likely to be extended beyond the domestic animal companion. In the next chapter we will consider how human relations with pets were transformed in the twentieth century. We will show that to understand human–animal relations in the twentieth century we need to examine more than just shifting values: the love of pets in the late twentieth century reveals changes in the ontological security of the individual, domestic social relations and community.

5 PETS AND MODERN CULTURE

> If you have no children, a poodle will do; last year, at the dog cemetery, I recognised, in the quavering oration which ran from tomb to tomb, my grandfather's maxims; dogs know how to love; they are more affectionate, more loyal than men; they have tact and an unfailing instinct which allows them to recognise Good and to tell good men from bad. 'Polonius,' said one grief-stricken woman, 'you are better than I: you would not have survived me; but I am surviving you.' I had an American friend with me: disgusted he kicked a cement dog and broke its ear. He was right: when you love children and dogs *too much*, you love them instead of adults.
>
> (Sartre 1967: 112)

Sartre's indignation was expressed in 1967, a time when many others condemned what was seen to be a pathological substitution of pets for 'real' social relationships (see Serpell 1986 for a review of these critics). Their comments must be seen in the context of an anxiety about the decline of certain forms of social relations (especially marital, family, neighbourhood and community), and in the context of social and political projects in the 1960s and 1970s which aimed to restore them. This scathing view of close relationships with animals has certainly changed since then, if not evaporated. Perhaps because we have given up all hope of a cosy community life, or because new factors have combined to make close relationships between adults more insecure, ephemeral or fugitive, a close relationship with pets is now seen as good for us and perfectly 'normal' and acceptable. Pets offer companionship for the lonely, prolonged life expectancy for the sick and therapy for the unhappy. Pets are acquired to become substitutes for a number of human relationships: to replace deceased partners; in place of children, loved-ones and friends, and, for many children, in place of siblings and parental company during work hours. This chapter will chart a process of social change in respect of pets and society, and in particular document and account for the radical rethink on the role and value of pets in late modernity.

The relationship with pets is the closest and most humanized of human–animal relations, and the changing nature of pet keeping can be related to important social and cultural transformations in modernity, particularly those affecting the individual and household. In many ways relations between people and their pets are highly individualized and personal. Even in families, individual members tend to have very particular relations with the family pet. Increasingly, more people live alone or can expect to at several points in the life cycle: the domestic unit is now fragile, insecure and ephemeral. Inspired by the writings of John Berger in the late 1970s, Thomas described contemporary pets in terms of the social plight of their owners: 'Sterilised, isolated and usually deprived of contact with other animals, the pet is creature of it's owner's way of life; and the fact that so many people feel it necessary to maintain a dependent animal for the sake of emotional completeness tells us something about the atomistic world in which we live' (K. Thomas 1983: 119). However, it is not merely social isolation or atomism or the need for emotional completeness that encourages pet keeping in recent years, or the manner in which it is done. During the 1960s and 1970s it was commonplace to bemoan the decline of community, neighbourhood, village and extended family, and many social ills, such as the privatized nuclear family, were attributed to their demise. Since the 1970s, the nuclear family has come under pressure and individuals at all stages in the life cycle face a more fragmented, insecure prospect. Here are the conditions favouring the elaboration of our ties with pets: while all around changes and 'all that is solid melts into air', pets provide a somewhat nostalgic set of old-fashioned comforts. They make long-term bonds with their human companions; they rarely run off with others; they are almost always pleased to see 'their' humans; their apparent love is unconditional (and therefore secured) and they give the strong impression that they need humans as much as humans need them. Teddybears also made a huge come-back among the baby boomer generation during the 1980s and 1990s, but postmodern individuals needed more than soft fur and cuddles at bedtime.

In Chapter 2 it was argued that key trends in pet keeping during the twentieth century may be explained by changes in the ontological security of the individual. Ontological security means knowing, almost without having to think about it, that key areas of one's life are stable, predictable and taken for granted. The stable, unchanging qualities of so-called traditional societies produced wide-spread ontological security, even if life was not free from risk. Risks tended to come from nature rather than society, from disease, flood, fire or famine. Society was governed by rules and reciprocal relations, by duties and obligations. Under normal circumstances, social relationships endured, households had continuity if not permanence, and access to resources and status was fixed if not equal. But in the twentieth century modernization removed many of the pillars of traditional ontological security. In the first half of this century, an attempt was made in most Western societies to restore ontological security through paternalistic welfare policies: the state attempted to guarantee health, education, housing and employ-ment for all citizens. Since the 1960s this policy has been eroded systematically and replaced by market individualism. People are less encumbered by high tax thresholds and less dynamic economies, but just as they may reach higher, they can also fall further – and without safety nets. In addition, changes in the labour market have undermined the stability of the single-wage family of the mid-twentieth century. Although few would want to return to it, the moral and economic ties that bound adults to a single household, even a mobile one, ensured more continuity than the contemporary family confronted by ease of marriage dissolution, career divergence between spouses, and the temptation of easier domestic relations. More people now opt not to marry and/or not to have children until late in their careers. Many decide not to have children at all. Women are pressured by dual workloads at home and in paid employment. Ontological security has been diminished: people cannot guarantee their jobs, partners, homes or parenthood. Even the security of their possessions is at risk as rates of theft and burglary rise and house prices crash on nervous property markets.

The extent to which changes in pet-keeping patterns and practices can be explained in terms of ontological insecurity provides a useful way of investigating the pattern and direction of change in the last twenty years or so. It will be argued that while pets may be kept as companions in lieu of a variety of human relations this only takes us so far in explaining recent changes in the composition of pet keeping. Certainly studies show that pets are now commonly kept by those who have recently suffered some kind of social crisis or by sole householders. Studies also show that such people have more emotionally intense relationships with their pets than others. Pets, but particularly dogs and cats, provide an enduring, stable and robust relationship, while placing few demands on their owners. However, it is not at all clear that the extension of greater care and humanity towards pets is simply because they are fulfilling surrogate human roles. Also at play are new attitudes to animals similar to those operating in other sites of human–animal interaction. At other sites, such as zoos and wild areas, members of the new service class have developed a more decentred and empathetic relation, replacing entertainment objectives with the morally charged rewards of good works, paternalism and care. While animals can provide some of the social and emotional needs that are created in late modernity, it is also the case that their human carers have learned to appreciate their animal pets as animals. This becomes quite clear in the celebrations of difference between breeds of dogs, cats, ponies, etc. and in the highly aestheticized nature of the breed associations, or 'fancies' as they are called. The classical argument that such animals are simply becoming ever more anthropomorphized may be exactly wrong. Rather, in considering their pets as animals with particular characteristics and needs, pet keepers are engaged in an exercise of decentring: attempting to understand the needs of others, realizing that the needs and interests of two species are not mutually exclusive and exploring the possibilities of mutuality. In sum, the human–animal relation is not one characterized simply by strong sentiments, but also unconsciously challenging and dissolving the human–animal boundary itself.

This chapter is divided into three sections. The first establishes the social and cultural foundations of pet keeping in modernity, and provides a basis upon which to measure change in the twentieth century. The second section reviews contemporary demographic trends and patterns of pet keeping in Britain, the USA and Australia, and sets out the key features of change. The third section looks at three key changes in more detail: human surrogacy, anthropomorphism in pet care and pets and therapy.

SOCIAL AND CULTURAL FOUNDATIONS OF PET KEEPING IN MODERNITY

The first and most obvious questions are: what are pets and how do they differ in their relations with humans from other animals? Keith Thomas defined pets as having three features not shared by other human–animal relations. First, pets are admitted into the human household whereas other animals are normally excluded. As householders, pets also take out membership in the domestic unit in which they live. Second, pets are given individual personal names, whereas other animals may be given generic species names (e.g. Jenny wren; Bruin the bear, and so on) or simple identifier semi-human names as is the case with horses, working hounds and cattle. According to Thomas the practice of giving animals human names only gained pace as recently as the eighteenth century;

> But there was a recurring tendency, which in the eighteenth century became very pronounced, to give pets human names; and the shift was indicative of a closer bond between pet and owner. When we find Christopher Smart's Lucy and Gilbert White's tortoise Timothy, and Southey's old spaniel Phillis, we know that we are confronted by a relationship of altogether greater intimacy.

(K. Thomas 1983: 114)

Third, pets, though edible, were never eaten. Without doubt this had to do with their special status as household members, their emotional closeness to household members and thus their quasi-human status. It might be argued that these species had no gastronomic history or that in the past they were too valuable as mousers, drovers or hunters to be frittered away as food. However, among hunter-gatherers, who have a long history of keen pet keeping, edible species frequently became pets but were never eaten, once given that special status. Moreover, occasionally their names were systematically woven into human naming patterns; they were given human mortuary and burial rites, were suckled and treated as very special children (Serpell 1986: 48–58).

One can elaborate on Thomas's definition. To begin with pets are also animals that have been specifically adopted by humans, rather as they might adopt a human child. Typically pets are preferred to be taken as baby animals, as soon as possible after birth. Once adopted, the pet retains its childish relation to the owner throughout its life, as though it never grows up. It certainly never assumes independence and leaves. According to Serpell, one of the universal appeals of most pets is their cuteness as babies. Accentuated heads and eyes, small features and limbs, soft skin and fur, slow uncoordinated movements are common among mammal babies and zoologists believe that they stimulate parental tendencies to feed, hold, protect and keep warm. It is well established that babies of one species stimulate such reactions in adults of others: cross-species suckling has been exploited for a long time by farmers, for example. A 3-year-old boy who fell into a gorilla enclosure at Brookfield Zoo near Chicago was rescued and cradled by an 8-year-old female nursing gorilla until human help arrived. According to primate researcher Kenneth G. Gould, 'This was good parenting, good gorilla group behaviour' (*Washington Post*, 23 August 1996: 1). On finding an abandoned baby mammal, hunter-gatherers frequently take it home to take care of. Among some groups such as the Barasana 'pet keeping remains one of their principal leisure activities' (Serpell 1986: 51). However, while this may be a universal response to baby mammals among humans, their qualities as adults may be appreciated by different cultures in different ways.

In England, for example, Thomas was able to show how the tendency to extend human emotional responses to pets was frowned upon and discouraged by the church and religious authorities in the early modern period. Indeed, as we have seen in Chapter 2, English attitudes to animals were strongly influenced by the anthropocentric dictums of the Bible. All animals were categorically different and for man's practical use. The idea of extending quasi-human qualities to certain animals was anomalous and dangerous. Those who harboured cats in their homes, for example, could be and were suspected of witchcraft. Nonetheless, the historical record is clear on the significance of horses and dogs in the lives of the English at most times. According to Thomas, the upper classes, perhaps freer from public scrutiny, developed an unselfconscious admiration for their dogs at a relatively early time. Dogs were certainly included as members of late medieval households. The Enlightenment created a more curious, open attitude to animals generally and, together with the pet-keeping practices of the social elite, this created the foundation for a wider expansion of pet keeping. During the late eighteenth century and nineteenth century when traditional status divisions were challenged by the new commercial and industrial classes, the keeping of pets, particularly high status pets, became important signifiers of rank. By the late eighteenth century dog and cat keeping had filtered down to all levels of society. According to the author of a 1796 Bill promoting the idea of a dog tax, there were about one million dogs in England (K. Thomas 1983: 105). By the mid-nineteenth century cats in London were estimated to be 'twice as numerous as dogs', or 'one cat for every ten people' (K. Thomas 1983: 110).

At different levels of society, Thomas provides evidence that dogs and cats formed emotional and enduring relations with their pets, but towards the end of the nineteenth century, with the creation of the Kennel Club, the burgeoning of dog and cat shows, the growth in the number of recognized pedigree breeds and breeders and the efflorescence of breed clubs, obedience competitions, magazines and books, it was clear that something besides the companionship of pets was at stake. While upper-class critics bemoaned the loss of vim and vigour of traditional breeds in favour of arbitrary differentiations, the middle classes had evidently moulded dog shapes and provenance in line with their own new social visions. 'Most late Victorian dog fanciers belonged to the urban business and professional classes. To many of them, the figurative dimension of dog fancying may have been the more important; it offered the vision of a stable, hierarchical society, where rank was secure and individual merit, rather than just inherited position, appreciated' (Ritvo 1987: 84). Summarizing for this period, pets were significant in society as much for their qualities as positional goods and entertainment value as showy, fashion accessories or intelligent competitors, as for their companionability.

This mix of qualities appreciated in pets became the hallmark of pet keeping in the first half of the twentieth century. The entertaining and decorative qualities of particular breeds of dog reached new heights in the 1950s when a variety of toy breeds became synonymous with luxurious and stylish living. Poodles, pugs, Pekinese and other Asian breeds were enormously popular, as were almost any other colourful and convenient species. Budgerigars and other exotic birds became popular in the post-war period as did coldwater and tropical fish. Asian breeds of cats which had been relatively rare in the early part of the twentieth century became fashionable as classy appendages for rich women, such as the Disney character Cruella DeVille.

CHANGING TRENDS IN PET KEEPING

Since the 1960s it is clear first of all that pet keeping has become more prominent in society and continues to be so. Evidence for this includes rising numbers of pets, the growth in the pet food and services industries, raised awareness of the health and therapeutic benefits of pet keeping and the growth in media attention given over to pets. Second, there is evidence to suggest that greater emphasis is given to companionability and rather less to the entertainment and decorative functions of pets. Third, surveys show that perception and attitudes towards pets are guided by life cycle and household. Fourth, much evidence shows that qualitatively the care of pets has become more empathetic and more sophisticated than was the case twenty years ago. All these indicators correspond with the notion that pets are required to play surrogate roles for humans whose ontological security has been diminished, and that general changes in attitudes to animals are affecting the nature of relations with pets.

Rising pet populations

In Britain, the number of dogs rose by 66 per cent between 1963 and 1991, from 4.4 million to 7.3 million. The rise in the number of cats was even greater, with a 75 per cent increase between 1963 to 1995, from 4 million to 7 million. According to the latest data from the Pet Food Manufacturers Association, cats now outnumber dogs for the first time, with dog numbers dropping 7 per cent from 7.3 million in 1991 to 6.8 million in 1995. Since the British human population has remained relatively stable over this period, these data suggest a significant increase in the two most important pet species. Between 1935 and 1986 the numbers of pedigree dogs increased by 237 per cent from 58,799 to 198,000. This growth continued apace during the 1990s, and by 1995 there were 264,000 registered dogs. Currently British sales of dog food are valued at £700 million and growing, while cat food sales are valued at £572 million (Canadian High Commission 1996). Although dog numbers have declined in recent years, dog owners continue to spend more on each dog; dog food sales have risen by £20 million each year since 1991. Altogether the British spent more on pet food in 1993 (£1.3 billion) than they did on fresh fruit and vegetables for themselves (£1.2 billion). Recent data on contemporary British spending on pets are not available but a 1988 estimate put it as £2.5 billion or approximately £150 per household per year. Europe is an enormous market for pets and pet foods, with at least four other countries ahead of Britain in terms of pets per household (Council for Science and Society 1988: 11). In 1996 the European pet food market comprised 456 companies that employ 21,000 employees and supply 54 million pet-owning households (Canadian High Commission 1996).

In Australia the rate of pet ownership in 1994 was much higher with 60 per cent of households owning at least one pet. Interestingly, in Australia dogs numbers have risen recently from 3 million in 1991 to 3.8 million in 1996, while cat numbers have declined from 2.7 to 2.5 million. This trend looks set to continue: of those Australians presently owning a cat 60 per cent intend to replace it when it dies but only two-thirds intend to replace it with another cat. Of the 33 per cent wanting to replace it with another species, over half intend choosing a dog replacement. Most dog owners on the other hand report an intention to buy another dog. Fifty three per cent of those not currently owning a pet but wanting one in the future would like a dog.

In the USA a similar proportion of households (59 per cent) own a pet, but predominantly a dog (54 million) or a cat (59 million) (Rachel Dickenson, *American Demographics*, January 1996).

In Japan, dogs and cats have only become popular household pets since the 1960s, although the keeping of birds and fish has a longer history. In 1993 there were an estimated 7 million dogs and 6 million pet cats in Japan and the numbers are expected to rise significantly (US Agricultural Trade Office 1993). As in Western countries, the sales of pet food have grown in recent years, often reaching double-digit annual growth.

New pet products and services

Since the 1960s pet products and services have undergone radical alteration, reflecting important changes between pets and humans. In the 1960s most dogs and cats were fed standardized canned food and dry biscuits that were barely more elaborate than agricultural feed. No references were made to the contents of the feed on the labelling or marketing, other than its wholesome, adequate composition. Everyone knew what cuts of meat the pets were getting (slaughterhouse by-products) and no elaboration could make them sound better. Instead harmless sounding brand names reflected on the basic unedifying types of human–pet relations of the day: from the regular (working-class) Pal and Chappie through to the premium (middle-class) Pedigree Chum. There were similar low-key marketing strategies for cat foods. In 1996, by contrast, Spillers, the pet food manufacturer, was employing different techniques in order to increase its share of a new market in gourmet pet foods. Behind a picture of the new cat food brand Purrfect was hidden a speaker coupled to a high-powered chip. A disembodied voice whispers, to unsuspecting consumers 'Indulge your loved one with a can of new Spillers Purrfect. But remember, it's just for cats.'

During the 1980s companies launched more premium and super-premium brands which, as the Purrfect voiceover suggests, were deliberately made tempting for humans. By 1989 premium and super-premium pet foods had increased their lead over standard and economy varieties by 47 per cent. By 1993 this lead had increased to 50 per cent, with sales rising by 10 per cent every year, which is not surprising given the seductive power of British television advertising. But the approach taken by the advertisers emphasized new relationships between pets and their companions. Cat food adverts, for example, played on the fact that women normally feed the household cats; that cats have a reputation for being difficult to please and are sensual if not sexual creatures. The resulting advert clearly made analogies between cats and husbands, pointing perhaps to the ambiguities and anomalies in human affections for animals. Some adverts referred to pet meals as though they were special dining occasions while others simply underlined how appropriate it is to give one's special companion special food. Some built on the human concern for health foods, including a range of vegetarian dog foods. However, it is a moot point whether vegetable proteins are inferior to slaughter-house wastes, particularly in view of the recent BSE scare. Since consumers are as concerned that their pets should not develop BSE as themselves, one upmarket manufacturer, Pedigree Pet Foods, is dropping all varieties that contain offal and spending £6 million on the relaunch over three months. In addition to the vegetarian dog is a variant vegetarian cat. In the Friskies Gourmet range, cat lovers can serve up a 'seafood supreme' or 'crunchy vegetable' dinner, again perhaps exploiting women's light and healthy dining preferences (Lupton 1996a). Vegetarian dog food reflects the significant growth in British vegetarianism: already sales account for 4 per cent of the market, worth £709 million. Finally, again in contrast to 1960s offerings, pet food manufacturers now provide variety: different meat (including duck, rabbit, chicken and turkey), different fish (including salmon, prawn, tuna and herring), and combination or recipe varieties.

Pet health products are also booming in the 1990s. During the 1960s such products were little more than veterinary items such as vitamin and mineral supplements, flea and worm remedies, combs and shampoos. By the 1990s the list of pet health products almost mirrors those available for humans. Dental and gum care for pets is big business. Pedigree Pet Foods have claimed success for their recently launched product Rask, a chew that reduces dental plaque. Since pets such as cats and dogs are in such demand for physical contact and proximity, their breath has required a degree of adjustment over the past thirty years:

> There can be few sadder sights than a much loved family pet shunned by those it has loved for many years. But it can happen when our pets grow older and their breath begins to smell. The good news is that the most basic method of oral hygiene can solve the problem. Up to 75 per cent of cats and dogs in Britain suffer from some form of periodontal disease – most, if not all of it preventable if pet owners took time to follow a regular dental routine.

> (*The Times Weekend*, 31 August 1996: 8)

New companies have emerged to provide pet dental products such as toothpastes with appropriate dog and cat flavours, dental brushes that fit over human fingers and other hygiene items. It is estimated that approximately £15 worth of products per pet is required each year, and owners are advised to commence brushing pets' teeth at an early age and to brush regularly, three or four times a week. According to Celia Gorrel, President of the British Veterinary Dental Association, 30,000 Britons regularly brush their pets' teeth: 'People are now often better at keeping their pets teeth clean than they are their own teeth' (*The Times Weekend*, 31 August 1996: 8). From the 1980s onwards, the idea that pet care and products are superior to those used by their owners is not at all unusual and further underlines the extent to which pets are treated specially as quasi-human children or partners. For example, the pet first-aid kits launched at the RSPCA Scruffits Competition for nonpedigree dogs were hailed as 'being of a standard higher than most human first-aid kits' (*The Times Weekend*, 3 August 1996: 8). During the 1960s flea treatments in cats and dogs were more or less the same as for farm stock, involving dips, sprays and powders. Since the 1980s flea treatment for pets has been made less stressful (e.g. flea collars, pesticidal tablets) and since 1994 nontoxic. According to the *Washington Post* (3 September 1996) the latest product, Program, 'prevents fleas from emerging from eggs or larva. It prevents the development of chitin, which is the key building block in the external skeleton of insects. Since mammals don't have chitin, the pharmaceutical is harmless to them. The result has been a 50 per cent increase over the past year in the dollars spent by pet owners for flea control products'. Although there has been a particular boom in pet products in the 1990s, data on trade value remain unpublished. In 1983 a Eurobarometer survey estimated British trade to be worth £130 million and a 1987 estimate put the trade through the 2,000 British pet stores at £150 million, also noting that 'a well stocked pet shop will sell at least 500 separate items' (Council for Science and Society 1988: 18). Pet health products have also ventured into alternative health treatments. At the 1996 Natural Pet Care Expo held in Annadale, Virginia, more than 250 alternative practitioners displayed their medicines and therapies, including acupuncture, aromatherapy, Chinese herbs, and psychics to enable owners to communicate with living and deceased pets (*Washington Post*, 14 July 1996).

In the 1960s pet services were more or less confined to grooming and kennelling. From the 1970s onwards, however, the list of available services has grown considerably. Most involve extensions of human facilities to pets and cover every aspect of a pet's life from cradle (literally) to grave. To begin with, would-be pet owners can enlist the help of a selection agency. Operating on similar lines to human dating and introduction agencies, they attempt to match owner to breed in order to make a happy union. This makes a great deal of sense, particularly in view of the rising numbers of discarded pets, especially dogs. In Britain alone, 500,000 dogs are taken into care each year, a large proportion of which being caused by incompatibilities (Council for Science and Society 1988: 44).

Selectapet is a computer-based cat and dog selection service working from Melbourne, Australia. A letter accompanying the results of their selection analysis identifies precisely some of the key components of change in our relations with pets:

> We realise that beauty is in the eye of the beholder, but do not dismiss a breed merely because you may not care initially for the look of the pet in the photo. You are choosing a companion with whom to share life's ups and downs, not a fashion accessory, and as such your choice should be based on your mutual suitability, rather than aesthetic appeal or any preconceived notions regarding a particular breed.

If the relationship breaks down there are a large number of rescue homes that will take unwanted pets, but increasingly owners may make use of a completely new service: the pet psychologist. Pet psychologists feature frequently on pet TV shows in the USA, Australia and Britain, some attaining minor celebratory status, and the number of private practices are growing. Rather like partnership mediators or guidance counsellors, pet psychologists help to identify the nature of the problem and what owners and pets can do to resolve it. Normally the problem is behavioural, but frequently the cause has to do with human interaction patterns that can be modified. A recent British TV pet programme, for example, showed a pet psychologist resolving the problem of a savage pet rabbit. The owners were desperate to cuddle their bunny but needed to modify their behaviour, particularly in order to make the rabbit associate handling with pleasures such as being fed titbits and ear massage.

The number of routine services available are legion: pet clothing, walking services, portraiture, dog horoscopes, charm schools and pooch playschools. In Old Town Alexandria dogs are treated as special citizens, again rather like children. According to the *Washington Post* (29 June 1996): 'a slew of Old Town businesses – shops, coffeehouses, banks, even the florist stand, the hair salon – provide doggie refreshments. Some merchants keep dog biscuits behind the counter. Others put the treats on the floor alongside a water dish. Bank tellers pass them out at their windows. One merchant has put up a "Bone Box" outside her store so dogs on an after hour stroll can still get their fix'. Clearly, the days when local businesses ingratiated themselves with cherished clients by giving their kids candy have been modified in some areas, especially retirement towns.

The death of a pet has always been traumatic, but whereas in the 1960s the passing may have meant a tear or two and perhaps a modest burial in the backyard, in the 1990s there is a pet mortuary industry offering everything from a funeral, a grave site and cemetery services through to bereavement counselling. These businesses are thriving on the increased emotional dependence on pets. Pet cemeteries were established throughout the 1970s and 1980s in most Western societies and they have thrived. Some, like the Rosa Bonmeur Memorial Park in California, contain thousands of pet graves including mice, birds, horses and exotic pets such as elephants and lions, alongside their owners. There are even older celebratory pet cemeteries designated as official historic sites, such as Aspin Hill Memorial Park, where the dogs belonging to J. Edgar Hoover are buried alongside Jiggs, the dog star of *Our Gang* comedies. In Australia the law prevents humans from being buried alongside animals, but in the UK there is no such impediment and new businesses offering such services have been very successful. The Rossendale Pet Crematorium and Memorial Gardens, for example, approved plans for 40 human burial plots in February 1995, with pet cremations averaging 500 per week and at least one burial. 'All the animals (with the exception of horses who are buried on beds of hay) are laid to rest in white silk-lined coffins. Each coffin, in polished hardwood, has an engraved plaque and silver handles. Owners can say their final farewells in the Chapel of Rest, next to the cemetery office . . . Prices range from $324 (£162) for a cat to $972 (£486) for a horse' (WHO, 8 May 1995: 34–6). The WHO article featured an interview with a prospective client and her husband who have elected to be buried with their seven spaniels, four miniature dachshunds, four cats and an African grey parrot. The couple have no children but were keen to deny that their pets were substitute offspring: 'My animals are my family, but I don't look at them as children.'

Companions and protectors rather than playthings and ornaments

Even though dogs and cats have always played companion roles, it is obvious from the previous section that, whereas in the 1950s and 1960s pets were frequently fashionable accessories or bought for recreational or entertainment purposes, from the 1970s onwards companionability is emphasized more and entertainment and decor rather less. The sorts of breeds that are bought and the naming strategies provide a register of change.

In Britain, the top ten dogs of the 1960s contained breeds such as poodles, Pekinese, pugs and other of the highly fashionable miniature and toy breeds. By 1987 none of these featured among the top ten registered dogs. At the top of the list were two types of dog, both related to the changing social conditions of individuals and households. The first group included dogs with heightened companionable and sociable characteristics, mostly former gun dogs such as Labradors, retrievers and spaniels. The second group included dogs with notably antisocial guarding or fighting breed characteristics, such as Rottweilers, Dobermans, Staffordshire bull terriers and German Shepherds. The selection of a large powerful guard dog during the 1980s related directly to rising house break-ins, burglary and theft. Such dogs also have a reputation for being extremely loyal to a single person or principal carer, a feature consistent with increased needs for companionship, particularly among people living alone.

The sociable group are active, lively and extremely human-orientated breeds that are popular with families, but particularly trustworthy with children. As we will see, providing animal companions for children is an extremely widespread strategy, related to the growth of smaller families, 'only children' and working parents. Data released by the Kennel Club in 1996 show that the companion breeds are still holding their place in the top ten. The number one dog is now the Yorkshire Terrier while the German Shepherd is the only remaining representative of the 1980s guard dog phenomenon. The number of cases of dog attacks rose during the 1980s and the guarding/fighting breeds were frequently the culprits. Much of the dog attack anxiety was fanned by intense media attention to the issue, but more reliable data are available from the British Post Office. According to a report of 1986, dog attacks on postmen increased from 3,992 cases in 1976 to 5,560 in 1986. Some areas such as Eltham near London have been declared 'no-go areas' (Council for Science and Society 1988: 57–8). Attacks on children may have deferred many from owning such dogs, but often the dog's owner or a co-householder were bitten, which rather defeats the object. According to Kennel Club registration data, the Rottweiler grew in popularity during the 1980s to a peak of 9,000 registrations in 1987. As they featured in more and more media attack stories their popularity plummeted: to 7,598 in 1988; 3,597 in 1990; 2,456 in 1993.

In the USA similar trends may be discerned from the American Kennel Club data. Throughout the 1970s the poodle was the still the most popular of the pedigree breeds. By the early 1980s it was replaced by a less ornate gundog breed, the Cocker Spaniel, especially known for its social and companionable qualities. From 1989 onwards the Labrador retriever, another gun dog, established itself as the most popular dog, while the Golden retriever rose steadily from tenth place in 1976 to fourth place in 1985. It is clear that the ornate toy breeds declined while companionable social dogs such as the gun dog breeds burgeoned.

Names are also an important guide to the social significance of pets. Like pet food during the 1960s, pets themselves were frequently given dog-specific names such as Rex, Fido and Rover; or cat-specific names such as Kitty, Tibby or Sooty. However, in Australia, the UK and USA companion animals are now more likely to be given human names. In Britain, for example, the 1980s marked a turning point away from the use of 'traditional canine' names, especially Shep, Brandy, Whisky, Rex, Lassie and Rover (Ash 1996). By 1995 the National Canine Defence League's survey found that the ten most popular dog names were all human. Moreover, many of them, such as Ben, Lucy, Sam, Sophie and Charlie, were also currently among the most popular names given to babies. In 1996 the most common name given to a dog by Australians was Sam, whereas in the past Dog was the most common name (*The Age*, 6 March 1996).

While Sam also appears on the US top ten dog names of 1995, along with Heidi and Coco, the extent of humanization is less evident. The top eight were still dog names: Lady, King, Duke, Peppy, Prince, Pepper, Snoopy and Princess. The US trend is not so much opposed to as different from British and Australian trends. Traditional US canine names included such names as Lassie and Rover, but in 1995 they were confined to 82nd and 161st place respectively (Ash 1996). The US listing, based on names recorded on dog licence applications, also contains a greater proportion of bizarre names such as Fag, Bikini, Beowulf and Twit. While these are clearly not so evidently humanized, they may well be more personalized, thus demonstrating a parallel trend: subsequent research, for example, may reveal that such names are similar in all respects to human nicknames, signifying close friendship status. A survey by the American Animal Hospital Association (1996) is more consistent with trends elsewhere. It claims that 'dog and cat owners have said good-bye to Lassie, Spot and Fido. Instead they prefer naming their pet Molly, Sam or Ann'. The survey of 1,206 pet owners found that '51 per cent of dog and cat owners give their pet a human name' and that 'of the top 10 names . . . seven are human names'.

Attitudes to pets

In the 1960s pet keeping was normally thought of as a harmless popular hobby or pastime holding no great social or cultural significance. As the zoologist Serpell remarks, 'almost nothing had been written about it, and there were few, if any, scientific studies' (Serpell 1986: vi). Pet keeping intrigued Serpell: 'it involves considerable emotional and financial expense, but does not appear to serve any obvious purpose'. One of the reasons why pet keeping was not being taken seriously, according to Serpell, was a widespread suspicion that it was somehow perverse, strange and wasteful. The perversity consisted in 'the belief or at least the suspicion that pets are no more than substitutes for so-called "normal" human relationships' (Serpell 1986: 19). His book is dedicated to countering such a view. However, in trying to dismiss the charge of perversity and strangeness, he also finds himself opposed to the idea that the growth of pet keeping is related to social change:

> The technological advances of the twentieth century have dramatically increased human mobility, and brought about the disruption or fragmentation of traditional family and community structures. This trend, it is argued, has increased the need for alternative sources of emotional support and companionship . . . the same argument has been used to explain the increasing significance of friendship in modern social life . . . This idea makes intuitive sense but unfortunately, it is lacking in any supportive evidence.
>
> (Serpell 1986: 121)

Serpell offers three reasons why such a theory might be dismissed. First, because hunter-gatherer societies keep pets and live in 'small, stable and relatively close-knit kin groups', a keen interest in keeping pets cannot be put down to a decline in community. Second, he argues that pets are actually less common among solitary and isolated households than among intact families with children. Third, he argues that pet keeping is no more common in urban than rural areas (Serpell 1986: 121). He does, however, concede the significance of some evidence to show that urban relations with pets do seem to be closer. But there are problems with Serpell's objections. First, all the available literature on hunter-gatherers shows not stable, close-knit groups but intensely flexible, unstable groups where frictions commonly result in band members leaving or bands splitting. Serpell's view is too romantic. Additionally, the theory he criticizes does not say that companionability is the only function or purpose of pet keeping. His wide sweeping review of the anthropology of pets reduces what is certainly a rich, symbolically complex set of human–animal relations into nothing more than a diversion or hobby. Pets can be entertaining distractions from mundane, day-to-day life or from serious social crises and conflicts: both occur within hunter-gatherer societies. One can mount the same reasoning to question his third objection: people in rural Britain may have the same number of pets, but their attitudes and practices do not have to be identical. One might intuitively expect a more instrumental and functional attitude from country dwellers. The reasoning behind his second objection is hardly convincing either. As a social group, the solitary or isolated include many of the elderly and young single people. There are good reasons why such a group may have low rates of pet ownership which have nothing to do with their attitudes to pets: a higher proportion of these life-cycle groups live in rented accommodation which frequently prohibits pet keeping; on average the single elderly have lower incomes than families and cannot afford to keep pets; the elderly are also more likely not to keep a pet for health and mobility related reasons; younger single people are typically more likely to be seeking the company and relationships of friends and lovers rather than animals. Family people may have different motives for pet keeping. Therefore rates of ownership cannot be used as indicators of motives for having or not having, a pet, or what is obtained from the relationship.

Serpell also seems to have ignored an important research finding that was published in an edited collection (Katcher and Beck 1983) to which he was a contributor. Salmon and Salmon (1983) found that Australian respondents stated benefits of pet keeping varied considerably according to life-cycle group. As we might expect, the benefit of friendship was expressed by 83 per cent of the widowed, separated and divorced, 75 per cent of young childless couples and 63 per cent of the singles, but only 44 per cent of young families and 47 per cent of adult families gave friendship as a benefit. Companionship was acknowledged by 100 per cent of old childless couples, 96 per cent of young childless couples, and 96 per cent of the widowed, separated or divorced, while only 87 young families expressed this benefit. Many respondents felt that a pet's childlike qualities were beneficial, but this too varied considerably: only 56 per cent of adult families and 59 per cent of young families gave this as a benefit, but 75 per cent of the widowed, separated and divorced acknowledged it, as did 65 per cent of old childless couples and 67 per cent of young childless couples. As might be expected, the majority of 'singles' are orientated to sociability with peers rather than families, which explains why only 44 per cent of this group expressed this as a benefit (Salmon and Salmon 1983: 258).

Since the publication of Serpell's (1986) *In the Company of Animals*, much of the research which he called for has begun and some of it confirms even more firmly the social foundation of much postmodern pet keeping. Albert and Bulcroft investigated the nature of attachments to pets, companionship, and anthropomorphism in a US sample. Their results were unequivocal:

> Feelings towards pets vary by a number of social/family variables, such as marital status, stage in life cycle. Number and presence of children, and type of pet. Pets are particularly important in the lives of single divorced and widowed people, and people in second or subsequent marriages. Newly-weds and emptynesters are also more attached to pets than are people in the 'middle stages' of the life cycle. Finally, pet attachment is high among people without children or without children at home. Given the demographic changes under way in America . . . it can be hypothesised that pets will become increasingly important in the urban households of the future.

> (Albert and Bulcroft 1988: 22)

The same demographic patterns were found for companionship and anthropomorphism. Although we have no time series data on attitudinal change, it would appear that the number of people most likely to form very close attachments with pets, to seek their companionship and to anthropomorphize their behaviour has increased (see Finch 1989). The nature and extent of human surrogacy and anthropomorphism from the 1980s is a major landmark in social history of the family and the home. Pets are able to provide their keepers with many social benefits which are no longer guaranteed by society:

> The protective and restorative effects of companionship derive not only from the practical or material assistance we obtain from others, but also from a much less clearly

defined sense of being valued or needed. By behaving towards their owners in a highly dependent, possessive and attentive manner, companion animals are particularly good at inspiring this sense of being needed and loved (Serpell 1986). The resemblance between pets and young children, in this respect, is difficult to ignore. Like children, companion animals need to be cared for and nurtured in order to survive; they enjoy being caressed, cuddled, and played with, and they are relatively uninhibited and uncritical in their overtures of friendship and affection.

(Council for Science and Society 1988: 31)

The social significance of pets has been acknowledged by journalists, but only so far through a continuous flow of stories concerning the eccentric and bizarre side of pet anthropomorphism. Pets have never made it into texts on the sociology of the family, despite the trickle of studies that emphasizes the extent of their involvement, their functions and growing importance (Soares 1985), and despite studies that found pets to be defined as family members by their owners. Voith (1985) found that 99 per cent of respondents bringing their pets to a veterinary clinic reported them to be family members, while 87 per cent of Cain's (1983) study gave a similar response. In many senses they embody the benefits of familial relations, in a pure and uncomplicated manner. Ironically, it is Serpell who puts this in the most succinct terms:

By seeking to be near us and soliciting our caresses, by their exuberant greetings and pain on separation, by their possessiveness and their deferential looks of admiration, these animals persuade us that they love us and regard us highly, despite all our manifest deficiencies and failures.

(Serpell 1986: 114)

IDENTITY

While companionship, love and familial relations with pets have reached new heights in late modernity, this does not exhaust their social use value or signi-fication. It is also the case that pets play an interesting role in the construction of self-identity in terms of lifestyle choices. Giddens argues that in modernity each individual faces choices whereas traditional society 'orders life within relatively set channels' (Giddens 1991: 80). He defines lifestyle choices – and everyone has to make them – as 'a more or less integrated set of practices which an individual embraces, not only because such practices fulfil utilitarian needs, but because they give material form to a particular narrative of self-identity'. Applied to the choice of pets in late modernity then, individuals appear to make choices in relation to two types of questions. First, there are functional questions: When do I need a pet (life-cycle stage)? What do I need one for (because I feel lonely; miss my children/husband; need protection, etc.)? Second: What sort of pet do I want? Which pet best fits my lifestyle? Which pet is 'me'?

We have already seen how the emergence of new British urban social elites at the end of the nineteenth century was accompanied by a restratification of the canine order (Ritvo 1987). By the early twentieth century dogs were clear markers of a complex system of social identity based on class. The Kennel Club and the pedigree system were new to this period and the relatively small number of recognized generic breeds in the earlier part of the century burgeoned from the late nineteenth century onwards (Ritvo 1987: 93). Ritvo's analysis of the Kennel Club, the steady increase in recognized breeds and their correct judging 'points' (body shape), the emergence of a cadre of pedigree breeders among the new professional and business elites, together with organized enthusiasms for particular breeds, emphasizes the ways in which pet species served to demarcate the very complex structure of social distinctions in modernity. Here was a clear case of completely new elite groups using the highly malleable body shape of dogs to create a more elaborate economy of dog symbols to suit more complex patterns of social stratification. However, while the pedigree system permitted more elaborate social rankings to be underlined metaphorically, the proliferation of different breeds indicated the operation of lifestyle choices in modernity.

One of the clearest expression of this sort of choice comes from George Eliot's *Middlemarch*. In this novel of 1872 Eliot 'employs the cultural shorthand of the canine to flesh out her characters and to set the stage for various conflicts of the novel' (Ray 1995: 3):

> Dorothea is, significantly, accompanied by a Saint Bernard. Her dog could be no other, considering her world view: a Bedlington terrier would not do, nor a collie, a Pomeranian or a saluki. She passionately wants 'to learn everything', to 'learn to see the truth by the same light as great men have seen it by'. Virtuous action is her ultimate goal: the contemplative life, she believes, must necessarily result in active and useful works. What better companion could there be for such a person than a Saint Bernard, a dog named for a hospice founded by a saint, a dog bred as a saviour of lost travellers, as a large comforter and companion par excellence? Her favouring of this breed over other breeds [especially the toy Maltese offered to her by Sir James Chettham] also heralds her choice of Casaubon, whom she perceives as saintly.
>
> (Ray 1995: 3–4)

Eliot's metaphoric device here presupposes a reader knowledgeable of the extent to which dogs served as props to social identity, and of the relatively fine brush strokes of signification that it permits. *Middlemarch* is a good early example of this, particularly because Eliot's Dorothea was painfully breaking out of traditional society roles and opting for a lifestyle based on choice.

Later, in the twentieth century, the common notion that dog owners come to resemble their pets conceals perhaps the owners' initial desire to find a breed consistent with their social identity. This practice has been observed by veterinary scientists:

> The breed of a dog that a person owns may be a projection of deeper needs and identifications. An insecure or paranoid person may want a powerful guard dog. Another person who is attempting to live up to an ego image of grace and agility may keep an Afghan hound or saluki. It is primarily because of these reasons that the pet often resembles its owner – it is something more than mere coincidence.
>
> (Fox 1974, cited in PetCare Information and Advisory Service 1977: 14)

No doubt the 'cultural shorthand of the canine' is both complex and prone to change. Certainly, no one has ever attempted to specify it, even in general terms, for any one society. Some breeds in Britain, for example, offer the possibility of identification with particular groups in society and may well aid processes of assimilation and belonging. Examples include: pedigree gun dogs among the rural middle classes (particularly black Labradors, spaniels, pointers or Golden retrievers); traditional poaching dogs such as lurchers among New Age travellers; toy breeds among the retired urban middle classes; and traditional fighting, racing and guard dogs among some sections of the working class. Regional identity and ethnicity are also expressed through dogs (e.g. corgis in Wales, Scottish terrier breeds in Scotland) and in the past some breeds were associated with particular trades or skilled workers. The Yorkshire terrier, for example, originated among Yorkshire weavers and for many years was more or less confined to their fraternity. Various working breeds such as barge dogs, sheep dogs and foxhounds were specific to particular occupational groups. In contemporary times dogs have also been used to specify masculinities and femininities. In recent years in Britain and Australia, for example, pit bull terriers complete with brass-studded leather collars have become familiar accessories to the physically tough 'bloke'; Apricot toy poodles have been popular among effeminate gay men. Standard poodles, Afghans, Pomeranians and salukis are feminine dogs, associated particularly with the urban, wealthy and young. Similarly pugs, schnauzers and chihauhuas are associated with older middle-class women.

However, dogs' shapes, colours, temperaments and sizes are so varied and malleable that individuals are able to make very finely tuned choices when seeking a dog consistent with or expressive of individual identity: Dorothea's St Bernard; Bill Sykes's bull terrier; Barbara Cartland's Pekinese; the Queen's corgis; Claude Greengrass's mongrel 'Alfred', etc. etc. As pedigree dogs have become more affordable and more widely distributed socially, the part played by dogs in the construction of self-identity has no doubt become more generalized, like a fashion option. However, dogs are not merely symbolic adornments. Pedigree dogs in particular have acquired standardized reputations in terms of temperament and character in addition to their looks. The acquisition of particular dogs enables their owners and others to impute a dog's breed character onto its owner. This has been noticed by analysts of the British 'dog attack' panics between 1988 and 1992:

> Because we identify with our pets and tend to project onto them our own fantasies and feelings, the aggressive dog inevitably reflects badly on its owner. The owners of the Rottweiler, German Shepherd or APBT [American pit bull terrier] thus become potential criminals themselves, whether or not they actually deserve the title.
>
> (Podberscek 1994: 240)

Cats' bodies are less malleable than dogs and, although there is a discernible range of shapes, colours and temperaments, breed variation tends to be less significant than species character in the popular imagination. Although many dog owners will also keep cats, some people only want cats. They are preferred for a number of their attributes, but among them are the symbols of social identity which they convey. Whereas dogs have accrued character traits along an essentially social register, cats are more socially ambiguous: they are in but not of the social, and have been attributed with characteristics consistent with that. Cats are mysterious, secretive, sexual (female), aloof, intellectual, independent and spiritual; they are of nature whereas dogs are of culture. These seemingly cross-cultural traits have seen them deified in Egypt, China and Thailand and burned as witches in Europe. In modernity, however, these attributes are assimilated by the owners and are not merely part of their aesthetic appeal. Because cats are seen as independent and single minded (whereas dogs are more conservative and conforming), they have enjoyed popularity among social rebels from the 1960s onwards. Cats symbolize the freedom from social constraint and the autonomy of the individual. Cat breeds offer variations on a theme: the long-haired, Persian-type cats are redolent of pampered (female) luxury; Siamese cats convey, with some help from Disney, association with powerful women, singlemindedness, even ruthlessness; black cats offer identification with spiritual and mystic forces (another form of female power). Indeed, some research suggests that women have a stronger relationship with cats than men (Mertens 1991).

THERAPY

While pets are now freely acknowledged as social substitutes for family, partners, children, and so on, recent research suggests that such bonds and relations are also functional for health and well-being. From the 1980s onwards, medical surveys and clinical studies have shown a variety of benefits from owning a pet, but the two most significant findings are that pet ownership is associated with better recovery from heart disease and lower instances of depression. It seems that both may be related to reductions in stress as a result of caring for and forming a close attachment to a pet. Since rising levels of stress are centrally linked to the social conditions of late modernity, and since stress is in turn linked to so many illnesses and escalating health budgets, it is not surprising that pet keeping as a relatively cheap, non-pharmaceutical, home-based intervention has been taken so seriously. Indeed, pets have been trialed in other situations where stress is a problem: in prisons, mental health hospitals and old people's homes.

The earliest studies of pets and health focused on the elderly, particularly because they are major users of medical resources. Akiyama et al. (1986–7) found that recently bereaved pet owners experienced considerably fewer common ailments such as headaches and constipation than recently bereaved non-owners. In another national sample of the elderly in the USA, Garrity et al. (1988) found that physical health was substantially better among pet owners lacking human support than among non-owners lacking human support. In addition, those pet owners who had formed strong attachments with their pets but who lacked a confidant were also less likely to suffer depression than non-owners lacking a social confidant. The ambitious claims made by early studies were later tested by more sophisticated methodologies, but most, such as that of Judith Siegel (1990) only confirmed or modified the earlier findings. Siegel found that in a prospective study of elderly persons in California 'subjects who owned pets reported fewer doctor contacts over a one-year period than subjects who did not own pets'. Siegel also found that pet owners required less medical intervention at times of stress than non-pet owners. Cynics may point out that these data do not show a connection between pets and better health, only a weaker propensity to seek the advice of doctors than non-owners. It may mean nothing more than that the lonely seek out the company of medical practitioners more than those with pets. However, some confidence in these claims comes from other studies that showed pet owners to enjoy better recovery from serious heart disease.

In a study by Friedmann et al. (1984), people with very high risk of heart attack (those with a diagnosis of myocardial infarction or angina pectoris) were the subject of a 19-month survival study. Ninety-five per cent of those with a pet (of any kind) survived this period as compared with only 74 per cent of those living without a pet. Moreover, the company of a pet proved a more sound predictor of survival than either marital companionship or social isolation.

Subsequent studies into the relationship between pets and health tend to confirm rather than dispute these findings. Prominent among them was an Australian physiological study which found that pet owners had lower levels of risk factors for cardiovascular disease, regardless of their smoking habits, body mass, socio-economic profile and other risk variables (Anderson et al. 1992). Further research has investigated the aetiology of the link, particularly between stress and illness reduction and pets. Friedmann et al. (1984) followed up their revelatory work on pets and heart disease with a study of the effects of pets on high blood pressure. Elaborate psychological tests confirmed that even the presence of an unknown dog could reduce blood pressure during a range of stressful circumstances. A recent study examined the relationship between pets and stress and found that while stress reactions can become locked into an individual long after exposure to stressful circumstances, contact with pets can break them down rapidly and reliably (Anderson et al. 1992).

It is not surprising therefore that many have called for a more systematic use of pets as a therapeutic intervention. While the prescription of pets has been seriously called for though not yet funded by any national health scheme, some success has been made in lifting the bans on pets in state-funded housing schemes and nursing homes. Moreover, Headey and Anderson (1995) have calculated the savings made on health budgets (both private and government) as a result of pet ownership in Australia. Based on survey findings suggesting lower numbers of doctor visits among dog or cat owners, they suggest the savings are in the order of $A790 million per year (if only the main pet carers are factored in) to $A1.5 billion per year (if half the benefits of pet ownership to main carers is extended to other members of the family). However, they conclude that the savings could be considerably more following a 'campaign to promote the benefits of the human–animal bond' (Headey and Anderson 1995: 7). But even that may not exhaust the total savings to national budgets if other non-medical applications are factored in.

It would appear likely that pets will be used more systematically in the care and treatment regimes of particular illnesses, especially heart disease. More generally, it may prove difficult to ignore their potential savings to burgeoning national health budgets. In the meantime, the number of smaller scale pet-based therapeutic schemes have grown considerably in most Western countries. Although most of these trace their descent to the post-1980s findings on pets and health, the idea that animals have therapeutic value dates back to the late eighteenth century. In England, the Quaker, William Tuke, established a liberal and permissive mental asylum known as the York Retreat. Central to treatment was the encouragement of active care and maintenance of small domestic animals such as rabbits and chickens. 'Tuke believed that contact with pet animals helped the insane to develop self-control by "having dependent upon them creatures weaker than themselves"' (Council for Science and Society 1988: 31). In 1867 a similar idea prevailed at a German residential treatment centre for epilepsy. Unlike many experimental therapies of this period, the 'animal treatment' at Bethel-Bielefeldt has stood the test of time and currently it is much expanded and elaborate: 5,000 mentally and physically handicapped patients engage in pet keeping, horse riding, tasks on working farms and maintaining a safari park (Council for Science and Society 1988: 31–2). Pet-facilitated therapy (PFT) is an established and respectable treatment approach, but its legitimacy derives not from the confidence and results of the early pioneers but from the work of the American child psychologist Boris Levinson and the subsequent empirical testing of his claims.

Levinson noticed that while he often had difficulty establishing communication and a working relationship with emotionally disturbed children, they frequently warmed to his pet dog. Levinson then began to use his dog therapeutically to act as a catalyst to social interaction and to speed up the treatment process. A series of papers followed in which Levinson attempted to explain their therapeutic potency. The catalyst effect was achieved for two reasons: first, because pets initiate or stimulate friendly, playful and unthreatening contact; second, because they prove a neutral, reassuring channel for the discussion of fears, worries and anxieties. Pets were always better at this than therapists because, however well intentioned and good their social manner, they can be perceived as judgemental or critical, whereas animals cannot (Levinson 1969).

Further papers explored the use value and function of pets in child development:

> Children, even in a world which surrounds us with machines and inanimate objects to which the rhythms must be geared, are still able to use pets to fulfil deep emotional needs and to serve as a bridge to human society. Since children learn best not by words but by active manipulation of and interaction with the world through their bodies, the non-verbal relationship with animals is a natural medium for exploring the animate but non-human world. The knowledge gained can then carry over to his [sic] dealings with humans, including himself.
>
> In the normal course of development, pet animals can help the child overcome his fears, gain empathy for others, achieve mastery and self-esteem, explore his sexuality, contain his aggression and deal with death. Pets can provide partial substitution for parents and peers when these are not sufficiently available . . . They also provide the child with a mirror wherein to see himself reflected as he relates to his pet.

> (Levinson 1980: 80)

Research in particular therapeutic settings has shown some promising results. Corson and O'Leary Corson's (1980) research looked at the effects of introducing PFT to hospitalized psychiatric patients who had failed to respond adequately to traditional forms of therapy. Only three out of fifty did not respond or show signs of improvement and the results indicated the potential for less reliance on pharmacotherapy. The therapeutic process was similar to that observed by Levinson:

> Pet animals and especially dogs offered patients and nursing home residents a form of non-threatening, non-judgemental, reassuring, non-verbal communication and tactile comfort and thus helped to break the vicious cycle of loneliness, helplessness and social withdrawal. Pet animals acted as effective socialising catalysts with other patients, residents and staff and thus helped to improve the overall morale of the institution and create a community out of detached individuals.
>
> (Corson and O'Leary Corson 1980: 107)

Subsequent research has examined the benefits of pets in prisons (Moneymaker and Strimpel 1991; Walsh and Mertin 1994), in communal housing for the elderly (Verderber 1991), in residential accommodation for former psychiatric patients (Nielson and Delude 1994), and in homes for elderly veterans (Robb 1983) and the reports are evenly favourable.

Although pets clearly have a therapeutic role in a variety of settings – even if that role is a secondary facilitating role – their value to inmates of institutions is more or less the same as for all people in late modernity. The lamentations of Sartre and Sennett for lost community in the 1960s have given way in the 1990s to a degree of acceptance of the unevenness of social contact, the unreliability of close emotional human ties and the spatially distanced nature of social relations and networks. Ironically perhaps, one of the first groups in society to feel the benefits of human–pet relations were members of royal and aristocratic households in the eighteenth century (K. Thomas 1983: 102–5). Members of such households might be regularly separated from loved family members for long periods, spatially distanced from other related households and required to distance themselves socially from most others around them. Then, as now, pet animals can provide companionship, love and attention to humans wherever it is required. In late modernity we are now self-consciously aware of their value and unselfconscious in acknowledging it. Royal enthusiasms for animal companionship are no longer such a mystery.

6 NATURALIZING SPORTS

Hunting and angling in modernity

While conflict over development has attracted most attention as an environmental issue, how best to open up natural areas to public consumption comes as a close second. The most colourful and heated consumption conflict centres on the issue of hunting and angling. Should natural areas be consumed passively, to see but not disturb its inhabitants, or actively, through a series of traditional food gathering and hunting relationships with natural areas? Given the historical trajectory of changing human sentiments towards wildlife, as set out by Keith Thomas (1983) and others, one might imagine that hunting and angling would have declined steadily over the twentieth century, especially over the second half. The romantic animal gaze so pervades Western cultures in late modernity that one might doubt that the older 'field sports' survive in any but the most conservative of backwaters. Indeed, almost every book published since the 1970s which reflects on modern relationships between humans and animals urges more restraint, more humanity, more paternalism and protection, more respect for animal life and rights. Yet despite this, both hunting and angling have remained popular sports in the West and have grown throughout this period. This chapter asks how this can be and investigates why these sports, which involve the participant in a close 'sporting' relationship with animals, have a particular appeal in late modernity and with whom.

Hunting and angling are therefore enigmas in modernity. While slaughtering, butchery and meat have become shrouded in guilt, shame, disgust and avoidance, these hands-on killing sports have enjoyed sustained popularity and growth during the twentieth century. While animals have been increasingly protected against cruelty and brutality (for example, in 1996 a Wild Mammal Act became effective against a range of actions against wild mammals in Britain), and subject to more sentimentalization, love and care, hunting and angling have remained exempt from all legislation until very recently. All too frequently debates about hunting sports focus on ethical questions and their political significance. This approach obscures the historical and cultural significance of hunting sports and their embeddedness in social networks and communities. It ignores the reasons that hunters give for their enthusiasms or the nature of their relations with prey and other species. It fails to reflect on modern hunting as a genuine and enduring form of 'natural relation' with the environment and hunters as actors in the environment. It reinforces a dubious 'great divide' between the modern and the pre-modern (hunting is only ethically supportable in the case of hunters and gathering cultures). It ignores continuities and similarities (James 1996) and the gendered nature of these activities.

A sociological account must seek to illuminate, describe and explain rather than judge and this chapter will profess a curiosity to hunting and angling in modernity appropriate to the anthropology of hunters anywhere. In this way, we can understand hunting and angling as both anti-modern, nostalgic and romantic discourses while at the same time being wrought as leisure forms by essentially modern social forces. Hunting and angling provide extremely good examples of the tendency in late modernity to increase the contact we have with nature in general and animals in particular, hence the title of this chapter, 'naturalizing sports'. If any sort of activity expresses an opposition to and a rejection of the social character of modernity it is angling and hunting sports: the complex division of labour in modernity gives way to the self-sufficiency of the hunter/ angler; the crowded congested city is opposed by the loneliness and isolation of the bush or wetland; the mechanical rhythms and noise of the factory are contrasted with the ebbs and flows of natural processes, seasonality and quietude of the wilderness; the *gesellschaft* of work and civil life give way to the frater-nities and *gemeinschaft* of 'the field'; the demand for progress and its blasé indifference to environmental effects is opposed by a conservation ethic, a love of specific country, of its flora and fauna and attentiveness to its detail.

According to their sporting literatures, there can be no greater absorption in natural environments than that of the hunter and angler who, in order to succeed against wary prey, must study and know their secrets and blend in rather than explore surfaces as mere tourists. The hunting and angling literatures of the twentieth century all attempt to express and explain these natural relations and knowledges and combine to form a consistent critique of modernity and the rejection of an exclusively modern urban social identity. Their arguments suggest the interesting possibility of developing multiple identities which include a working identity in a number of natural environments. These predispositions have made hunters and anglers sensitive to and aware of environmental destruction in late modernity. We find in their literature and journals a growing concern for animals and an increasing tendency to champion them (see Figures 6.1, 6.2). To all intents and purposes, theirs is a sustainable but harvestable environmentalism with room for humans active in the food chain and not merely voyeurs of a remote 'nature' – increasingly rendered off-limits to humans. As Berger (1980) argued, it is not a contradiction for hunters (anywhere) to love and kill animals. Hunters frequently express moral superiority over the urban meat consumer who prefers to avoid all reference to the conditions of life and death of the animals they so lustily consume. Equally, lacking such refinements and squeamishness, hunters and anglers are likely to be seen as base, cruel and barbaric by urbanites. It is not surprising therefore that hunters and anglers find themselves increasingly in conflict with middle-class urbanites over their continued rights to hunt and fish.

In August 1997 one of the largest groups of protesters ever assembled in Hyde Park, London, gathered to protest against proposed legislation to ban hunting foxes and other mammals with hounds. Although explicitly directed against the hunting of foxes, hunters and anglers knew that this was the first part of an agenda to ban all hunting sports. The crowd was composed of hunters and anglers and while speeches identified the conflict as based on urban versus rural claims for an appropriate human relation with wildlife in which an urban majority were imposing their views on the countryside, it was more accurately a conflict between traditional human–animal relations (subscribed to by both urban and rural people) and a mix of new urban sensibilities and the discourse of animal rights. Equally, many states in the USA and Australia have commenced legislations to restrict hunting sports. Some of these concern practices such as baiting for bears which have very few supporters anywhere, but others involve less contentious practices such as duck hunting. The ban on duck hunting in several Australian states suggests that this movement will seek to expand its range. When it attempts to ban more popular activities such as deer hunting in the USA and fishing generally, the scope for major social conflict is considerable.

We will return to the issue of social conflict in the final section of this chapter. Before that we will first complete a brief survey of contemporary hunting and angling cultures in the USA and Britain where the most extensive data sets have been collected. The social composition of these sports offers important clues as to their significance in late modernity. In the second section we will consider the various appeals of these activities through anti-modern, neo-Darwinian, ecologistic and masculine discourses.

SOCIAL COMPOSITION OF HUNTING AND ANGLING IN THE USA AND UK

In the USA, hunting and angling have a place in national culture alongside other components of the American Dream. A popular hunting and angling fraternity is central to the American (male) national identity, particularly because it puts into practice so many values of American individualism: freedom of movement and access to natural resources; the appropriation of natural bounty, self-provisioning and self-reliance; male bonding and male companionship; the aestheticization of American nature; the essential healthiness of the great outdoors. Importantly, hunting and angling enable modern American men to touch base with their historical roots as an open, frontier, country culture involved in a struggle with natural forces. This is what distinguishes American from European heritages, since the European landscape and nature have since at least the medieval period been tamed, tightly controlled, socially differentiated and crowded (Nash 1967). Whereas hunting and angling in Europe so frequently express the social and spatial organization of landscape and nature in terms of class, in America they express nation. Perhaps this is why they are so popular and ubiquitous, and why they have such a robust and growing following. As national identities are under threat everywhere from globalization, it is no surprise that the particular and distinctive components of a nation's nature become the setting and underpinning for a reconstructed national social identity.

Data on hunting and angling in the USA reflect its privilege and longstanding position in national life. The National Survey of Fishing, Hunting and Wildlife Associated Recreation was first administered in 1955 and has been regularly conducted ever since. In 1991, 35.6 million Americans aged 16 years old or over

(19 per cent of the population),went fishing in the previous year. This compares with only 14.1 million hunters representing 7.4 per cent of the population. In terms of participation, these sports are more significant than any other sporting activity. On average American anglers fish on 14 days per year and spend on average $674 per year on fishing, while hunters hunt for 16.7 days per year on average and spend an average of $872 per person. The markets for both activities are thus very significant: $24 billion for angling; $12.3 billion for hunting. Hunting and angling are remarkably evenly distributed across America. Participation rates for angling range from a low of 13 per cent in the mid-Atlantic region to a high of 27 per cent in the West North Central region; participation rates for hunting range from 4 per cent in New England and Pacific to 13 per cent in West North Central.

While hunting and angling are clearly masculine sports, angling has a significant female participation rate, which for hunting is very insignificant. In 1991, 28 per cent of American males aged 16 or over fished, while only 14 per cent hunted. However, 10 per cent of American women aged 16 years of age or over fished, as compared to only 1 per cent who hunted. Hunting and angling also differ considerably with regard to income, education, race and urban–rural demography. Angling participation increases with income in all except the very highest income band where it decreases only slightly. Hunting participation rises sharply with income towards the middle-income bands and then decreases by a similar rate as income rises. This suggests that in the USA fishing may be a higher status activity than hunting. Such a conclusion is supported by data on education. The highest participation rate (21 per cent) was found among people who had 1 to 4 years of college education and the rate among those with five or more years college education was only slightly less at 19 per cent. Americans with eight years or less education had the lowest participation rate of 11 per cent. While American anglers are predominantly white (92 per cent), 10 per cent of the black population fish as compared to 20 per cent of the white population. Hunting is more exclusively white: 97 per cent of all hunters are white and only 2 per cent of black people hunt as compared with 8 per cent of white people. The largest proportion of anglers (32 per cent) lived in the large Metropolitan Statistical Areas (MSAs) as compared to only 22 per cent of hunters, while the largest proportion of hunters lived outside MSAs (44 per cent) as compared to only 30 per cent of anglers. It is also perhaps significant that the vast majority of anglers (87 per cent) are freshwater or inland anglers: America was until relatively recently a rural culture orientated towards the land and the interior. The aestheticization of American nature favoured forest, high country, lakes and streams over sea and coastline; thus it is not surprising that freshwater angling has built up such a strong following.

Even though there are clear social differences between hunters and anglers in the USA, 9.7 million people (5 per cent of the population) participated in both activities. However, there are important social divisions within each of these activities. Hummel, for example, underlines the social division between bass and trout anglers in the USA and strongly suggests that these are based on class (Hummel 1994: 44). Fly fishing for trout, especially in more recent years, has become an elite sport for a fraction of the upper middle class, with a considerable appeal among urban-based, college-educated men. The success of Norman Maclean's (1976) *A River Runs Through It*, Raines's (1993) *Fly Fishing Through the Midlife Crisis* and Gierach's (1986) *Trout Bum* exemplify the appeal of fly fishing among this social class.

Despite the clear exclusivity of fly fishing in the USA (or perhaps because of it), it is attracting a growing following. 'By one estimate, there were a hundred dry fly purists in the United States in 1929 . . . By 1986 there were an estimated one million fly fishers, and in 1992, the number had risen to three million' (Raines 1993: 235). This rapid growth in recent years is mirrored in the British data which are considered below. Quite why so many are drawn to an activity like fly fishing in postmodern times will be considered in the next section.

Bass fishing in the USA is characterized by many opposing values. It is orientated to a democratic and inclusive style of fishing. The goal is to catch the biggest or the most fish in competitions using the very latest in electronic technology; satisfaction comes from the quantity of the catch and the rewards are based on public displays of skill and esteem. If not an exclusively working-class pursuit, bass is certainly the most popular species fished for in the USA. Some 19 million people fish for black and white bass, representing 54 per cent of all freshwater anglers. Its appeal is based on its relative ease of capture, the commodification of bass fishing tackle (which almost constitutes a separate aesthetic as an 'accessory sport'), and the fact that the fish is found in all fifty states.

Hunting in the USA cannot be broken down into similarly opposed sociations, perhaps because hunters occupy the broad middle ground of American society. There is some patterning, however. The lower income hunters are predominantly rural while the higher income hunters tend to be predominantly urban. There may be some correlation between big game hunting and the higher income groups and a greater participation of lower income groups with small game hunting, but such patterns are overshadowed by the dominance of deer hunting. Of the 14.1 million hunters in the USA, 10.7 million (or 76 per cent) are deer hunters. Compared to angling, hunting is less differentiated in terms of methods and ethics. Most hunters use a gun, and all shoot to kill – to do otherwise is considered unethical. Those who prefer to shoot with a bow, crossbow or antique firearm do not assume superiority over those who do not. There is no evidence that some species are considered inferior, less noble or less acceptable socially than others.

However, the economics of hunting has changed considerably in recent years. It has altered from a largely spontaneous, self-directed recreation to an organized service industry catering for relatively wealthy urban hunters who lack the time and commitment required to achieve success on their own. The industry has packaged hunting into a form of social Darwinian nature tourism. As reliable quantities of game exist only in the less habitable areas, hunters now fly into wilderness hunting lodges and rely completely on guiding services and lodge accommodation in tourist-style packages. Hummel (1994) described four contemporary forms of hunting services currently available in the USA. For $800 plus travel costs it is possible to have seven days moose hunting in Ontario,

Canada. The outfitter flies parties to cabins in the wilderness, provides fully equipped do-it-yourself accommodation and boats and checks on the hunters twice a week.

Second, Hummel described a commodified bear-hunting experience. For $800 for five days (plus travel) black bear hunting is widely available. No doubt this is cheaper because baits are set to encourage the bears to feed in predictable and convenient locations and hunters are guided to perfect shooting sites in which to take their trophy head.

The third form of commodified hunting documented by Hummel involved private syndicates of hunters purchasing hunting grounds by the acre/year from a landowner and equipping the lease with accommodation, animal feeds and services. Birds, deer and rabbits were kept on the lease by feed supplementation and the populations of game were very high. This system is clearly intended to concentrate the best hunting and restrict access to the few who can afford it in a way similar to the management and sale of shooting on English estates.

However, the fourth form, the commercial game ranch, is completely new. Large ranches are stocked with exotic trophy animals and hunters are able to order in animals not currently stocked and pay only for those they shoot:

> The owner contends that modern-day hunting in the wilds is so costly in time and money and the success rates are relatively low, especially in something like elk hunting (7–17 per cent). The ranch offers a hunter the specific animals s/he wants to pursue, when s/he has the time to pursue them. The hunter pays only for what is shot. The guide and lodging/meals fees are relatively modest. The trophy fees (price of the animals) are substantial but less than the cost of wilderness hunting trips with their marginal expectations of success.
>
> (Hummel 1994: 102)

In other words, this is convenience hunting. These ranches are now numerous and successful in the USA and hunting magazines and web sites offer a completely global stock of animals and fast service. At one web site, a ranch advertising guided boar shooting concludes, 'To reserve your hunt just phone . . . and ask for Ron.'

In the UK, hunting and angling are more socially differentiated, reflecting the very different history of social organization and ownership of land and resources. In Britain hunting and fishing rights were historically commodified and reserved for a landowning class in specific game laws, while in the USA, partly in reaction to such inequalities in the old country, provision was made for universal access to vast areas of resources. This is why hunting and angling are more popular and less differentiated socially in the USA. The social history of hunting and angling in Britain continues to influence the attitudes, meanings and practices in these sports in a number of ways.

Angling is an ancient British sport and the subject of one of the earliest printed books in the English language (de Worde 1496). Throughout the early modern period almost all of the fishing in Britain was owned as a separable commodity from the land, although of course in most instances fishing (or riparian) rights were held in common with the land it bordered. Riparian rights could be bought and sold separately, and owners could give permission or licence to whomsoever they chose. However, the highly stratified nature of British society ensured that access to fishing was restricted to the landowning classes and their social networks. The poor were allowed to fish in some areas as a form of charity, but historically, angling is associated with the gentlemanly class, which is why it has such a strong following among the middle and upper classes, a sophisticated literature, and also why fishing tackle was the basis of a high quality craft industry.

Isaak Walton's *The Compleat Angler* (1971, 1653) provides an important ethnographic guide to English angling culture of the seventeenth century. It is clear that the anglers were a gentlemanly fraternity who considered angling to be an aesthetic art, a celebration of creation and a therapeutic activity. It was associated with the clergy and emerging forms of civility in the post-civil war period and contrasted strongly with the noise, violence and commotion of hunting. In Walton's time the strict social division between game and coarse angling did not exist. Anglers fished for all species in their season, and aimed to be all-rounders. Some, like Walton's friends Cotton and Venables, were dedicated fly fishermen but such specialism did not become the basis of social division in their period. It was in the nineteenth century that a major bifurcation occurred. Although the gentleman angler continued to pursue all species, fly fishing, particularly the emergence of dry fly and nymph fishing became the basis of upper-class exclusivity. From the middle of the nineteenth century the numbers of anglers grew, putting considerable pressure on many waters. Part of this pressure was due to rising wages among the lower classes and cheap access via rail to all parts of England. In response, exclusive and expensive clubs and syndicates swallowed up the best of the trout streams, particularly in the south. Middle-class anglers also travelled widely into Scotland, Wales and Ireland in pursuit of other 'game' fish, salmon and sea trout, staying in expensive purpose-built fishing hotels. These acquired the fishing rights to very large stretches of water and in effect kept them for the exclusive use of their guests. In this way, they preserved something of their historic exclusivity in angling, but in so doing they more or less confined themselves to the salmon and trout species.

By 1870 working-class anglers were also forming into clubs and purchasing the cheaper coarse fishing leases on the slower rivers and lakes. Thus, well before the turn of the twentieth century there was a rigid class division expressed in angling. Coarse fishing was predominantly bait fishing while game fishing was predominantly artificial lure and fly fishing. Rather less is known about the social history of sea angling. It had a considerable following among the middle class in the better seaside resorts, especially pier fishing, and there was considerable interest in the game fish of the sea (tuna and shark especially). However, sea angling rapidly became a working-class province, particularly when the price of fishing tackle and seaside holidays dropped.

In 1994 there were 3.3 million anglers in Britain representing 7.2 per cent of the population aged 12 or over. Angling grew to 8.2 per cent of the population in the 1980s but the current numbers of anglers are still greater than they were in the

1970s. Of these 2.3 million are coarse anglers, 0.8 million are game anglers and 1.1 million are sea anglers. Over the past twenty years the number of coarse anglers increased by 22 per cent and game anglers by 26 per cent, but sea angling declined by 14 per cent. This is a significant overall increase and we will return to examine its cause below. As in the USA, angling is a predominantly male sport: 88 per cent of anglers are male and 12 per cent female, and these proportions have not changed in the past ten years, despite considerable effort by the tackle industry to encourage women anglers. Angling is evenly distributed between the social classes but it is most popular among the skilled working classes (17 per cent of households contained at least one angler) and least popular among the professional, management and executive households (9 per cent) (National Rivers Authority 1994: 13). Other evidence suggests that the latter group contains very significant variations however. According to Savage et al. (1992), one middle-class group, which they called 'ascetic', are particularly low consumers of angling, although otherwise very high consumers of nature activities such as bush walking and camping, while another group consisting of middle-class managers are particularly high consumers of angling and shooting:

> They seem more prone . . . to seek 'escape' in the form of modified versions of country pursuits earlier adopted by the landed aristocracy. For the managers at least, the pursuit of a cleaned-up version of the 'heritage' or 'countryside' tradition seems apposite.
>
> (Savage et al. 1992: 116)

It may be that a more affordable form of game fishing is being appropriated by this group to provide clear markers of status, alongside other activities such as golf, squash and tennis.

Angling in Britain has retained the fraternity and organization which characterized the earlier period. In 1994, 51 per cent of all anglers belonged to a club, with club membership highest among game anglers (62 per cent for salmon anglers, 55 per cent for trout anglers) and lowest among sea anglers (48 per cent). The working-class tradition of organized coarse angling was also significant with 56 per cent belonging to a club. 'Only 30 per cent have never belonged to a club' (National Rivers Authority 1994: 15).

Coarse angling is predominantly a skilled working-class sport and is divided into two principal groups. First, there are those oriented to competitions, or match fishermen, whose aim is to catch the heaviest weight of fish, usually dominated by roach and bream. This is the traditional organized working-class form of angling dating back to the nineteenth century (Lowerson 1988). The second group can be described as specimen hunters, or specialists, and they aim only to catch good sized examples of one species of fish. Every species has its followers and dedicated organizations but the biggest by far is the carp. Thirty-six per cent of those coarse anglers who expressed a species preference in 1994 preferred carp. In 1970 carp barely featured among preferred fish species and the field was dominated by roach (39 per cent) and pike (29 per cent). But in the past twenty years the demand for carp fishing has increased substantially, alongside other

FIGURE 6.1   *Yes – a living fish and the promotion of catch and release (instructions from the contributors' guide for* Freshwater Fishing Australia*)*

FIGURE 6.2   *No – piles of dead fish lying around (instructions from the contributors' guide for* Freshwater Fishing Australia*)*

specimen hunting. It has generated a more environmentally sensitive and ethically elaborate form of angling that reflects new values, particularly the significance attached to the interests of the fish (Figures 6.1 and 6.2).

Hunting in Britain is considerably less popular than angling, and aside from the continuation of small game hunting by a rural working class, it has remained an upper-class sport and a central feature of their domination of the British country-side. Perhaps because hunting is an essentially private activity or an exclusive service industry, data are less available or reliable than in the USA. Hunting in the UK is also at the centre of a growing controversy in which the sport has attracted sufficient public opposition for anti-hunting legislation to commence. Under such circumstances, accurate information is becoming restricted.

For at least 900 years hunting in England has been a rural activity closely linked to an agricultural landscape. Wilderness forests had long since given way to smaller, tightly controlled and scattered woodlands which could hold small populations of deer and other game such as wild boar (Darvill 1987). These animals became the exclusive province of royalty and the aristocracy. Other hunted animals such as hares, rabbits and game birds were scattered among the patchwork of open agricultural land, fallow, commons and wetlands and were reckoned as part of the value and price of any given landholding or estate. As such, hunting became a landholders' sport, and the entire tradition and industry is dominated by their patronage. The pattern of landownership was stable until the eighteenth and nineteenth century when the enclosure acts concentrated more land in fewer hands and the captains of industry began to seek a status and life style commensurate with their new wealth (Tester 1989). In order to move in the best circles and to be accepted, a rural estate was a minimal requirement. It was also important to become proficient in rural sports since so much socialization and conversation focused on them. By the mid-eighteenth century, deer had become scarce and unavailable in many districts. Fox hunting, which had barely featured before, rapidly became popularized and fashionable. It had all the pomp, ceremony and ritual of the deer hunt, and could therefore claim kinship with the sport of kings. There was no better way of emphasizing the total control of the landscape by one social class than to dress in bright red and to ride to hounds wherever they chose. Indeed, by the late eighteenth century it was the most popular sport of all, winning support from royalty, clergy and the military who could at least claim some functional purpose for encouraging fast riding. Shooting and deer stalking were a feature of many Scottish estates and became an attraction in the form of hunting tourism among the middle classes by the twentieth century, when hunting continued more or less unchanged. Attitudes to hunting as an elite pleasure of the landowners remained:

> Britain's landowners are often conscious of their land less as a source of wealth or power than as their personal playground. Outsiders may be struck by the degree of wealth and power which the ownership of land may bestow. But, traditionally the British landowner has not cared to be seen to be concerned about such things. For him, the habit of thought persists that the serious business of life is play.

(Shoard 1987: 266)

However, changes that affected other groups in society were to modify and challenge their exclusivity. The growth of the salariat and rising real wages meant that shooting in particular became affordable by more than just the rural gentry. Rough shooting for species such as pigeons and rabbits, prone to population explosions as the countryside shed more and more people, became cheaply available. Ferreting, a working-class sport became more popular, as did hare coursing. Indeed, up until the 1970s there was a considerable efflorescence of interest in rural hunting skills and people from a wide variety of backgrounds and incomes became involved. In part this was because the old estates were struggling financially and began to sell their shooting, particularly pheasant shooting, as a serious business. This provided shooting opportunities to the middle classes seeking traditional forms of status display.

A similar trend occurred in the Netherlands where the hunting population is better documented through state regulation. Between 1900 and 1940 the numbers of hunters rose from 7,000 to 12,000, but the main boom occurred after 1945 when numbers increased to 41,000 by 1977 (Dahles 1993: 3). European Community calculations showing the amount of hunting grounds available to each hunter reveal the sort of pressure that popular post war hunting has placed on the countryside. In the Netherlands there is 1.2 sq km per hunter left, but in Denmark there is only 0.25 sq km, in West Germany 1.0 sq km, in the Republic of Ireland 0.6 sq km and in the UK only 0.3 sq km.

The popularization and democratization of hunting was assisted by countrymen broadcasters such as Jack Hargreaves. His *Out of Town* show featured among the top-rated television programmes in the 1960s. Post-war nostalgia for a 'traditional' countryside created the conditions for yet another rural invasion, this time by the middle-class commuter. Like those before them, they were seeking the romantic English countryside, this time in the form of a quaint cottage, access to village life and a modified set of rural leisures. Some proportion of the gentrifiers took up hunting (following Savage et al. 1992, we might suppose many of these to have been managers), while others were clearly anti-hunting (Savage's middle-class ascetics). According to Dahles:

> The popularity of hunting in the highly industrialised and populated countries of north-western Europe cannot sufficiently be explained by external factors such as population growth, increasing welfare and leisure . . . The taste for hunting did not grow in the Dutch population in general but only in certain social groups that I would call the 'new leisure class': middle class and middle aged professionals living in a rural community where they exert a strong influence on local politics and policy.

> (Dahles 1993: 5)

From the late 1970s onwards the English countryside was no longer dominated by the post-war nostalgia as characterized by Jack Hargreaves, but became the focus of a conflict over usage. New smallholders consisting of artists, writers and intellectuals found themselves in conflict with the local fox hunt if they refused permission to cross their land. Shoard (1987) and Lowerson (1980), for example, document the conflict of interests between landowners wishing to preserve their private hunting and angling pleasures and walkers and ramblers seeking to preserve legal access to the countryside along traditional footpaths.

If deer hunting dominated twentieth-century American hunting culture, fox hunting is easily the most significant hunting culture in modern Britain. Although hunting in Britain is typically understood as riding to hounds, fox hunting is still the most prominent hunting sport. There are now only four deer hunting packs in England which kill a total of 150 animals per year and the number of harrier packs has declined from 101 in 1905 to 40 in 1935 and to 27 in 1981 (R.H. Thomas 1983: 48). Beagling is a slower but cheaper method of hare hunting and it has increased modestly in the twentieth century from 69 packs in 1932 to 76 in 1981. The spectator sport of hare coursing, where two greyhounds compete to catch a released wild hare, has declined considerably from its mid-nineteenth century heyday when there were 382 hare coursing clubs in Britain to a mere 20 clubs in 1978. Membership is down to around 800 people who kill approximately 600 hares a year. Otter hunting was terminated by a law in 1977 to protect dangerously low numbers of wild otters. Four of the remaining eleven hunts turned their attention to introduced 'pest' species which occupied similar river habitats – the mink and the coypu. By 1982 there were twelve packs dedicated to mink hunting.

In comparison with other chase hunts, fox hunting remained vibrant throughout the twentieth century. In 1982 there were 194 hunts officially recognized by the Master of Foxhounds Association. The numbers of participants increased during the post-war period and remained large with over 50,000 people hunting at least once per season. 'A third of the hunts have over 100 horses out at the major meets and a handful have over 200' (R.H. Thomas 1983: 54).

These changes notwithstanding, fox hunting remained firmly dominated by landowners and the rural gentry, if only because to own a horse required reasonable access to fields and stables and the income to support a riding sport. It became the focus of more conflict among the new social composition of the English countryside and the object of public accusations of cruelty and disruption from hunt saboteurs. The rural elites had always been able to dominate the rural working class because they employed them, but the new educated service class represented a more robust opponent. Fox hunts became battle grounds and throughout the 1980s were a regular media issue. We will return to this in the final section. While it is relatively easy to understand the origins of the anti-fox hunting position, it is less easy to understand the continued attraction of fox hunting in the late twentieth century.

THE APPEAL OF HUNTING AND ANGLING

I fish because I love to; because the environs where trout are found, are invariably beautiful, and hate the environs where crowds of people are found, which are invariably ugly; because of all the television commercials, cocktail parties, and assorted social posturing I thus escape; because, in a world where most people seem to spend their lives doing things they hate, my fishing is at once an endless source of delight and an act of small rebellion; because trout do not lie or cheat and cannot be bought or bribed or impressed by power, but respond only to quietude and humility and endless patience; because I suspect men are going along this way for the last time, and I for one do not want to waste the trip; because mercifully there are no telephones on trout waters; because only in the woods can I find solitude without loneliness; because bourbon out of an old tin cup always tastes better out there; because maybe one day I will catch a mermaid; and, finally, not because I regard fishing as being so terribly important but because I suspect that so many of the other concerns of men are equally unimportant – and not nearly so much fun.

(Robert Traver 1960, in Paxman 1995: 3)

There is room here only to assemble the briefest set of factors that account for the appeal of hunting and angling in late modernity. Even to aim for a general account must be treated as at least limited. More detailed studies of hunting and angling, such as Tester (1989) in England, Dahles (1993) in Holland and Franklin (1996a) in Australia, find that hunting in each of these countries can only be understood in reference to specifically national discourses relating to the natural world and human–animal relations. However, most share at least some common features: anti-modernist themes; neo-Darwinian themes; ecologism and conservationism; masculinity.

Anti-modernist themes

As Rojek argues in *Decentring Leisure* (1995), the ordering processes of modernity were not instituted without resistance and subversion. In a previous paper (Franklin 1996a) I analysed the most famous book on angling, Walton's *The Compleat Angler* (1653) as a subtle critique of the post-English civil war puritan order. Taking entire days off from business to sit on a river bank, during which one's time alternates between quietly contemplating nature, god and fellowship on the one hand and enjoying the tension and excitement of fooling wary and nervous trout on the other, was clearly a subversive thesis in its time. Moreover, Walton and his friends liked to end their angling day in the after-glow and throng of a public house where drinking, smoking, discoursing and singing were recommended to his readership. Indeed, Walton singles out the one-dimensional character of the puritan dissenter, 'men of sowre complexions; money-getting men', as a major social problem of the age. Angling was to deliver a return to a sane, peaceful, slow, aesthetic of Arcadian Christianity. That this book has been in continuous publication since 1653 is a testament to the appeal of its nostalgic rural idyll. It is in comparison with the ordering of everyday life that angling and hunting find much of their appeal:

No life, my honest scholar, no life so happy and so pleasant as the life of a well-governed angler; for when the lawyer is swallowed up with business, the statesman in preventing or contriving plots, then we sit on cowslip banks, hear the birds sing, and possess ourselves in as much quietness as these silver streams, which we now see glide so quietly by us.

(Walton quoted in Paxman 1995: 16)

It is interesting that the *Compleat Angler* is an instructional book, addressed to the beginner who might be considering taking up a rural sport. Moreover, the beginner Walton addresses is clearly an urbanite expecting some therapeutic value from a 'natural' relation. Walton preached the therapeutic virtues of acquiring natural history and an appreciation of the aesthetics of wild flora and fauna; the benefits of quiet contemplation and meditation that the intensely engaging patience of angling provides; and the healthiness of an outdoor pursuit requiring an early rise, a healthy jaunt through the countryside and plenty of fresh air. Angling and hunting books have extolled these virtues ever since and, we must conclude, have held their attraction with most discernible groups of city dwellers from businessmen and professionals through factory and office workers, commuters and the new service class. In addition to tangible benefits, these sports were framed in such a way as to engender identity formation among their aficionados. Thus the angler was not simply someone who enjoyed angling; an angler was someone who rejected the modern world in some way and belonged to a fraternity, a leisure cult that worked only in order to angle. The rhetoric of the angling journals and memoirs are always couched in these terms, but also in terms of a passion that opposes the rationality of modernity. In the quote above Robert Traver calls it 'an act of small rebellion'. The centrality of passion to these sports is taken a step further in the second type of discourse which frames their appeal. From the seventeenth century onwards angling and hunting had expressed themselves as a foil to and a refuge from modernization. In the nineteenth century, following the revelatory work of Darwin, the animality of humanity was seen as overconstrained and weakened by civility and the city. From the late nineteenth century urbanites began to be anxious about their lack of contact with nature (see, for example, Stratton 1986).

Neo-Darwinian themes

Neo-Darwinian themes emerged in the nineteenth century and provided a fresh layer of appeal and justification for these sports. This anti-modern discourse preached the unnatural living conditions of the city and the restraints of civil life. It was argued that modern humans descend from former hunting cultures and are naturally predisposed or inclined towards hunting. Because of certain natural inclinations associated with the physical and mental requirements of hunting, a sedentary life in the modern city which lacks the excitement, physicalities and tensions of hunting is inherently unhealthy. Mental and physical imbalances can be restored by making genuine contact and relations with the natural world, by relearning those (hunting) skills that establish these links and by unleashing those primeval passions (tracking, stalking, 'fighting' large fish, killing) against natural prey animals. Cartmill (1993) argues that neo-Darwinian arguments were substantial and influential in the first half of the twentieth century and lay behind some of the more sinister and bizarre pre-Nazi writings and the conservative outdoor movements in the USA and UK. They were famously popularized by the adventure-books-for-boys genre and by Hemingway, and accompanied by supportive anthropological literatures which argued for a somewhat bloody and violent reinterpretation of the archaeology of early hominid ancestors. Following World War I, Cartmill (1993) shows how in a war-weary Europe and USA, neo-Darwinian interpretations lost ground and were substantially toned down. Moreover, a misanthropic anxiety developed in reaction to the destructive pace of long boom development, Korea and Vietnam and the falterings of welfarism. As ecologism gained pace in a new relation with nature, it was mixed with humanistic displacements: animals especially became the focus for show-case demonstrations of a softer, caring, sustainable and custodial humanity. The appeal of angling and hunting was deeply influenced by this. The excitement of hunting and angling, together with the possession of the mysteries of the sport for the participant, continued to be couched in neo-Darwinian terms (as healthy and worthy pastimes, for example), but in the second half of the twentieth century this was mixed with a softer, less bloody purpose.

Ecologism and conservationism

In the face of scathing criticism from animal rights activists, the hunter's claim to be motivated by a passion for ecology, a love of nature (and animals) and a need to conserve animal habitats often seems, at best, feeble, but it is not only in conflictual situations where that claim is made. Indeed, the hunting and angling literatures from the 1950s onwards are characterized by these themes, and there is an underlying anxiety that habitats survive only through the vigilance and diligence of organized field sports. Out of these tensions some interesting ironies have emerged. As we have seen, the British coarse anglers were keenly aware of the dangers of an industrialized landscape to wetland habitats and developed, from the late nineteenth century on, a custodial, caring attitude to their fish such that almost all forms of violence or damage, short of not catching them at all, were minimized (Franklin 1996a). By 1950 eating the fish had all but disappeared; by 1970 some of the more excessive hardware such as gaffs, gags and snap-tackle were being questioned; the 1980s saw the rise of the barbless hooks, fish friendly nets and handling materials and the end of live baiting. In addition, anglers became better acquainted with aquatic and wetland environments and more concerned with waterways, management regimes and land practices that border the waterways. They formed organizations to lobby for stricter laws, to buy out salmon netting rights and to prosecute polluters. Similar developments occurred in hunting. Ecologism and conservationism encouraged custodial relations and identification with particular tracts of country, which engendered naturalized social identities. At a time when a strong spatial–local component to social identity had been undermined (Savage et al. 1992), the 'spatial locatedness' of and belonging to hunting and angling may have had considerable appeal. While the persistence and growth of hunting and angling sports, together with their extension to new groups in society, may appear to run contrary to the key trends in the twentieth century, they now operate under very different conditions and in some areas practices have changed considerably.

Contemporary opinions on hunting depend, for example, on the political economy of hunting in particular countries. In the USA and Australia hunting has a nostalgic quality relating to nation formation in rural and often difficult circumstances. Seen as part of the self-provisioning practices of pioneer ancestors, hunting has occupied an almost hallowed corner of the national psyche and social identity. In France, Britain and the Netherlands, by contrast, hunting is largely associated with historic or traditional social elites and, if anything, is resented as symbolic of domination and oppression. However, the extent to which traditional class divisions colour contemporary debates depends on how hunting has been commodified and regulated in the twentieth century. The Netherlands and Britain, for example, were set on very different trajectories as a result of different types of state regulation. In Britain hunting remained a private matter, with shooting and hunting rights more or less in the gift of farmers and landowners. The state only intervened to protect certain wild species. In the Netherlands, however, under the Game Act of 1954, hunters were more regulated. They had to pass wildlife exams, obtain a licence to hunt and show that they had specific hunting lands under ownership or lease. Hunters were given responsibility for keeping agricultural pest species (rabbits, foxes, crow, etc.) under control in their hunting grounds and maintaining game species in check so that agricultural compensation to farmers from game damage to crops was minimized. This responsibility, with its links to national interest and wildlife conservation, has blurred the moral rectitudes of hunting in the Netherlands:

> Hunting, not shooting, is defined as 'harvesting' a small amount of game which has been maintained by intelligent management of the resource of cultivated nature. The changing attitudes among Dutch hunters reflect the decline of the game population and the scarcity of hunting grounds in times of increasing numbers of aspiring hunters. This is why modern hunters have to accept tasks which are imposed on them by the Game Act: they are becoming professional wildlife managers, subscribing to the demands of modern nature conservation . . . Dutch hunters derive a new identity from this legal assignment, presenting themselves to the world as wildlife managers. In the light of increasing opposition against hunting, this image forms the front stage in the presentation of self, a strategy of survival.
>
> (Dahles 1993 :3)

It is not entirely clear therefore that hunters can only be presented in an anti-animal manner and it remains to be seen how hunters elsewhere manage their reputation collectively and with what measures the state decides to intervene. In cost-cutting times, state governments would be foolish not to consider the benefits of harnessing hunters' enthusiasms for tasks under their budgetary responsibility.

The changing public view of hunters and anglers from cruel sportsmen to the softer image of conservationists has also emerged from private sector interests. For example, by the 1970s bass fishing competitions in the USA were the single largest organized angling enthusiasm. They involved large-scale competitions for major prizes, there was a large popular support base from every US state and the commercial value of the tackle, media and administration was very significant. In 1986 it was rumoured that the key administrator for BASS, the main bass competition organization, sold his interest in the venture for $17 million. As bass fishing competition fever spread in the post-1945 period it came under increasing criticism from local anglers who complained that fish numbers were declining. To prevent the competition from further damaging comments the organizers instituted the rule of catch and release. All fish had to be measured and released alive. This competition rule became instantly popular and influenced attitudes to fishing generally (see Figures 6.1, 6.2).

Masculinity

It is tempting to interpret hunting and angling sports as masculinity cults in modernity. They are almost exclusively male in composition and predicated on the notion of men's separation from day-to-day life, especially from contact with women and the domestic sphere. They frequently refer to themselves collectively as a fraternity; at the local level they form the basis of exclusively male clubs and associations; they are strongly associated with male bonding between close friends, fathers and sons. There are rituals of initiation such as the giving of a fishing rod or gun to a son, 'first trip', 'first head' or 'catch', 'blooding', and so on. There is the notion of apprenticeship and master–pupil relationships and there are unmistakable mysteries associated with them, frequently focused on penetrating the barrier between culture and nature. According to Morris, for example, angling is a 'sport that has, with rare exceptions, been written about primarily by men and whose traditions and legacy to date have been exclusively male (Morris 1991: ix).

While this interpretation is compelling it remains poorly understood and researched. However, Dahles (1993) and Raines (1993) have both tried to understand why these sports are so exclusively male. Dahles's analysis, which follows an Eliasian path, is based on her participant observation of Dutch hunters as they underwent their training courses and participated in hunting in a variety of contexts. In-depth interviews were also conducted with two principal informants. For Dahles, hunting is strongly ritualized, forming 'a world apart that distinguishes itself from "ordinary life"' (1993: 2). However, it is not primarily directed at maintaining a separate men's cult, rather, the reason hunting 'attracts a large number of men . . . is related to the intrinsic attraction the quest for game has to offer' (p. 3). As with other anthropological studies of hunting, Dutch hunters 'emphasise that they pursue hunting "for the love of animals"'. However, Dahles is at pains to point out that only those animals with special game qualities (aggression, courage, vigour, strength, cunning, fighting spirit) are loved and valued by hunters. These animals, especially males of the species, provide a spirited fight with or a powerful flight from the hunters. Wild boars, especially the males with their formidable tusks, are valued above others; male deer species are also valued and again their value is related to the size of the antlers. Hunting is conceived of as a staged, mimetic form of combat in which only worthy opponents can be counted:

> Transforming the landscape, manipulating the game, submitting oneself to self-inflicted restrictions are strategies to delay the killing and heighten the attraction of shooting. The

more the game rises to the challenge and the more it makes high demands on the hunters' proficiency with the rifle, the more it is appreciated. It is no coincidence that the characteristics which are highly valued – aggression, courage, vigour, strength – are associated with manliness in our society. Hunters, mostly men, measure their strength or cunning by comparing themselves to their animal competitors. For this reason, sportsmen prefer those animals which behave like an equal (human) opponent – a male wearing 'weapons' and fighting back. Their opponents become enemies as shooting is a metaphor of warfare.

(Dahles 1993: 6)

Preferences are not only given to male game animals, wild animals are preferred over stocked or semi-tame, and migratory animals over non-migratory. These ranked preferences are mirrored elsewhere (in the USA and UK) in terms of, say, wild pheasant and other game over stocked pheasant; wild trout over stocked trout; and migratory fish species (e.g. steelhead salmon, Atlantic salmon and sea trout) over non-migratory fish species. Also widely emphasized are preferences for fighting qualities, physical size, and difficulty of capture.

The connection between hunting and angling and warfare and fighting is a relatively easy one on which to elaborate. Rifle know-how/can-do has been encouraged by most nation-states as a means of maintaining a semi-trained militia. Fox hunting was encouraged by the English army, keen to exercise those riding skills which were useful to cavalry warfare. Hunting was encouraged because it made hunters used to and familiar with bloodshed and killing and hunting and angling also honed survival and outdoor skills useful to the military. Hunting and angling also take place in set pieces of male cooperation: expeditions in which equipment must be prepared, rations put by and prepared by men; where strategies must be agreed and planned which involve travel and nights away from home in the field of combat. In other words, the gendering of hunting and angling has been socially constructed as male for the same reasons that men were trained for military service. The nature of these sports is received always in a gendered form and only boys are socialized into its cultic practices and pleasures. For boys it may form part of those rituals which separate them from the domestic sphere of the mother and initiate them into the social world of men. The experience and appeal of male company during these expeditions is therefore separable from the social conditions (military societies) which favoured its emergence. Raines (1993) concentrates on this dimension by considering a variety of explanations for male separation and camaraderie in hunting and angling. Three types of account are considered.

First, Raines (1993) considers those accounts that emphasize men's need to be intimate with one another. While both genders need to seek intimate and private relationships with the same sex, only women are able to do this in a routine manner, through their cooperation in domestic settings and in problems relating especially to their gender. Men lack such routinized encounters with each other and have to invent an excuse to be alone. During such trips men can seek a form of support from one another that is difficult to achieve elsewhere.

Second, Raines (1993) considers Fiedler's (1967) claim that hunting and angling trips have a sublimated homoerotic content and consequently enable such attractions and fantasies to be played out. Raines rejects this on the basis that there are sufficient alternative opportunities without the need to create a special function for hunting and angling. Third, Raines considers seriously that the male content of these sports derives simply from male selfishness, dereliction of duty and reliance on women to maintain home and family in their absence. Hunting and angling would not be the only sports which create 'widows' and many studies, such as Dempsey's *Smalltown* (1990), attest to men's ability and propensity to create free 'play' time away from their homes, justifying it in terms of their primary labour market roles.

The origins and persistence of hunting and angling as a masculine domain clearly require further research. Despite the history of male domination in these activities, Raines is ultimately persuaded that things are changing. Women are enrolling in increasing numbers in fly-fishing schools and the number of women anglers has been rising steadily over the past twenty years. Again the angling industries have made a major effort to extend their market to women in recent years. Morris's (1991) collection of essays by women anglers demonstrates that there is nothing intrinsically masculine about the attractions and appeal of angling: given the opportunity to learn and sufficient time, women appear to enjoy exactly the same things that have preoccupied men for centuries. As we have seen in the UK, the increase in women's hunt memberships remains one of the more significant changes in the late twentieth century.

CONCLUSION

This chapter has addressed the apparent enigma of a popular Western enthusiasm for hunting and angling sports. While it has been taken for granted that the act of hunting and angling provide an exciting, self-contained contest similar to other sports, this chapter has attempted to understand why such sports persist against a generalized increase in sentiments towards animals. Hunting and angling sportspersons are, as we have seen in the first section of this chapter, neither marginalized socially nor insignificant numerically. Such enthusiasts are evenly spread over space and across socio-economic groupings. Some middle-class consumption groups are highly motivated against these sports, however, while other middle-class groups include large numbers of aficionados and provide very significant leadership in the burgeoning of field sports over the past fifteen years. Some of these sports are declining relative to their recent past (e.g. otter hunting and fox hunting) while others are increasing (e.g. fly fishing), but all the evidence points to a significant growth in popularity since 1945. Since the ethical debates raised in the 1970s (e.g. the publication of Singer's *Animal Liberation*) have now turned into physical, political and legal confrontations, it seems very compelling to stop and consider why these sports are so ubiquitous and the subject of so much passion.

This chapter has argued that far from opposing the hunters to the environmentalists, it makes far more sense to see them as an opposed form of environmentalism. An attempt has been made, albeit briefly, to sketch out some of the more important sources of their passion and the content and focus of their attraction to an active consumption of the environment. Far from being a conservative, violent culture, in many ways it is anti-modernist, nostalgic and romantic. This is a long-standing legacy from ideas which grew popular in the seventeenth century and have been overlaid with later influences, particularly from the extension of Darwinian thought onto nineteenth-century theories of human health, well-being and leisure.

While the animal rights organizations are clear on their reasons for wanting a ban on hunting, these are not completely shared by other anti-hunting groups and sympathizers. Although most anti-hunters believe hunting is cruel, unpleasant and unnecessary, they do not all believe that it is unethical to kill animals or to maintain active and close relationships with them. Indeed, it must be supposed that many anti-hunters are animal lovers who want to enjoy seeing and to have access to wild animals as a leisure activity. Hunting not only kills the animals they want passively to consume in their leisure, but historically has also kept wildlife observers off key hunting ground for their own safety, leaving their quarry undisturbed by visitors. Seen in this light the conflict is less an ethical issue than a competition for access, consumption and control over wildlife and wildlife habitats. In Britain, traditional hunting cultures were predicated on private ownership of land and game and in the past draconian laws were upheld to maintain that privilege. In the late twentieth century organized wildlife enthusiasts have lobbied for more and more land to be set aside as sanctuaries, and for more and more species to be protected from the routine predations of game management. Through organizations such as the Royal Society for the Protection of Birds (RSPB), which are supported by a burgeoning population of birdwatchers, traditional hunting and shooting preserves and practices are facing a considerable threat. The long-term aims of the RSPB are to use its considerable funding to purchase and protect key habitats, to keep hunters under surveillance and to prosecute infringements against protected birds.

The anti-hunting lobby consists of an uneasy alliance between those who are ethically opposed to hunting and those who find themselves in competition with hunters over access to animal-related leisure pursuits. For the millions of amateur and occasional naturalists, birdwatchers, tourists and schoolchildren (for whom nature study is a curriculum activity), access to wild animals is seen as a democratic right, part of the national heritage and a matter to be decided by parliamentary debate rather than by privilege and landownership. Already matters relating to hunting are regular items for electoral decision-making in the USA. Hunting law reform, for example, was placed on the ballot in many states in 1996: Michigan, Washington and Idaho all voted to ban baiting and hounding of bears; Alaska voted on whether to ban same-day airborne hunting of lynx, foxes and wolverines; Massachusetts and Colorado decided whether to allow the trapping and snaring of small mammals, and Oregon voted on whether to uphold a ban on bear baiting and hound hunting of bears and mountain lions (Washington State 1996; Woodbury 1996). In Britain the passage of the Wild Mammals (Hunting with Dogs) bill will be carefully scrutinized by lobby organizations and the media and is guaranteed to produce further conflict whichever way the vote goes. In the longer term, if most forms of hunting are banned, the animal rights organizations will pursue angling and other forms of leisure which disturb or control wildlife – including wildlife parks, zoos and certain national park activities (e.g. pest control, culling, etc.) While such activities as fox hunting in the UK and baiting for bears in the USA may be seen as the thin end of the wedge, there are good reasons to suppose that the less despicable forms of hunting, particularly those which include wildlife management criteria, and angling will not be so easily abolished. Unlike bear baiting and fox hunting, these are very popular activities which are related to popular and democratic rights. The public is out of sympathy for the privileged fox hunter defending a legacy of popular oppression and exclusion from rural sports, and the rich game hunter who kills bears simply for a trophy. However, those activities which enable people to maintain a viable and long-term relationship with animals are more likely, given the conclusions made here, to find themselves under increasing pressure from demand rather than criticism.

7 ANIMALS AND THE AGRICULTURAL INDUSTRY

From farming to animal protein production

INTRODUCTION

This chapter aims to clarify the changing nature of twentieth-century animal husbandry using modernization theory as a guiding framework. In a sense this chapter is the first of two which deal with our relations with animals as food. It focuses on the production side of the relationship, while Chapter 8 explores the consumption side. These two facets of our relationships with farm animals have become increasingly separate as people of the twentieth century have become spatially detached from the animals they consume and emotionally reluctant to recognize the embodied nature of meat foods. Indeed there are many tales of urban children in the late twentieth century who did not know that meat came from animal sources or even what they looked like. The approach used here is predominantly political economy and it aims to show how the social organization of animal production has changed from a local–national to a global–international scale; from a government area of modernist social policy to one dominated by large corporations seeking to maximize profitability from animals strictly as commodities; and from a traditional set of localized farming and breeding practices to a series of methods continually revised and changed by experimental–empirical procedures, governed and monitored by computer systems and highly segmented between scientists, technicians, corporate sponsors and producer units (formerly farms).

Nowhere is the changed relation between humans and animals in modernity clearer than in transformations in the agricultural industries. In many (but not all) pre-industrial societies, animals tend to be more significant for their labour power than for their meat. Throughout India, for example, cattle were the principal means of ploughing; they were used in other processes such as winnowing and flour making and, along with other animals, for transport. The fact that they are sacred and eaten only by a few in India has been explained, albeit controversially, in terms of ecological imperatives: if cattle were eaten during times of food shortage there would be nothing to plough the soil and commence the food production cycle (Harris 1965). Although meat eating became more widespread and consumed in greater quantities in medieval Britain, oxen were traditionally not eaten because they too were important in ploughing and other heavy agricultural tasks (Dyer 1988; Harvey 1993). Dogs and horses were also significant sources of power prior to the utilization of water, wind and steam power (K. Thomas 1983). In modernity, however, animal labour power was quickly eliminated while the modernization of meat production and the democratization of meat consumption became one of the most significant projects of the nineteenth and twentieth centuries. From the nineteenth century onwards the highly visible, urban-centred sentimentalization of animals has been accompanied by its opposite: a willingness to exploit animals in increasingly intensive, controlled industrial meat, egg and milk production systems, deliberately obscured from the sensitive and critical public gaze. The former relationship between the farmer and farmed has changed: the microchip and process system has taken over almost all of the caring, monitoring and management of animals to the extent that farmers have become technicians, often dependent on expert back-up from system suppliers.

Cheap meat has become ubiquitous and the problem in late modernity is not the social provision of sufficient protein but the personal regulation of animal protein/ fat intake. In this shift of emphasis, human representations of farm animals appear to have changed from those based on husbandry and the associated anxieties of potential shortage to those based on industrial mass production, superabundance engendering blasé indifference and, later, anxieties about overconsumption and contamination. In representational terms, the farm animal has changed from a saviour of health and security to one associated with risk and pollution. However, older representations continue to persist. Children's books still feature the farming idylls of pre-Fordist agriculture: free-ranging mother hen and chicks roaming safely around the open farmyards; the shepherd on personal terms with his sheep; contented cows keen to be milked at the end of another perfect day; the cock crowing the dawn of another. The distance between representation and reality is not a refusal to acknowledge and accept new conditions of animal protein production, but the impossibility of recommending the new intensive production systems as suitable human moral tales for children. In late modernity, the mythic farmyard of children's books is replayed in the proliferation of hobby farms, backyard menageries and city farms, and through the purchase of free-range eggs, hormone-free beef and 'stress-free' meats of all kinds. While battery egg production has been the basis of a moral issue for many years, the public has been carefully screened from other forms of food production systems and, as a result, has continued to accept intensification uncritically.

However, a series of health rather than moral issues, emerging first in the 1980s, has refocused attention on the food industry. The food scares of the 1980s and 1990s are just beginning to be associated with the unregulated extension of intensive livestock production. The claim in October 1996 that an unknown number of Britons have contracted the brain disease Creutzfeldt-Jacob Disease (CJD) as a result of eating meat infected with bovine spongiform encephalopathy (BSE) will no doubt bring about far-reaching state and consumer led changes in the industry. There is also some concern that BSE may already have jumped the Atlantic and infected beef cattle in the USA and South America (Rifkin 1992).

This chapter will describe the origins and development of the intensive livestock industry, relating it to the changing conditions of capitalist investment and trade and agricultural competition and technological development. These changes will be illustrated with examples from egg production, broiler meat production, intensive pig units and feedlot beef production. The Western meat industries became politically powerful lobbies and, as a result of efforts to expand production and consumption, they have had a significant impact on the world food economy, not least in redirecting grain surpluses into intensive meat production and promoting new meat products.

While the beef industries have been commercially successful, they are at the same time vulnerable to shifting consumer behaviour, particularly in the past twenty years in relation to health risk issues. Up until recently health fears involved animal fat consumption, heart disease and cancer. While these had a dramatic impact on meat consumption, the industry was able to restructure its products and marketing and, as we will see in the next chapter, these anxieties have been stabilized. However, the more recent meat scares, particularly BSE and *E. coli* bacterial infections, identify risk factors within the very nature and management of the industry.

PRE-FORDIST LIVESTOCK PRODUCTION

While Fordist livestock production methods spread throughout Western nations from the 1920s onwards, intensification of production lagged behind other areas. Arguably there were two principal livestock systems in existence before the intensification of the industry. Small-scale mixed farming on relatively stable and sustainable pastures characterized most of Europe from the thirteenth century until the nineteenth. It was also based upon stable legal systems for the ownership, transmission and purchase of land, a rural social hierarchy composed of large estate landowners, a landowning yeomanry of small farmers, tenant farmers, a significant rural working class, and a growing demand from urban centres. As a polity it was tied to national and state military interests and managed for long-term domestic needs.

The second system was extensive cattle ranching and sheep grazing on relatively unstable and unsustainable grasslands, which characterized much of the land taken over by European colonization of the southern USA and South America, Africa and Australia from the sixteenth to the nineteenth centuries. It was based variously on militarily acquired and colonially organized land, extractive-exploitative colonial social relations (frequently involving slave labour), rural peasantries or displaced and unwanted, unutilizable indigenous peoples, and a landowning class of cattle and sheep barons, self-styled on various European aristocracies. As polities, these were initially loosely tied to parent country interests, shipping wealth in the form of gold, silver and other valuables to boost war-torn exchequers in Europe and as such the lands were frequently exploited for short-term gains. As they became more independent as colonies, with growing immigrant populations, their interests were increasingly tied to local and longer term investment and need. However, the extensive nature of exploitation in the previous period continued to influence independent national production. The ranching system of livestock production was the only feasible one, for example, given the very large units of landownership and relatively small numbers of owners and hands on each ranch. Overstocking and overgrazing quickly downgraded native pasture. The ranching system tended to require the availability of new lands over time in order to replace exhausted pasture, particularly for beef. As a result, in the USA and South America, for example, the industry has continuously looked for new grazing lands, creating them out of virgin rainforest where necessary.

In eighteenth-century Britain and Europe most farms were relatively small and mixed, even if the ownership of land had become more concentrated after the Enclosure Acts. Most farms in most districts produced a similar range of products and marketed them locally. This is why there are so many different local types of cheese in France and England specific to different localities, and also different varieties of chicken, pigs, cattle and sheep. Different farming districts developed their own relatively isolated tastes, breeds and husbandry that were, in part, developed in relation to changing geographical conditions. The relative isolation was a function of limited transportation options prior to the railways. The emergence of local farming cultures was a function of the stable and sustainable nature of the agricultural system. It was possible to drive cattle and sheep over long distances (albeit at some considerable cost), but it was impossible to transport perishable goods such as milk and animals such as pigs and poultry. The small mixed farm was in many respects an efficient use of local resources, particularly the grazing of areas of grassland that would be suitable for little else (Johnson 1991). However, with the building of extensive railway links specialization became a more profitable option as local conditions favouring a particular livestock production gave the producers a competitive edge on national markets. Over time, natural advantages produced a new specialist geography of British livestock production; 'this trend has continued right up to the present day, with cattle and sheep production being favoured in the wetter Western half of Britain, while the intensive pig and poultry units tend to be situated in the east, where the cereal crops used to feed them are grown' (Johnson 1991: 33).

The ranching system grew out of specific conditions of colonial agriculture. The social and environmental transformations of an extensive cattle industry can be illustrated with American examples from the sixteenth through to the twentieth century (Cockburn 1996). The Spanish conquistadors in Mexico were followed by colonist pastoralists who quickly took over agricultural land such as the famously fertile area of irrigated intensive agriculture in the Valle de Mezquital in highland central Mexico. Spanish livestock began grazing this valley in the 1520s, shepherded by African slaves. By 1565 there were 2 million sheep in the valley and between 1576 and 1581 the local Indians were decimated by an epidemic brought by the colonists. In this way fields became pastures and as the sheep multiplied on the highly fertile soils they grew to very high stocking levels of 20,000 sheep per station. Under this pressure local pastures collapsed, leaving behind scrubby thorn desert. By 1600 'sheet erosion scarred the hillsides and covered the flat and sloping lands with slope-wash debris', home only to the desert mesquite, the Mexican symbol for arid poverty (Cockburn 1996: 33–4). This is largely how cattle spread into the Texas range lands and most other areas of South Western USA.

The Texas ranching system was establishrd hy herds migrating from exhausted grazing on the ranges of Tamaulipas (exhaustion took place between 1795 and 1825) along the Mexican Gulf coast and moving east from Louisiana. Over the course of the next fifty years the ranching system was 'wiped out by ecological maladaptation'. According to Jordan (1993), free grass on the ranges encouraged overstocking and the grass species were fragile rather than tough as supposed:

> The resulting cattle glut both severely damaged the ranges and, by 1886, led to a crash in beef prices. Livestock dumped on the market because the depleted pastures could no longer support them further depressed prices. Even so, thousands of additional cattle died due to the deteriorated condition of the ranges.

(1993: 80)

By 1887, after severe weather, the boom was over, millions of cattle had died and the pasture was severely degraded. A similar pattern and time scale accompanied the grazing of California's open ranges, where there were some 3 million cattle by the 1860s. Between 1862 and 1865 bad weather conditions again demonstrated the fragility of the landscape and its inability to sustain cattle in such numbers: 'In less than a century, California's pastoral utopia had been destroyed; the ranchers moved east of the Sierra into the Great Basin, or north, to colder drier terrain' (Cockburn 1996: 35).

However, it was just when these American range lands were collapsing during the 1870s that technology, in the form of refrigerated ships, first made it possible to extend US beef markets into Europe. Several pressures grew apace to intensify the livestock industries as markets globalized, but it was, of course, the application of Fordism to agriculture that modernized our relations with farm animals.

ANIMAL PRODUCTION AND FORDISM

With the arrival of meat ships to Europe from the USA and Australia in the 1880s, it became possible for Europeans to eat considerably more meat, providing the price was right. Increasingly, therefore, the livestock industry attempted to raise profitability and consumption. The solution to the problem was to intensify production, to centralize operations, to shed labour and to rationalize the production system. But the Fordization of the livestock industry was more than just the application of principles. There were five interlinked factors that affected the progress of intensification: mechanization, vertical integration, governmental leadership, industrial representation and lobbying, and environmental factors.

Profitability from livestock grew during the latter half of the nineteenth century and throughout the twentieth century. Specialization encouraged the development of specialist mechanization: milking machines, combine harvesters, chicken batteries and pig-rearing plants. Farming was no longer a distinct and autonomous industry. Competitive advantages could be gained by grain elevator, meat packer and canning and refrigeration companies, by purchasing their own supplier farms or contracting farmers to produce directly for them. Large grain farmers became millers and animal feed suppliers and offered cheap agricultural credit to the livestock farmers in return for feed purchasing contracts.

Profitability was also raised by shedding more and more agricultural workers. Although grazing is an efficient use of otherwise low yielding land, continually moving animals 'by hand' was very costly. The greatest profits were to be made from keeping the animals in one place and bringing in feed and water via a conveyer system that at the same time took away waste. This also had the advantage of minimizing unnecessary and wasteful animal movement. Once part of a control system, livestock production became an experimental science and all aspects were changed in order to improve yields and profits. During the twentieth century, for example, electric power grids made intensive systems available to all localities. Temperature and light could be controlled; prophylactic disease controls could be implemented; selective breeding optimized meat gain, environmental tolerance or egg output; chemical and hormone additives were used to fine-tune animal health, and so on. It became possible for the farmer to spend less and less time with his animals.

It is naive to suppose that the intensification of livestock production was simply a matter of market forces finding the cheapest, most effective means of producing meat. For that to have happened would have required the support and encouragement of governments. Meat was a very popular food in the West, associated historically with high status, land ownership and wealth. Modernizing and democratizing governments of the twentieth century increased animal protein output targets: first, in order to eradicate malnutrition, especially in children (free school milk in Britain was one such programme that lasted until the 1970s); second, to raise 'standards of living'. Meat consumption norms rose in the twentieth century so that by the 1960s meat was included in three meals per day for most people. Meat consumption was a key metaphor of social progress. However, governments were very dependent upon science to support major agricultural and food policies and their beliefs had played a major role in changing livestock practices in Western and developing nations:

> The role of livestock products in world food consumption has been a matter of controversy; until the 1960s it was believed that some animal protein was necessary for healthy growth, and so it was thought that the reduction of malnutrition in the developing countries required an increase in livestock production and consumption. Since then it has been established that protein from plant foods – providing a variety of these is eaten – is sufficient for health.

> (Grigg 1993: 66)

As late as 1967 the Food and Agriculture Organization (FAO) of the United Nations was underlining the global necessity of increased animal protein production:

> Proteins of animal origin – meat, cheese, eggs, fish – when they are available provide a concentrated form of readily assimilated amino acids in suitable proportions for human

needs. The shortage of animal protein, however, is one of the most serious of all the world shortages. Standing as testimony to the gravity of this shortage, as they have increasingly over many generations, are the impairment of growth and development of children and the widespread occurrence of such deficiency diseases as marasmus, and kwashiorkor, appallingly common in today's world.

(Food and Agriculture Organization 1967: 7)

Even when it was widely recognized that famine could easily be averted, in some cases by redirecting agricultural efforts away from livestock production to more efficient plant protein production, Western countries maintained support for the intensification of animal protein production. For example, in a report from the US President's Science Advisory Committee, *The World Food Problem*, it was argued that livestock intensification was a more viable long-term option, and that with new recycling methods it was not necessarily the least efficient option:

Meeting the world needs for quality protein is complicated by the fact that human dietary habits are difficult to change. There is no doubt that human diets can be adequately supplemented with properly processed oilseed meals, microbial protein, and synthetics; however strong preferences have developed for traditional foods. Consequently, people are extremely reluctant to accept what they consider to be aesthetically inferior substitutes. On the contrary, animal products are highly desired and are readily consumed by most people throughout the world; consequently, it is not realistic to ignore the potential for expanding the world production of animal products to meet some of the world needs for high quality proteins. In the long run, it may be far more realistic to increase animal production in certain areas than to alter food preference patterns developed over many centuries.

(United States of America 1967: 247)

This report ignored the fact that pulses and pulse-grain proteins were the most ubiquitous global forms of high quality protein, extensively eaten in Africa, Asia and South America, and that part of the global food problem was caused by the replacement of such crops by monoculture for world markets driven largely by the Western livestock feed industry. It is possible that this report simply failed to take in all the evidence, but the significance of plant protein foodways in developing countries had been extensively documented by anthropologists. It is equally possible that this panel, composed largely of agricultural scientists were simply and unwittingly extending Western orthodoxies. However, it is equally plausible that since very large US interests were at stake in changes to global foodways and taste, solutions advantageous to US trade and market development were given strong support (United States of America 1967: 247).

In order to counter the argument that animal protein production is less efficient than plant protein production, the report points out that it 'applies only if the entire diet of the animal is composed of foods eaten by people. Livestock thrive on many feeds, forages, wastes, by-products, and even chemicals that are not suitable for human food' (United States of America 1967: 248). In recommending agricultural wastes and waste from the animal industry itself ('such as meat scraps, tankage, bone-meal, animal fats, and even animal manures'), it points out that already in the West a very large proportion of the feed given to intensively reared animals is 'forages and by-products not generally consumed by people'. Thus in the USA '70 per cent of an average dairy cow's protein intake is derived from forages, 60 per cent of a beef steer, and 80–90 per cent for sheep and beef brood stock' (United States of America 1967: 249).

The European Community's Common Agricultural Policy (CAP) has also encouraged the intensification of the livestock industry, in two principal ways. First, it has significantly inflated land prices throughout Europe:

> The inflation of land values by the CAP inspired philosophy of production at any price has encouraged farmers who wish to expand to make more intensive use of the land they already have, rather than buy or rent more costly acres. Intensive, silage-based dairy operations are thus favoured compared with keeping the cattle on open pasture, while large pig and poultry units can be built on very little land indeed if the animals are intensely housed.

> (Johnson 1991: 181)

Second, the manner by which increased production is induced through grants and subsidies favours the purchase of all equipment, buildings and materials required by intensive production. Such support for intensification is further compounded by member state tax laws. For example, in Britain tax breaks accrue to expenditure on plant and buildings rather than land.

Thus a combination of market forces, environmental barriers, scientific opinion (and interest) and governmental policy serves to encourage intensive livestock production on a global scale. In the post-World War II period, when trans-national corporations became as significant as nation-states, it is possible to see the development of the livestock industry as a highly organized global business. According to Le Heron and Roche (1995) and others writing from a political economy perspective, intensive livestock production (and especially grain-fed livestock production) constitutes part of what they call a food regime. 'Food regimes . . . link international relations of food production and consumption to forms of accumulation and regulation under capitalism since the 1870s' (Le Heron and Roche 1995: 23):

> The first food regime, anchored in the white settler colonies and their ties to the metropolitan heartlands of Britain and the US and spanning from the 1870s to World War I, created an international division of labour that fostered spectacular aggregate gains in agricultural production and a reliable source supply of unprocessed and semi-processed food and products to the growing metropoles. The first regime gradually disintegrated as metropolitan agricultures increasingly competed with cheap imports and trade barriers were erected. The second food regime rising after World War II and lasting until the early 1970s centred on investment circuits related to two internationally organised agro-industrial complexes, those of grain-fed livestock production and fats, and durable foods. It incorporated developed and developing nations into increasingly specialised and geographically segmented commodity production systems and added a new layer of complexity to the international geography of investment and labour characterising food production.

> (Le Heron and Roche 1995: 23)

A significant component of the post-World War II food regime was the beef industry, but intensification of the beef industry leading to the feedlot system began much earlier with the cycle of British investment in the Western ranges of the USA and their environmental collapse around 1900 (Rifkin 1992: 86–99). In the early nineteenth century the British were almost alone in Europe in their love of beef. By the 1860s British manufacturing became more concentrated and highly profitable, raising living standards and disposable wealth. Domestic beef production was not able to track demand and an anthrax epidemic of the 1860s devastated European and British herds. In trying to secure better beef supplies, British investors looked to Australia and Argentina and particularly to the USA. From the 1860s shipments of live cattle and salted beef commenced. When the Western ranges opened the British invested heavily in railways linking the West to Eastern ports and in new shipping and refrigeration technology to bring Western range cattle to England as fresh beef. By 1880 steamers left the USA on a daily basis ferrying beef to Britain. The excitement and relief created by this major breakthrough fed a major investment bubble in British land investments in the Western ranges:

> They set up giant cattle companies across the plains, securing millions of acres of the best grasslands for the British market. While the west was made safe for commerce by the American frontiersmen and the US military, the region was bankrolled by English lords and lawyers, financiers, and the businessmen who effectively extended the reach of the British beef empire into the short grass of the western plains.
>
> (Rifkin 1992: 89)

Large numbers of companies with substantial landholdings and millions of head of cattle organized themselves into powerful political associations, notably the Cheyenne Club, Texas Livestock Association and Wyoming Stockmen's Association. By the mid-1880s, when 'much of the American West belonged to British and Scottish bankers and businessmen', the British taste for 'fatted' beef began to influence the course of US beef production.

Based on previous practices of finishing range-reared cattle with surplus corn, the Western range and the corn-growing areas to the east became linked in one extremely powerful investment–production matrix. Government policymakers were quick to formalize what was an efficient use of two major agricultural regions. 'Let the vast areas of pasture in the border states and territories be employed with breeding and feeding the cattle until they are two years old, and then let them be sent forward to the older sections to be fed on corn and rounded up to the proportions of foreign demand' (the 1876 US Commissioner of Agriculture, cited in Rifkin 1992: 94). The same British financiers who bought up the Western range made parallel investments in the corn-belt states. By 1900 with the range lands overstocked and overgrazed, the feedlot system became a solution to an environmental barrier to growth. The corn belt continued to produce surpluses and to turn even more of its output into beef. Such was the power of this beef lobby that it secured a national grading and price system favouring grain-fed or 'choice' beef as the most popular among producers, and over time with US consumers. Even so, in the growing US market of the mid-twentieth century only 5 per cent of beef consumption was grain fed. In the post-war period when agricultural yields increased by 240 per cent, huge surpluses of grains made it possible to expand feedlotting on a very cheap basis. Thus, between 1950 and 1990 when the national herd increased from 80 million cattle to 100 million, the majority were grain fattened:

> By 1989, about half of the nation's output of grain-fed cattle had been 'finished' in 198 giant automated 'beef factories' scattered throughout the Western states. Some of these commercial feedlots handled more than 50,000 cattle. Special federal tax incentives in the 1970s encouraged even more investments in feedlot operations. Affluent Americans, including well-known personalities like John Wayne, invested in limited partnerships 'which brought livestock, placed them in feedlots, and then sold them for club members'.

> (Rifkin 1992: 98)

In the 1990s livestock consume almost twice as much grain as is eaten by Americans, and the feedlot system has spread to other former ranching countries such as Australia. Not simply a means of drawing together two strands of a national agriculture, feedlotting is now tied to global grain markets. As beef eating is strenuously marketed and exported to new areas such as South-East Asia and Japan, its effect on agricultural policy, prices and foodways has become profound on a global scale. As Rifkin concludes, 'The grain-fed beef complex has forced a fundamental change in the dynamics of human social relations at the most basic of all social levels' (Rifkin 1992: 99).

Under these conditions, livestock husbandry in modern Western nation-states was less a matter of choice facing individual farmers than a system imposed on them by market conditions, purchasing contracts and governmental directives. To some extent the degree of intensification of production was determined by how much different species could 'take'. Unfortunately for chickens, calves, geese, cattle and pigs this was a great deal. These animals were particularly tolerant of confinement, crowding and artificial manipulation of daylight, temperature and reproduction; or at least sufficient numbers could tolerate stressful conditions for intensive operations to remain profitable. Sheep and goats, however, do not thrive under such conditions and are only profitable as free-range animals. The next section outlines some of the new intensive livestock systems as they are commonly deployed. To the extent that these livestock production systems are highly mechanized, rationalized and require the minimum of human labour, it is clear that the principles of Fordist manufacture have been adopted. About 90 per cent of all eggs in Britain and the USA are produced in batteries; close to 100 per cent of broiler chickens are reared in intensive sheds, and around 50 per cent of pigs are reared from sows kept in close confinement. The consumption side of Fordist animal production, where the main beneficiaries of mass production are ordinary working people, is obscured by the issue of animal welfare and rights. However, the success of Kentucky Fried Chicken, British Rail's bacon rolls and McDonald's and other retailers of intensive livestock products tells a more positive story. This food is carefully marketed to allow its consumer to identify with the pleasure and success of modernity. In their recent libel case against two British critics, McDonald's did not object to the label 'junk food' being applied to their products (Vidal 1997: 115). Presumably this is because junk foods are what people prefer and what give them pleasure, even when they know they do not maximize their potential nutritional intake. The association of indulgence and indulgent pleasures with these foods is the main appeal. It is because they are bad that they are craved. Quite why this is so is a theme that will be taken up in a later section, but it is clear that the mood of badness and self-indulgence, combined with modernist appeals of cheapness, quantity and speed of service, provide a solid barrier against which the ethical counter-arguments frequently wither and die – in practice.

What follows is a brief description of the production processes of intensively produced eggs, broilers, pigs, veal and beef. Every effort has been made to avoid emotive language (although pure description of the process may be read emotively), because the purpose of the description is to show, first, how far Fordist techniques have been applied and, second, to enable readers to understand the background to some of the risk factors which will be discussed later in the chapter. Most of the material has been drawn from veterinary and agricultural texts and, not surprisingly, descriptions tend to be fairly standardized. The most used texts were Cockburn (1996), Fox (1984), Johnson (1991), the Report by the Senate Select Committee on Animal Welfare (1990) and Rifkin (1992).

Battery egg production

Although free-range and deep-litter egg production has grown in recent years, battery production still accounts for over 90 per cent of the laying flocks. In Britain, for example, it accounts for some 35 million birds and in the USA for some 300 million. Although it is not a new technology and dates back to the 1920s, it is only in the last thirty years that it has dominated production. In 1961, for example, less than 20 per cent of eggs came from batteries while 50 per cent came from deep litter and 30 per cent from free range. Increased land prices, the extension of electricity and the development of antibiotics favoured the extension of battery farms.

Typically, five hens are kept in each cage measuring around 45 × 50 cm with approximately 450 sq cm of floor space. The cage has a wire mesh bottom for excrement to fall out (onto a pit or conveyer belt) and slopes forward to ensure eggs roll out to a collection rack or conveyer belt. Cages are stacked three to five tiers high along each side of a long narrow building. Ideal conditions for egg production can be produced with temperature (21°C) and light (17-hour days) control systems. Costs are kept down by intermittent lighting: egg production is maintained by giving artificial light for only 15 minutes per hour during the birds' day. A variety of lighting options can be used to control egg size.

The battery system has several advantages over other methods. First, labour costs are substantially reduced: in 1961 almost all egg producers kept flocks of less than 1,000 birds and required a minimum of one stockman, but with the battery system approximately one stockman is required for every 30,000 birds. In 1983, 43 per cent of birds were kept in flocks of over 50,000. Critics argue that the birds cannot be so well observed and checked for health in batteries, but in cost terms this is not a significant disadvantage. Second, the hens require less food and it is more efficiently portioned out, reducing the distributional effects of 'a pecking order'. Third, it is potentially cleaner and more hygienic and particularly useful against diseases spread through droppings. Fourth, despite the various privations, battery hens lay at the same rate as free-range hens, about 250 eggs per year.

Although the advantages clearly outweigh the disadvantages to the producer, the battery farm also provides ideal conditions for disease. As Fox (1984: 2) argues for all intensive livestock methods, 'when things go wrong they go wrong in a big way, and the animals cannot do anything to help themselves'. A variety of infectious diseases is endemic in this system, some of which effect the egg quality and others which are dangerous to consumers because they are passed on inside the egg (e.g. salmonella). In order to manage infections the hens have to undergo systematic and frequent vaccinations and a 'battery' of antibiotics is continuously given; almost 100 per cent of US hens are routinely given anti-biotics. However, even the most diligent management cannot eradicate diseases caused by caging and lack of movement. A degeneration of the liver resulting from these conditions causes a large number of deaths. Another set of problems known as vices – feather pecking, cannibalism and vent pecking – relate to the boredom of the hens and is controlled by debeaking or beak trimming.

The life cycle of the battery hen is either one or two years. For the first 6 to 8 weeks the chicks are kept in a cage or deep litter brooder in groups of 40–50. From there they are transferred into smaller groups until they are old enough to lay. Their peak laying age is between 18–76 weeks. After this they may be kept for a second year, during which time they lay fewer, larger eggs, or they are sent to slaughter (for soup, stock, pies and baby food).

Broiler chickens

Broilers' lives are much shorter than layers, even though under 'normal' conditions both might live for 5–6 years. The oven-ready broiler chickens of 2 kg (4–5 lb) that have become commonplace in the West over the past thirty years are only 6 to 7 weeks old when sent for slaughter. Thirty years ago the same weight was achieved only in birds of 14 weeks old, and the improvement is the result of selective breeding and antibiotics. Between 1955 and 1988 chicken consumption in Britain, for example, increased tenfold from 50 million to 500 million birds. In the USA chicken consumption has grown from 34 lbs per person per year in 1960 to 90.5 lbs in 1994.

After 6 to 8 weeks in the brooder the birds are delivered to broiler sheds and kept in large flocks of 10,000–75,000 on deep litter. On arrival they have approximately 900 sq cm of floor space, reducing to less than 700 sq cm on 'maturity'. To encourage feeding they are kept under 24-hour continuous lighting, although this is dimmed after a while to avoid excessive aggression. Food and water are supplied automatically and husbandry has been reduced to system maintenance, flock checking and the removal of dead birds. The role of the traditional farmer is further reduced through a centralized management scheme:

A central company supplies all feed and chickens to farmers, who simply raise the chickens to slaughter age. The company supplies all veterinary field advisers and ready mixed food; computers are used in the food mill to work out the most economic diet on the basis of current market prices. Larger companies also do their own screening for pesticide contamination.

(Fox 1984: 29–31)

Arsenic and growth hormones are added to the feed in order to stimulate appetite and pesticides are used to control external parasites. Controlling disease in such conditions is extremely difficult. Over the past twenty-five years vaccines have been developed and administered to prevent Newcastle's disease and infectious bronchitis but total immunity is never achieved and high incidences of coli-septicaemia have been attributed to handling of the birds during vaccination. 'There is a growing trend to let an epidemic on a broiler farm take its course and, rather than treating afflicted birds, destroy all or salvage what remains for slaughter. Medication in feeds (except for coccidiosis) may soon be dropped for both economic and health reasons' (Fox 1984: 38).

A number of other problems result from this production system. First, meat quality is affected by cheap feeds containing fish meal, leading to a fishy taste in the chicken. Second, it is impossible to stop chickens eating their own dung and dirty litter and this also affects the meat quality. Third, rapid growth and lack of exercise leads to several leg and foot disorders, with 'older birds spending most of their time sitting with their weight supported by the upper legs and the breast' (Johnson 1991). Fourth, urine-soaked litter results in ammonia burns and birds whose skin and flesh has been discoloured in this way have to be discarded or used for chicken joints or pieces. Stressful levels of ammonia in the air also cause blindness and growth reduction. Fifth, large numbers of chickens kept in this way are prone to mass hysteria. One poultry specialist told Fox of a case he was called out to deal with:

It was like an ocean wave that swept from one end of the house and then to the other with birds piling up six or ten deep against one wall and then they would roll and tumble the length of the house 'til they piled up at the other end. This had been going on for several days until the farmer called me, and he looked like his birds: he couldn't sleep for the noise.

(Fox 1984: 33)

Sixth, broilers tend to be bruised and have bones broken while being caught for slaughter. In order to be cost effective, teams of 'catchers' have to work fast, grabbing up to four birds at a time and bundling them into crates.

Once mature, at the correct contract slaughter weight, an entire shed of broilers is caught packed and transported to the slaughterhouse where they are shackled onto to a conveyer belt and processed automatically into dressed and packaged oven-ready chickens. The slaughter process requires that they pass into an electric stunning bath before being automatically killed by a throat cutter. From there they pass to the scald bath prior to plucking and gutting. According to the Farm Animal Welfare Network (1995), when the necessary stunning current is applied it results in a high rate of bone breakage and splintering. Since this is dangerous to consumers, they claim the industry reduces the current so that the chickens may have their necks cut and enter the scald baths fully conscious.

While such organizations seek to bring ethical standards into modern farm practices, it is the case that by placing large quantities of animals in semi-automated manufacturing systems housed in discreet buildings in the countryside, farmers and consumers have been significantly insulated and distanced from the consideration of individual animal suffering. Arguably, it is only the battery hen that has attracted widespread human sympathy, leading to changes in consumer demands for free-range eggs. Why is it that the hens whose lives are much longer and whose purpose is not to be eaten but to lay eggs attract more sympathy than the broiler? In part it is because more adverse publicity has been mounted against battery farming, but this in itself may be a function of the tendency to judge the condition of animals in human terms. Thus the Farm Animal Welfare Network pamphlet on the poultry industry deploys terms of human suffering to describe the lives of the battery hen: 'they're *imprisoned* in battery cages for *life*' [my emphasis]. There are also subtle references to the unnatural and indecent harnessing of sexual behaviour such as egg laying: 'Battery hens become highly stressed and aggressive during the prelaying period because of lack of privacy and nesting materials . . . Hens will overcome an amazing range of obstacles to reach the seclusion of a nesting box. For the abused battery hen there is no hope – she must lay in a crowded cage, on the bare wire floor' (Farm Animal Welfare Network 1995: 2).

In the same document the language used to describe the broilers is, unintentionally no doubt, less humanized. In fact, in this and other documents the sympathy of the readers for such animals is blurred by the language of human deviance imputed to the birds: 'Selective breeding for "*greedy*" birds, and the addition of growth-promoters to the feed, have ensured an end-product twice as heavy at seven weeks as *chickens should be* – and were, before the poultry and *drug* industries *moved* in. The result? PROFITS for producers and SUFFERING for the *sick and deformed* birds' (Farm Animal Welfare Network 1995: 4; my emphasis). Further this text appears under the heading 'Baby Giants', suggesting anomaly and disorder. Drug-crazed and greedy, deformed and unnatural in genetic make-up, practice and body, this highly manufactured animal accrues the aberrant qualities that derive from its origins in the wicked manipulation of nature. So far removed from true nature, humans can react to it with the same moral indifference as other manufactured 'products'. The mythical Western farmyard supplied chicken meat only for special occasions, at Easter and Christmas especially. It was most commonly supplied by male cockerels and their reputation for proudness, fighting, strutting and crowing was associated with troublesome young men. This deviant behaviour may account for the less than sympathetic human attitude towards them. However, broiler chickens are male and female, but their confusion with cockerels and errant maleness may further reduce the extent of human compassion.

Another animal that has an ambiguous moral reputation is the pig. On the one hand it has a negative reputation for greed, laziness and dirtiness, but on the other it is considered intelligent, docile and gentle. Like the broiler it has not been liberated from intensification as much as laying hens. Free-range pork and bacon have a limited if growing demand, but the vast majority are reared intensively.

Pigs

Pig production has grown dramatically in most Western countries since World War II, and that growth is entirely attributable to more intensive systems which yield pork and bacon at considerably lower cost. Although the traditional pasture system continued during this period, the trend was towards more total confinement systems and larger scale operations. For example, in the USA which has a pig population in excess of 85 million, the numbers of new confinement systems rose from 8,700 in 1963 to 30,000–40,000 in 1973. By 1980, 63 per cent of all pig husbandry facilities were of the total confinement–environment control type, while only 27 per cent were raised on dirt lots with some shelter. Systems varied in the type of flooring given but the majority favoured partial slats (to allow excrement to fall through) with liquid manure waste disposal systems. In the USA the traditional 'hog belt' is in the Midwest and throughout the twentieth century the agribusiness supported and protected a large number of medium-sized hog farmers. However, from the 1980s, following the example of the broiler chicken industry, some hog producers began to break away to become concentrated in larger units and in states that would establish a legal framework suitable to greater intensification. One such state is North Carolina, where the freedoms given to the industry through lobbying and industrial representation in state legislatures have resulted in severe environmental damage:

> The coastal plains and piedment of North Carolina are now pocked by vast pig factories and pig slaughterhouses. People living here sicken from the stink of twenty-five foot deep lagoons of pig shit which have poisoned the water table and decanted nitrogen and phosphorous-laced sludge into such rivers as the Neuse, the Tar-Pamlico and the Albermarle. In North Carolina it is as though the sewage of fifteen million people were flushed into open pits and sprayed onto fields, with almost no restrictions. That is where the seven million pigs worth of manure goes.
>
> (Cockburn 1996: 37–8)

The production system starts with breeding sows, which are kept in production with the minimum of time between pregnancies. Whereas they were once allowed outside between or during pregnancy, today they are kept confined indoors all of their lives. Similarly sows were once put to the boar when in heat, but today most are artificially inseminated. This means that the sows can be kept in their stalls (either entire enclosures 2 ft wide or open stalls with the sows tethered by the neck or girth), where they cannot turn around, for all of their pregnancy. Shortly before farrowing they are taken to the farrowing crates, which allow space for the piglets to move away from the sow. This prevents piglet crushing while allowing access to the piglets. Piglets are weaned very early at three weeks and kept in groups of between twenty and twenty-five for three weeks in a heated cage prior to the fattening stage. After weaning the sow is 'dried up' through a 24-hour period without water or food, which very quickly brings her on heat. For the next five days she is either served by the boar or inseminated, and the process starts over again.

For the next five or six months the piglets are fattened ready for slaughter. It takes four months to produce the best pork, while bacon is usually from six-month-old pigs. After the nursery cages, the piglets are moved to 3×12 m pens in groups of around 75, and from there to smaller group pens of 40–45 pigs. The buildings are windowless and with full light and temperature controls. Feed, waste flushing, water spray and so on are fully automated and human contact is minimal, save to check for health and mortalities. The feed frequently includes high doses of antibiotics and growth-stimulating hormones.

As with poultry under intensive systems, pigs are more prone to a range of infectious diseases and system-related problems. In some systems where manure is composted below the pigs, temperatures become too high and the air too ammoniated, causing stress to the pigs, reduced feeding and growth. Research has shown that slatted flooring produces poor health and stress, and in such conditions the pig social hierarchy breaks down, leading to aggression and tail biting. Research has also shown that if pigs are kept in groups of more than thirty, it becomes impossible for them to memorize the social rank order, leading to confusion and similar behaviour. Infectious diseases are endemic and require efficient hygiene systems and increased use of antibiotics and vaccine. Key infectious diseases include swine vesicular disease, Aujesky's disease, transmissible gastroenteritis and streptococcal meningitis. However, the total confinement system has produced new difficulties: 'With a continuous farrowing operation . . . the indoor environment may build up a heavy contamination of *E. coli*, viruses, transmissible gastroenteritis, trophic rhinitis, and internal and external parasites' (Fox 1984: 75). The growth of total confinement systems has increased the mortality of pigs from 2.9 per cent in 1963 to 6.1 per cent in 1979 and, since the continuous use of sub-therapeutic doses of antibiotics masks the existence of diseases such as *E. coli*, it is entirely likely that increased levels of food poisoning in humans can be traced to these systems.

Veal

Like laying hens, calves used for veal meat have incurred much sympathy and consequently consumer avoidance is significant. This is partly connected with sentimentalization of the calf, typically associated with babyhood, innocence and beauty. But in part it also relates to the deliberate suffering inflicted on such animals (known to call for their mothers for many days following early separation), and the production of a food which only the wealthy have traditionally eaten. Whereas the mass production of bacon and chicken has a populist, democratic appeal, even under more intensive systems, veal is still one of the most expensive meats and associated with the menus of elite restaurants rather than the diner. Annual consumption of veal in the USA was about 1.9 kg per person, as compared with 43.4 kg of beef (Fox 1984: 81).

Under the European veal production regime, which is replacing the traditional US veal method, calves are separated from their mothers almost as soon as they are born and placed in wooden crates, during which time they are fed a low iron mix based on skimmed milk. The point of the exercise is to produce a soft, white fillet of meat. While the calf would ordinarily commence its high-fibre grass diet within a few weeks of birth, this no-fibre diet leads to immediate health problems. The veal calf is by definition unhealthy, if not sick. Mortality rates of 20 per cent have been recorded for this system with diarrhoea and pneumonia being the principal diseases. The traditional US veal regime required less isolation, with veal calves being raised in pens in groups of six to eight, and research by the US Department of Agriculture found that they required five times less medication than the stall-fed calves (Johnson 1991). Nonetheless, it is still more profitable to produce veal in this way and, partly as a result of demands for white meat in the past twenty years, veal production has increased.

Beef and dairy cattle

One of the most important changes in the livestock industries in the recent past has been the intensification of beef and dairy production. In the USA, home of one of the principal extensive or ranching systems, beef production has grown as a result of new intensive feedlot systems. The feedlot is generally a fenced-in area with a concrete feed trough along one side. Almost all work associated with the feeding and maintenance of the animals is automated. Grain surpluses stimulated vertical integration between the grain elevators and animal feed industries that manufacture feeds or 'forage' suitable for cattle to eat without any need to graze. Aside from turning low-priced wheat into a value added product, the so-called marbled, grain-fed beef attracted higher prices and was popular in valuable new export markets such as Japan. Grain-fed cattle eat corn, sorghum and other grains, but increasingly these are supplemented or replaced with cheaper materials including manure from chicken houses and pig pens, industrial sewerage and oils. Research is currently investigating the usefulness of cardboard, newspaper, cement dust and plastic.

In the USA calves are allowed to stay with their mothers on the open range for 6 to 11 months prior to transportation to one of 42,000 giant automated feedlots where they are fattened up and readied for slaughter. Some of the feedlots are massive: the largest 200, for example, feed nearly half the cattle in the USA. Weight maximization is achieved with growth-stimulating hormones and antibiotics. Anabolic steroids are given in slow release capsules implanted into the animals' ears. They release five times the normal rates of oestradiol, testosterone and progesterone which combined increase weight gain by 5–20 per cent, feed efficiency by 5–12 per cent, and lean meat growth by 15–25 per cent (Rifkin 1991: 12). Under such cramped conditions the cattle are prone to infectious and other diseases, for which antibiotics have been administered in large doses. The cattle are also contaminated by build-ups of herbicides and pesticides which have been sprayed on the feed crops. According to the National Research Council of the National Academy of Sciences, beef is the most herbicide contaminated food and ranks third in terms of pesticide contamination (Rifkin 1991: 13). As Rifkin notes, all factors relating to weight conversion are addressed. Flies, for example, which can bother the cattle and keep them from their feed, are kept down through pesticides. 'In the biggest feedlots, where 50,000 head or more are sequestered, managers sometimes turn to aerial spraying. Crop-dusting aircraft fly back and forth over cattle pens and spray feedlots with insecticides, drenching the facilities with toxic rain' (Rifkin 1991: 14).

In Britain and elsewhere, dairy and beef cattle used to be kept off the pasture during winter in order to avoid labour costs, feed costs and damage to the land. Instead they were kept in barns or yards with a deep straw bedding. As a result of recent agricultural changes, less straw is being produced and, in order to avoid rising prices as well as the labour costs of the mucking out system, farmers have kept cattle inside on wooden slats or concrete. Increasingly, cattle are being kept in yards throughout the year, while pastures are ploughed and planted with fodder crops. Such changes substantially reduce transportation and labour costs.

While beef cattle fatten very quickly on the feedlots and continue to do so despite increased health problems, milk yields drop considerably among sick cows and much research has gone into finding high protein feeds that do not create digestive difficulties and pain. Silage feeds tend to produce more urine and, under crowded conditions, infectious diseases such as mastitis, requiring more or less continuous doses of antibiotics, are endemic.

The intensification of the livestock industry has more or less revolutionized all major meat production. Only sheep and goats have yet to be intensified, but they are not major meats in the West. While enormous gains in terms of output and security of supply have been enjoyed for many years, the disadvantages of the system in terms of health risks to humans and degradation of the environment are only just beginning to be appreciated. In this chapter we have seen the socio-economic foreground to this development. The application of Fordist principles to animal protein production revolutionized Western diets, changed forever the global pattern of food production and profoundly altered relationships between farm animals and those in daily contact with them. Although the spatial distance between food animals and their consumers has been extended in late modernity, the changing conditions of animal husbandry have been revealed to a popular audience in a series of media exposés, first, by animal rights activists on moral grounds and, second, by health authorities following the discovery of significant risk factors in contemporary production and processing systems. This highlights a critical feature of animal husbandry in late modernity. It has been detached from its place in the modern order as a pillar of human and social progress and become symptomatically disordered and chaotic. Out of the social demands for meat have grown very powerful meat and livestock corporations that now operate purely to advantage their industries rather than human diets. As we shall soon see, the deregulation of the public sector has also affected the animal and meat inspectorates which formerly safeguarded the public from the potential risks associated with animal production and processing. In the next chapter the risk to human health is considered in more detail, alongside a sociological consideration of animals as food.

8 ANIMAL FOODWAYS

ANIMALS IN THE HUMAN DIET

Animals are included in all but a few human diets. Indeed, it has been argued that the origins and development of our species is related to climatic changes that favoured larger areas of open grassland, an associated growth in the number of grassland animals and opportunities for early hominids to scavenge and kill them (Pelto 1976). Whatever the cause, the archaeological record is clear: most hominid species were gatherers and hunters. Contrary to assumptions dominant until recently, other contemporary apes are also animal eaters. Baboons have been observed to eat at least 47 species of animal, including infant gazelles and antelopes. Chimpanzees are highly organized in their hunts and are known to eat at least 23 species of mammals including several species of monkeys and baboons, pigs, small deer species, rats, mongooses, and chimpanzee and even human babies (Harris 1990: 37). Marvin Harris argues, on the basis of a range of indirect evidence, including archaeological remains and the observation of apes and humans, that early hominids such as australopithecines 'had a special fondness for meat' (Harris 1990: 36).

This special fondness for meat, accompanied by more elaborate sharing and heightened communitas during meat meals, is a common human characteristic. Indeed the anthropological record suggests that humans everywhere have elaborated complex ritual and religious rules and procedures for the eating of meat – again, in contrast to most other foods. However, meat is not like other foods. First, apart from a few locations, meat is not a staple; for most people, meat is an occasional food. In most hunter-gatherer societies meat makes only a minor calorific contribution. This is the case among cattle herders such as the Nuer in the Sudan and pig farmers in Melanesia. Second, the killing of an animal for food, whether the result of a hunt or the slaughter of a domesticated animal often produces more than the domestic group or residential group can eat (Rival 1996; Sahlins 1974). Meat frequently provides the basis for social meals or gifts and is associated, therefore, with corporate social relations. Third, meat is widely valued over other foods. Pigs, cattle and sheep are the principal units and stores of wealth in many areas of the world. In this way meat is the very consumption of wealth and is involved centrally in systems of exchange, blood and bride payments, rites of passage and politics. Fourth, meat is widely associated with power, status and masculinity. In many societies there are roles in the production of meat that more or less exclude women, including hunting, butchering, sacrificial preparation, herd protection and corralling. In addition, the acquisition of skills associated with these activities forms key masculine rites of passage, and thus male identity is tied to the production of meat. Fifth, because meat has become the focus of such social significance, its preparation in terms of slaughter or sacrifice rituals, involving ritual specialists and elaborate rules, is of considerable communal concern. Sixth, the animals that provide meat, alongside other animal species, belong to complex sets of relations between humans and animals, and are not understood as separate abstractions such as 'nature' or 'food'.

According to Ingold (1994), hunter-gatherers consider human and animal worlds to be indivisible and interactive. Animals are understood as sentient beings with interests, spirits and particular relations with humans, including kinship. Humans and animals inhabit the same plane of existence. Thus, the killing and eating of animals has important moral and ethical implications and is frequently governed by the same or similar types of rules and procedures in operation between humans. Moreover, meat cannot simply be an abstract category of food since it derives from particular animals with specific meanings and relations to the hunter-herder. For example, the manner in which the Huaorani eat monkey meat differs very significantly from the manner in which they eat pig meat. This reflects their admiration, familiarity and reverence of monkeys, whom they track on a day-to-day basis, and their disgust and hatred of wild pigs, whose herds turn up suddenly and dangerously. The two categories of animal have a meaning which is not simply the metaphoric extension of human relations onto nature. According to Rival (1996), it is far more complex because these meanings are based on day-to-day, close relations with the animals and their constant observations and reflections on them form the basis of Huaorani aesthetics. Values that emerge from observation of nature are adopted back into human affairs and influence taste. In the West this relationship with food animals has been gradually eroded to the point where meat is separable from the animal it comes from and its abstraction into a comestible commodity is an important product of modernization. Moreover, as we shall see, the separation is very strictly maintained in a series of avoidance rituals. At a global level the cultural specificities of meat are striking and relate to particular geographies, histories and polities. It is only by taking these into consideration that such variations as meat avoidances in India and the centrality of meat in Germany and the USA can be understood.

The global consumption of meats varies by region in terms of calorific consumption and the species consumed. At various historic conjunctures, different regions of the world can be classified in these terms. Thus in the early part of the twentieth century subarctic regions were characterized by very high levels of wild marine mammal meat consumption. At the same time, across Western Europe, cattle, sheep and pigs formed the principal species but consumption varied according to class and income. In Japan, meat from mammals was minimal while fish and marine animals were very significant in the diet. In Melanesia, animal foods were relatively insignificant in the diet and only the pig was an important meat animal. Sheep and goats were important meat animals in the dry regions of the southern Mediterranean and Middle East. The majority of the population in mainland South-East Asia are Buddhists and reluctant to take the life of any animal (Grigg 1993: 73).

In the 1980s global variations in meat consumption were still very significant though the pattern had changed. According to the FAO (1989), foods from animals comprise 15.7 per cent of the global average per capita calorific daily intake. In the developed world animal foods comprise 30.8 per cent of daily calories compared to 8.9 per cent in the developing world (Grigg 1993: 67). In the developed world meat comprises 13.1 per cent of daily calories compared with 4.3 per cent in the developing world. This contrasting pattern of consumption reflects relative wealth rather more than food preferences:

> Animal foods are, with few exceptions, more expensive per calorie than are plant foods. This is because human beings can either eat plants directly or eat animals which feed upon plants. There is a great loss of energy between these two levels in the food chain, and so it takes six or seven times as much land to produce one calorie of animal food as it does to produce one calorie of plant food . . . In Europe in the early nineteenth century, most of the population were poor, and got 70 per cent of their calorific intake from cereals and roots. With the increase in incomes in the nineteenth and twentieth centuries, the consumption of livestock products rose until in the 1980s they provided one third of all calories in most developed countries, whilst the contribution of cereals and roots had fallen to less than 30 per cent.
>
> (Grigg 1993: 66–7)

Consumption is still influenced by histories of taste and among the developed nations, for example, there are important differences. Europeans and those regions dominated by European migrants tend to favour beef, but eat substantial quantities of poultry and pig meat. However, the main pig-meat eating areas are confined to the USA, UK, Germany, Spain, Greece and Scandinavia with Italy, Australia and France eating substantially less. Such patterns reflect differences in the development of mass meat production in the twentieth century. Of all developed countries only Australia and New Zealand eat significant quantities of sheep meat, reflecting the cheap meat by-product of the extensive wool industries that were established there in the nineteenth century. In Australasia 168 calories from sheep were consumed per person per day, as compared with 22 calories in Western Europe, 1 in the USA, and 9 in the other developed countries. In Japan, none of these meats are eaten in very significant quantities, with fish and shellfish continuing to dominate their protein intake. In contrast to the British, who have a reputation as a fish-eating nation but eat only 4.8 kg per person per year, the Japanese currently consume 85 kg of fish and shellfish per person per year (Franklin 1997). However, their consumption of meat is rising, not in relation to income but in relation to westernization, the growth of Japanese international tourism and the fashion for exotic foods. In 1955 the average Japanese ate 12 gms of meat and 14 gms of milk per day, but by 1990 they were consuming 71 gms of meat and 130 gms of milk (Japan Statistical Association 1993: 18). Although Western cultures continue to be significant consumers of meat and market their animal foods culture elsewhere in products such as McDonald's and baby milk formula, meat eating has undergone very significant changes over the past twenty years. The next sections consider these transformations in relation to overall levels of consumption, the presentation of animal foods, ethnic and gender variations, the growth of vegetarianism and the association of animal foods as health risks.

ANIMAL EATING TRENDS IN THE WESTERN DIET

The modernization of meat production in the West over the course of the twentieth century was a key marker of economic and social progress because it made a former 'positional' good available to everyone. Historically, in Europe especially, meat eating was associated with wealth and status. Only the wealthy could afford a meat-rich diet and their main means of displaying status was in lavish feasts, the centrepieces of which were always a procession of meat courses. Viewed from a different perspective, the modernization of meat meant that it became, if not a feature of every meal, a daily food for most people, as opposed to the occasional 'special' meal. In Australia and the USA, extensive livestock industries produced cheap meat on a scale never imagined by Europeans. New meat-rich diets appeared first in the USA, Australia and Argentina, but they were export industries whose wealth hinged on reaching large population centres. A popular meat-eating cuisine dominated the middle decades of the twentieth century. Although it was a stratified market with the rich still getting the better cuts, in dietary terms it was more homogeneous with animal fats established at relatively high levels across all income groups. New fat-rich products were innovated by the food industries in order to render more of each animal profitable. It is precisely for this reason that the icons of meat in high modernity are not roast joints, steaks or chops, but the American hamburger and hotdog, the German frankfurter and the British sausage. The animal in meat was distanced by these and other developments. Animal slaughterhouses were modernized and removed from sight. Butchers shops were transformed as consumers changed from wanting to see the meat taken from the dressed carcass to wanting to see nothing of the animals at all. Supermarkets and fast-food diners catering to families that no longer had a full-time mother/cook enabled consumers to avoid purchasing and handling meat altogether by selling meals rather than ingredients. The restaurant trade also changed the presentation of meat. Increasingly consumers ordered the more delicately chopped and multi-ingredient dishes from China, India and South-East Asia in preference to the large meat portion centred dishes. As tastes refined and diet and cuisine became decentred through increased foreign travel, the necessity of meat to a meal came under scrutiny. Vegetarianism also spread as young educated consumers began to see diet and cuisine as a global and environmental political issue. Famines, wars and the encroachment of graziers onto tropical rainforests all contributed to this politicization, but it was particularly in relation to more substantial, immediately tangible risks that popular modern meat culture began to break up.

CHANGING MEAT CONSUMPTION IN WESTERN DIET

From the historical record it is not clear exactly when meat became such a centrepiece to the Western diet, nor when it became a preferred food. In medieval Britain meat eating was tightly controlled by the Church and state and the cheaper and plentiful marine fish were imposed on fish days that accounted for about half the year (Harvey 1993: 39). Harvey's study of the diet of a Westminster Benedictine monastery in London between 1100 and 1540 is useful since the monastic diet was typical of the upper strata of society. In the early period, flesh meat was forbidden to all but the sick, but later in the period meat was permitted to be eaten in specially constructed buildings. Typical of the gentry of their day, the monks ate large amounts of meat, averaging just under 2 lb (908 gms) per person per day. In addition his data show that outside the fasting periods of Lent and Advent when fish alone was permitted, the monks completely substituted meat for fish. At this time the meanings of meat were very different. As with all foods in this period, meat was closely associated with the effects it had on the body and constitution. Meat had an adverse physical and moral effect: 'the fasts of the church had a two-fold object: to mortify the flesh by removing the immediate pleasure of meat eating; and to reduce carnal passions, which were held to be inflamed by too meaty a diet' (Wilson 1976: 31).

Dyer's study of harvest workers diet at Sedgeford, East Anglia provides the best evidence for working-class attitudes to meat at this time. As a result of labour shortages after the Black Death, harvesters had to offer better wages and conditions to workers. The meals given to harvest workers before the Black Death were basically bread with very small accompaniments of meat and fish; afterwards the ratios reversed:

> For every 2lb of bread they ate in the thirteenth century, the workers received an ounce or two of meat and about 5 ounces of fish. A century and a half later, for every 2lb of bread workers were allowed a pound of meat and 3–4 ounces of fish.

> (Dyer 1988: 27)

Meat continued to be consumed as a central item to British meals rather than a minor accompaniment, and although the supply tended to fluctuate it increased in line with population increases. American consumption of meat followed the rather frugal pattern of British consumption until about 1860 when cattle were developed that could exploit the rich grazing on the Texas range lands. The sudden expansion of production at first benefited the growing populations of eastern US cities but during the 1870s the USA began exporting to Britain where concerns were beginning to be aired about a protein shortage (Bartrip 1988). Australia, the USA and later Argentina were all competing to export meat to the population centres of Europe. In the last quarter of the nineteenth century, canned meat, cold chill meat and frozen meat technologies were developed to facilitate this (Mcnamee 1966: 80–5). American bacon and hams followed beef and together with secure supplies of mutton and lamb from Australia and New Zealand meant that meat consumption was set to rise in Europe and to approach levels of consumption in the exporting countries. Growing consumption is illustrated by growth in the number of butchers shops in the UK, for example, from 67,691 in 1851, to 109,015 in 1901 (Mcnamee 1966: 83). It is also reflected in the rapid increase in animal herds in the exporting countries. The Australian cattle herd increased from 3.8 million in 1865 to 12.3 million in 1895 (Mitchell 1995: 302).

Precise meat consumption data for the mid-nineteenth century, prior to the imports of American and Australian meat, do not exist. Perren (1978) estimates that the average Briton ate approximately 87 lb of meat per person per year in the period 1831–40. Shortly after foreign imports began in the mid-nineteenth century consumption rose in proportion to imported supplies. Thus consumption grew from 90 lb per year in the period 1861–70, to 110 lb in the period 1880–84 (Perren 1978: 3). Some indication is also given by Smith's report *On the Food of the Labouring Poor* to the Privy Council in 1863. According to Smith the annual consumption of meat ranged from 22 lb per person per year (6.75 oz per week) in some southern counties such as Dorset and Essex, to 88 lb (27 oz per week) in Lancashire and 113 lb (35 oz per week) in Northumberland (Mcnamee 1966: 79). By the turn of the century average meat consumption in the UK had grown considerably and was approaching American levels. In 1904 the average Britain consumed 120 lb of meat per year (37 oz per week) as compared with 150 lb in the USA, 100 lb in Germany and 80 lb in France.

During the twentieth century, Western nations were now clear of any concerns of protein shortage (except during war time) and three key trends can be discerned. First, there was further growth in meat consumption to the 1960s, the result of the intensification of meat production in feedlots, intensive rearing plants, genetic engineering and improved health controls on the one hand and rising real wages on the other. Second, an uneven reduction in meat consumption occurred during the 1970s and 1980s. The decline is uneven in two senses. The connection of high fat meat consumption with cardiovascular disease meant that it affected red and fatty meat more than white and lean. In addition, the new service class reduced their consumption of meat more than others. They were more responsive to health issues and risk, but this highly educated group was more reflexive and decentred in its attitudes to meat and a variety of influences combined to reduce overall consumption. Third, from the 1990s onwards it is possible to discern a moderate growth in some meats alongside continued decline of others. This was the result of the restructuring of the meat industry (providing lower risk products; risk-sensitive marketing and information) and consumer readjustment (finding more lower risk meats, using meat in different ways such as in Asian and Mediterranean cuisines; widespread checking of personal cholesterol levels).

Twentieth-century meat consumption shows a clear growth trend up until the late 1970s. For example, in Britain meat consumption grew from an average of 135 lb per person per year in the period 1909–13, to 143 lb in 1934 (Russell 1941: 7). In the wartime year of 1942 meat consumption dropped to 85 lb, but afterwards rose sharply from 97 lb in 1950 to 117 lb in 1960, to 128 lb in 1970 and to the high point of 131 lb in 1979. In the USA by 1980 meat consumption had grown to 228 lb per person per year, and in Australia (apparent per capita) consumption of meat in 1978–9 was 224 lb (Australian Bureau of Statistics 1992: 5; Ministry of Agriculture, Fisheries and Food 1992: 98; Perl 1980: 99). Australian meat consumption was particularly high by global standards in the nineteenth and early twentieth centuries, meat being the most readily available protein. As other foods became substituted for meat, consumption declined.

Meat consumption expanded partly because in addition to its status as a favourite food in the West and its association with wealth, status and the popular luxuries of modernity, it was assumed to be essential for a healthy, robust life-style. The *Complete Book of Meat* (Gerrard and Mallion), a handbook for students entering the meat trade, was published in 1977 with a second edition in 1980. Coinciding with the high point of meat consumption in the West, there was little mention made of the risks of meat eating, a theme that was going to dominate the meat industry in the 1980s. Instead, the authors are very confident of the health-giving properties of meat and clearly intended their students to maintain a hearty confidence in meat as a food:

> Meat is considered to be one of the most nutritionally complete of all of man's foodstuffs . . . Human flesh has a chemical composition hardly distinguishable from bovine, ovine or porcine flesh (ox, sheep, and pig respectively). It therefore follows that meat, being the flesh of animals and compositionally identical with the flesh of man, must be a well-nigh perfect source of the materials necessary for tissue growth and repair. Thus we utilise the flesh of animals in order to manufacture and sustain the flesh of man. It is a matter of converting one form of flesh into another.
>
> (Gerrard and Mallion 1980: 418–19)

Their assumption about the necessity of meat for a healthy diet is typical of the period, arguing that meat is only lacking in some essential vitamins: 'This perhaps is the secret of a good diet, plenty of meat but with a few vegetables too!' (Gerrard and Mallion 1980: 438).

Cardiovascular disease grew directly as a result of the new meat-rich diets. Although increases in animal fats rather than meat were responsible for this disease it can be directly attributed to increased meat consumption since in the UK, for example, milk, cream and cheese consumption remained stable over the post-war period. Since cardiovascular disease kills people at a relatively young age and since its medical costs are so high, there was a concerted effort to reduce animal fat intakes in the modern Western diet. Health education programmes, dietary guidelines and health promotions were successful in changing behaviour and meat consumption fell. From the high point of 131 lb per person per year in 1979, British consumption fell to 120 lb in 1985, to 110 lb in 1990 and to 108 lb in 1995 – a decline of 18 per cent in fifteen years. In Australia apparent consumption of meat fell from 224 lb in 1978–9 to 183 lb in 1988–9. In the USA consumption of red meats declined by 10 per cent from 184 lb in 1980 to 165 lb in 1994 (Australian Meat and Livestock Corporation 1996: 37). Since the 1970s US beef consumption has declined while the consumption of other meats, particularly poultry, has grown. From the high point in 1976, beef consumption declined by 31 per cent from 94.4 lb to 65.1 lb in 1993. In 1976 Americans consumed 52.2 lb of poultry per person per year, but by 1991 it had grown by 73 per cent to 90.5 lb. (Texas Cattle Feeders Association 1996).

The decline in meat consumption varied significantly between different groups in society. Table 8.1 shows the relative decline in meat eating among British income groups between 1980 and 1990. The highest two income groups have reduced their intake by over 25 per cent while the lower groups have reduced by only 12.5 per cent or less. The most significant decline (29 per cent) occurred among the A2 group which would include a substantial proportion of the highly educated new service class, or the ascetic and postmodern lifestyle groups (Savage et al. 1992). This finding is mirrored in a recent study of meat consumption in the UK. While 28 per cent of the population reported to be reducing meat consumption, 38 per cent of social class II (semi-professions) were reducers as compared with only 28 per cent of social class I (professional and executives), 28 per cent of social class III (skilled workers), 20 per cent of social class IV (partly skilled working class), and 11 per cent of social class V (unskilled working class) (Richardson et al. 1994: 60–1).

Despite the overall decline, some meats deemed unhealthy have declined more than others deemed low risk. Thus, in Britain poultry consumption (low risk) has increased by 24 per cent between 1980 and 1990, while over the same period bacon and ham (high risk) declined by 18 per cent, pork (high risk) by 23 per cent, mutton and lamb (high risk) by 40 per cent and beef and veal (high risk) by 35 per cent (Ministry of Agriculture, Fisheries and Food 1992: 98). This demonstrates that the decline may have more to do with the cholesterol, salmonella and BSE health scares than with animal sentiments. During the 1990s, meat marketing has been keen to develop and market lower fat carcasses, low-fat cuts and low-fat recipes. But in addition, different meat industries now compete against each other in terms of claims about low risk and other nutritional factors, whereas before, this line of marketing was unnecessary.

As the Japanese diet became more westernized and acquired a taste for beef in particular, Western diets were continually changing and searching for new exotic foods. Alternative meats and other proteins were high on their list since a large number wanted to cut down their consumption of the traditional fatty meats. In addition to the growth of chicken and later turkey meat in the 1970s, other 'safe' types of meat have since become established. Prominent among these are emu and kangaroo meat, farmed deer and other traditional game animals, rabbit, pheasant,

TABLE 8.1   *Meat consumption in Britain, 1980–90 (lb per person per year)*

| | Income groups | | | | |
	A1	A2	B	C	D
1980	142	139	128	129	127
1990	105	99	112	112	109
Decrease %	26	29	13	13	14

Source: Ministry of Agriculture, Fisheries and Food, 1992: 102

quail, partridge and grouse. Indeed, declining income and profit from traditional livestock farming has encouraged the trialling and restructuring of the industry.

THE PRESENTATION OF ANIMAL FOODS

Changes in the presentation of meat reveal very clearly the sorts of change in human–animal relations identified in Chapter 2. Because meat is an animal body rendered into human food, part of the rendering to produce a socially acceptable food involves a range of representations. This was the central point made by Lévi-Strauss in his essay 'The Raw and the Cooked' (1964). In this section we will not attempt a structuralist deconstruction of meat in modernity, but an historical analysis, linking a series of critical transformations to key social change in modernity. In viewing changes in the presentation of meat we can see the influence of modern and postmodern sensibilities at work. We can see the increasing uneasiness with animal slaughtering, the sight of dead animal bodies and even recognized parts of dead animal bodies. From the Middle Ages when the sight of an entire animal on the feasting table was the triumphant centrepiece of the social meal, to the Fordist family whose principal meals involved a recognizable part of an animal, to the postmodern meat artwork in nouvelle cuisine, the presentation of meat in our meal has changed dramatically. In addition to the dining table, there are other places where the display of meat has changed: the siting and design of slaughterhouses, the retail presentation of meats in butchers' shops and supermarkets and the presentation of meat in the restaurant and fast-food trades.

From the early modern period onwards, meat has been the centrepiece of domestic family meals. The most important social meals required meat as a centrepiece, in the form of a recognizable animal part in the case of pig, cattle or sheep, or an entire chicken, goose or turkey. Less significant meals were marked by a smaller, less distinguishable part of the animal such as a chop, rasher, fillet or chunk. The serving of meat provides important clues as to its role and meaning. Its 'superiority' over other foods was marked by four principal observations. First, it was brought to the table last (the recognized order for the highest status in processions) and with a certain degree of pomp and ceremony. As it was brought to table there was cause to acknowledge it and make appreciative comments. Second, it was placed on the plate before other foods (perhaps seated on the plate), again mimicking other ritual orders of rank and status. Third, unlike other foods which were put on the plate by the diner, meat was served to them by the carver who sat at the head of the table. Finally, the carver was normally the male head of household, while other foods were usually associated with women. The issue of gender and the status of meat will be examined below, but this highly organized presentation highlights the overt connection between an animal and meat as food.

The origins of ritualized meat eating are not difficult to fathom. Following Elias (1994) and Mennell (1993), they can be explained at one level as the diffusion of elite table rituals and manners to most ranks of society. The social elites were a significant landowning and farming group and the production of meat and hunting of game were central concerns in their lives. The connection between the meat on the table and the animals from which it came was thus a very personal one. In its specific form among the middle classes, however, there was always something to celebrate about a full and brimming table of food during times when supplies were never fully guaranteed. But having plenty of the most favoured food was particularly significant. The overt connection between an animal and meat celebrates not only plenty, but in the modern period progress. The controlled production of plenty was a vibrant, passionate concern and the urgency of the cause was underpinned by the direct symbolism of the undisguised animal. However, it will be argued in this chapter that the significance and meaning of meat ultimately derives from its association with vitality, strength and health. The unambiguous assumption made by people in the West, and most other places besides, was that the strength and vitality of animal can be assimilated into the human body through digestion. Meat is like no other food, because only meat is like humans corporeally. Because animals are made of similar material, the consumption of their flesh is the clearest, most direct mode of maintaining the human body. It is significant perhaps that the most highly valued meats derive from animals whose bodies are both bigger and stronger than the human body. Such assumptions made meat eating compelling in the quest for health and strength and any regrets about killing and slaughter were mitigated by self-interest and preservation.

The centrality of displaying the animal origins of meat continues to the present day, but since the 1970s there has been a discernible decline in its frequency and the ubiquity of its social distribution. Beginning perhaps with the new educated middle classes, the connections between health and strength and the necessity of animal foods began to break down rapidly in response to advances in medical and nutritional science, persistent food crises and famines in the Third World, the discoveries of risk factors in meat consumption and generalized reflexivity in relation to the body and health. Reflexivity over dietary matters produced rapidly changing patterns of behaviour and consumption. It is possible from the 1960s onwards to compress arguments from many sources into a growing critique of meat. In every case the arguments undermined the necessity of meat eating on health grounds and, on the contrary, for the first time in the West, extolled the virtues of new environmentally efficient sources of protein such as lentils and chickpeas, soybeans and quorn. While there is some evidence to suggest that beliefs about the health-promoting qualities of meat continued, the new debates aroused doubts and anxieties that promoted changes in the way meat was consumed. Once the connection between meat and robust health was questioned, there was very little to stop growing animal sentiments from further eroding the desirability of meat. However, meat eaters found that meat was socially acceptable in a more disguised, modest form and the meat trade was quick to exploit this.

First, as we have seen, it was consumed in smaller quantities and not required to centrepiece meals. Second, partly in order to make good the decline in meat consumption, meat corporations in the UK and Australia, for example, promoted a new way of eating meat that completely changed its presentation. Recognizing that the animal–meat–health connection was no longer made by many consumers, it marketed new, non-animal symbols: taste (i.e. that lamb and beef taste better than tofu and lentils which were now widely considered Spartan and boring); healthy low-fat animal protein (in smaller leaner quantities there was no health risk); meat as a superior source of iron (which in Australia targeted women and children, raising consumption significantly); variety (meats in smaller cuts can be part of healthier varied food intake, including boutique meats such as emu, kangaroo, venison and game); ethnicity (since the dramatic growth in overseas tourism large numbers of peasant cuisines were added to middle-class diets and their low meat content was consistent with new dietary norms); and nostalgia (the new meat abstainers were vulnerable to temptations based on foods of their childhood and recidivism among vegetarians was common). Third, beef and other red meats declined, as we have seen and white meats, particularly poultry, have grown significantly. Again, the ease with which the animal origins of poultry could be disguised was part of its recent success. New terms such as chicken nuggets, fish fingers, seafood sticks and 'foreign' terms such as schnitzel and goujon further disembodied the animal origins of meat. The industry is now confident of a revival for what it calls new meats:

> Consumers are attracted to new meat, i.e. lean and served in small portions. New meat is perceived to possess practical and emotional values which consolidate the product's relevance and appeal for the modern consumer. At the practical level, meat continues to be seen as part of a modern meal, convenient and offering variety. Television advertising has turned the product around from a static, old fashioned commodity into one which is innovative and trend setting.

> (Food Australia 1991: 479)

As a result of these changes the retailing of meat has been transformed. The traditional butcher's window, complete with whole game birds, rabbbits and hare (partly plucked or skinned) 'hanging' over a range of roast cuts, chops, fillets and offal on the refrigerated window display and with sides of beef, lamb, mutton and bacon 'hanging' in the space behind the counter has become a thing of the past. Increasingly, even in butcher's shops, carcasses are less frequently hung on view and neat trays of smaller, leaner cuts dominate (Figure 8.1). In addition less meat is left in body sections, showing skin, bone sinew and fat. Fat in particular is meticulously removed as if it was an impurity.

New also are the stir-fry mixes, marinaded meats, curries, satays, hamburgers, schnitzels and other ready to cook meals using meat from lean fillets. Supermarkets are now the largest retailers of meat in the West and the term butcher or butchery has disappeared from stores in favour of terms such as 'fresh meat departments'. However, most meat is now packaged into small portions and sold from refrigerated cabinets much like any other supermarket food. Altogether these changes distance the consumer from all connections with the animal of origin and reduce meat to a more abstract notion of animal protein. These changes have also progressively distanced the consumer from those who butcher, cut and serve meat (Walsh 1989). This abstraction is possible in part because the business

FIGURE 8.1   *In the past butchers' windows displayed an animal's whole or part carcass. This window display is designed to appeal to the anxious consumers of the risk society (Adrian Franklin)*

of killing animals for meat has become removed not only from residential and industrial areas, but increasingly from attention (Figure 8.2).

Once delivered to the slaughterhouse, animals are kept for a brief period in lairage before being driven into the pens prior to stunning and bleeding. The pens are carefully concealed from the public, but such are the sensitivities to modern slaughtering that even the awaiting creatures are not allowed to see or hear an animal being slaughtered. Indeed all sorts of devices have emerged to conceal and obfuscate the business of killing animals for meat. The word slaughterhouse is rarely used, for instance, outside the industry. The normal term *abattoir*, from the French *abatre*, to fell trees, euphemistically avoids the act or process of killing. According to Vialles (1994: xiv–xv), the language of slaughtering involves several 'vegetalizing' metaphors. 'It is a question . . . of aligning the animal (in the special form represented by cattle) on the tree, of 'gathering' meat as one gathers a vegetable, almost of reducing the carnivorous aspect of human eating to its vegetarian aspect.' Inside abattoirs a complex series of actions render the animal into the edible. Each of these actions is separated, often with dividing walls, screens and doors. While the stages in the process are closed off from one another, the act of killing is obscured by the combination of two actions. First, the animal is stunned in the unclean or animal section of the abattoir. The stunned body is then hung on chains and taken on overhead rails into the next section where a different man cuts the arteries of the animal with a knife in order to bleed the body.

FIGURE 8.2 *Animals now appear to many only as pre-prepared meals*
(Adrian Franklin)

The first man does not really kill, he anaesthetises. The second does not really kill either; he bleeds an animal that is already inert, and, in the terms that are in constant use, 'as if dead'. The result of dissociating death from suffering in this way is as follows: since anaesthesia is not really fatal and since painless (or supposedly painless) bleeding is not really killing, we are left without any killer at all, nor do we have any one person who 'really kills; by separating the jobs, you completely dilute the responsibility and any feelings of guilt, however vague are held in check.

(Vialles 1994: 45)

From this point on, the animal passes through a into a very strictly separate 'clean' area called the slaughterhall where various processes, flaying (skinning), gutting and so on, are completed. The animal has passed from a site where its death occurred without a killer, onto a new site where other men confront it not as an animal but a carcass that needs to be disassembled ready for the table.

Ultimately a fully automated process will no doubt complete this process of separation. Such a technology is not that far away. In Australia the company Fututech is developing a semi-automated slaughtering system, which according to Mayrhofer 'will offer a more humane process for the animals, better conditions for the workers and saving of up to 30 per cent for the Australian meat industry' (Mayrhofer 1991: 44).

MEAT AND GENDER

The association of masculinity and meat, notably red meat, has been noted by many (Bourdieu 1984; Charles and Kerr 1988; Lupton 1996a, 1996b; Mennell 1993; Twigg 1983). The traditional meaning of meat in the West, as a giver of strength, health, muscle power, vigour and virility, is strongly suggestive of this association. The association of masculinity with meat eating is also to be found in day-to-day norms and assumptions. Jane Grigson tells of another English food expert who 'remarked that fish could not be served when men were present, as they needed steak or some other good red meat' (Grigson 1994: 1). Twigg notes 'the common expectations of waiters that the steak will be for the man and the fish for the woman' (Twigg 1983: 24). Bourdieu's study found similarities among the French working class. Fish is deemed inappropriate for French workers while red meat, and especially second helpings of red meat, are quintessentially male dining norms. A 1983 survey in Australia, for example, found that while the average man ate 73 gms of beef and veal and 23 gms of pig meat per day, the average Australian woman ate only 42 gms of beef and veal and 13 gms of pig meat. While men eat more of all meats, there is less differences between men and women in the consumption of lamb (men 32 gms, women 22 gms) and poultry (men 29 gms, women 21 gms) (Cashel and English 1987: 186). Another study of meat pie eating in Australia found that while men eat an average of 2.9 meat pies per month, women were only eating 0.9 pies per month.

Charles and Kerr's study of British family eating shows a firm belief that men should have more meat than women (Charles and Kerr 1988: 110–12). A recent Gallup poll in Britain also found very significant gender differences in meat avoidance. While vegetarianism increased from 2.1 per cent of the population in 1984 to 4.5 per cent in 1995, 'women are leading the trend and there are now more than twice as many vegetarian women than men. The number of women aged 25 to 34 who no longer eat red meat has increased by nearly eight times compared with 1984' (Fletcher 1995). Among the under-24 years old group, 'one in four women no longer eat meat and most believe a vegetarian diet is healthier' (Fletcher 1995).

The animalic potency of animals has been particularly assimilated in masculine needs, drives and passions:

> Thus meat is associated with animal strength. Through the direct, though nutritionally incorrect, equation of muscle with muscle, it has been particularly associated with body building and athletic strength. Victorian training diets put an almost exclusive emphasis on meat, and this belief in its necessity is still widely held today, so much so that Wilf Paish in his *Diet for Sport*, feels he has to repudiate the misconception: 'Probably the most hallowed of the time honoured fads is the need for the pre-match steak or even the large emphasis on beef-steak in the diet of sportsmen'.

> (Twigg 1983: 23)

It was long believed, for example, that full masculine strength depended upon a good meat diet. The German and US armies in World War II both maximized wartime meat production in order to supply their armies with meat-rich diets (Fiddes 1991: 11). Twigg (1983: 23) elaborates on this, noting the widespread belief that meat can make men 'angry and fiery tempered', the ritual meat-eating practice of the athlete before a race and even the pre-launch steak of the astronaut. Such beliefs work in the opposite way for men deprived of meat, but especially for male vegetarians. Tester quotes a meat-eating reporter attending a Vegetarian Society Conference in England:

> It is irrational and unacceptable, but most of us attribute to people the qualities of what they eat. Just as vegetarians must have thought me 'tainted' – yellow toothed and intangibly dirty, so I watched for signs of 'zestlessness' – for sagging thighs and weak chins. In fact for the most part they looked very healthy.
>
> (Tester 1992: 145)

Historically the potency of meat was such that it was held to be too strong for certain types of people, 'commonly children, certain groups of women, the sick and those in bookish and sedentary occupations' (Twigg 1983: 24). As we have seen above, the Benedictine diet and early modern views of health saw meat as an arousing food promoting carnal drives. Twigg gives further examples of meat avoidances in order to contain masculine drives:

> John Newtin the hymnographer, when a captain of a slave ship and experiencing the throes of evangelical conversion, made a point of dropping all meat from his diet to prevent his lusting after female slaves. In a similar vein, educationalists in the nineteenth century and into the twentieth often recommended a low meat diet for adolescent boys as a means of combating masturbation.
>
> (Twigg 1983: 24)

The association of masculinity, meat and sex drive is particularly strong in the USA, where Feirstein's *Real Men Don't Eat Quiche* became a best seller. The following passage, quoted in Fiddes, illustrates it well:

> There was a time when this was a nation of Ernest Hemingways. *Real Men*. The kind of guys who could defoliate an entire forest to make a breakfast fire – and then wipe out an endangered species hunting for lunch. But not any more. We've become a nation of wimps. Pansies. Quiche eaters.
>
> (Fiddes 1991: 146–7)

The single most significant reason for the decline of red meat eating among men is its connection with coronary heart disease, a cause of early mortality that affects men far more than women, though recent studies also suggest a correlation between meat eating and cancer (Thorogood et al. 1994: 1667). As we have seen, the consumption of meat by middle-class men has declined the most. Meat and its association with a variety of risks will be examined further in the final section of this chapter. Paradoxically perhaps, it is on women that the meat corporations have concentrated substantial marketing in the past few years. While there was always room to expand the market by encouraging women to eat more meat, advertisers were up against the dominant food beliefs and the association of femininity with moderate consumption or avoidance of meat. Since the 1970s, however, women have arguably become as much concerned with their health as their femininity. In particular, women have become more aware of specifically female disorders as related to diet. Notable among these is iron deficiency resulting from menstruation. Since iron deficiency can affect women acutely and chronically and is regularly a problem during pregnancy, the avoidance of red meats, which are one of the best natural sources of iron, does not make sense from a health perspective. Recent meat advertising has singled out women consumers and is claiming unanticipated success.

THE EMERGENCE AND MEANING OF VEGETARIAN DIETS

We saw in Chapter 2 that the earliest forms of vegetarianism in the modern West were explicitly linked to the extension of thresholds of repugnance towards animal violence in the nineteenth century. Prior examples of meat avoidance, such as the rules of the Benedictine Order, were related to the effects of meat on the human body and carnality, rather than human–animal relations. In addition they were partial and directed by the church calendar.

Later transformations in vegetarianism were consistent with the general direction of change in human–animal relations in the twentieth century. The very earliest emphasized vegetarianism as the biologically appropriate form of human diet, backing such assertions with a range of anatomical, anthropological and archaeological evidence (Cartmill 1993; Tester 1992). Linked to this were claims that meat was more difficult to digest and related to several modern diseases. Killing animals was considered morally repugnant but the polluting, unhealthy aspects were more prominent. Here again we see an example of the tendency in the later nineteenth and early twentieth century to privilege human interests over animals. Animals were not yet the subject of strong human empathy and de-centredness. Rather the physical contact with animals (killing and especially eating them) was seen as potentially polluting. Later forms of vegetarianism dropped the scientific and archaeological emphasis and the anthropocentricism. Salt's vegetarian position 1892 reverses the emphasis: human physical drives and wants for meat must be controlled by civilized people as a result of the clear and imperative rights of animals. Early twentieth-century vegetarianism was confined to a small body of intellectual and working-class, non-conformist Christian groups. Vegetarianism held little appeal to the masses. They equated meat with health and success and food, especially meat, was frequently in very short supply.

It was not until the late 1960s that meat began to drop in price and become a taken for granted, everyday staple. By the 1970s the West was experiencing food gluts and meat was widely eaten, as we have seen, three times per day. At the same time, famines became regularized in the Third World. Concerns about food safety and the condition of intensively reared livestock and animal experimentation became consolidated. The necessity of meat for health, growth and vitality was no longer believed, at least by the emerging new service class. Among this group, vegetarianism provided a physical and spiritual means of protest and direct political action on a range of modern ills, not least of which was the health of the protester. Increasingly, from the 1960s onwards, the decentred, reflexive nature of vegetarianism extended to the interests of farm animals, to a global human community for whom the majority faced insecure and unbalanced food supplies and to health and environmental issues in the West. These issues found a spiritual and political home in the rising numbers of health food stores. In Britain, for example, the number of health food stores grew from 100 to 800 in the 1960s. 'By the 1980s, 1200 such shops were taking £80 million a year' (Driver, 1983: 104). However, since the 1980s vegetarianism has become more complex than a mix of animal sentiments and concern over food production in late capitalism.

First, the link between heart disease, cancers and animal fats led to an overall reduction in meat consumption. Among meat eaters, part of this reduction was achieved through adding some vegetarian meals as part of their overall diet, which removed meat from its symbolic place at the centre of meals. During the 1980s it became de rigueur for the best restaurants and cafés to offer vegetarian options. By the mid-1980s this demi-vegetarianism was evident in the new lines sold by supermarkets and fast food outlets. Survey evidence also shows that people have periodic and occasional vegetarian diets (Richardson et al. 1994). Through regular health checks, people became conscious of their own cholesterol level and ate accordingly.

Second, people became more 'fat' conscious, and the health risk from fatty foods became confused with the fashionably thin body. The desirability of thinness coincided, not surprisingly, with greater food security and food glut in the West and impacted most on young women. While the health risk from eating animal fats impacts most on men, it is among women, particularly young women, that vegetarianism has most appeal. According to a British survey conducted by the Meat and Livestock Commission, one in four 16- to 24-year-old women is now vegetarian as compared with only 4.5 per cent for the total population. Among the vegetarians in this sample, moral and ethical issues were less significant than health issues: 45 per cent of vegetarians said that they gave up eating meat for health reasons, while 16 per cent gave taste as a reason and only 13 per cent gave moral reasons for their choice. Another survey by the catering firm Gargener Merchant found that teenage girls were the most keen to avoid meat and that 44 per cent of all vegetarian children were girls aged 13 or 14 (*Electronic Telegraph*, 11 July 1996).

Third, the puritanical, Spartan nature of earlier vegetarianism has given way to a less strict version where occasional lapses are tolerated, if not endemic, and vegetarianism could be incorporated into a healthy, safe and delicious cuisine. This was pioneered by the Moosewood Restaurant of Ithaca, New York, who relaxed the meaning of vegetarianism and encouraged a broad, middle-class clientele:

> There is no specific dogma attached to the Moosewood cuisine. Moosewood cooks prepare meals which are nutritionally balanced and aesthetically pleasing, using – in addition to vegetables, cheese, eggs, nuts, beans, grains, bean curd, and fresh fish (served on weekend evenings). Perhaps most of Moosewood's customers are not strict vegetarians (or vegetarians at all), but they are drawn to the restaurant for the experience of a meal cooked with skill and care.

> (Katzen 1977: viii)

In Britain vegetarian restaurants prospered. 'Enterprises such as Cranks   note the belated admission of self-mockery to the vegetarian canon – found a ready market in cathedral cities and country towns as well as the metropolis' (Driver 1983: 104). Later, Colin Spencer's *Gourmet Cooking for Vegetarians* (1980), emphasized the potentially indulgent side to vegetarian cuisine, adding alcohol, cream, spices and French sauces to a full range of dishes. By the 1990s vegetarian cuisine was a mainstream dining option in the West and, as Driver admits, 'the professional vegetarian no longer sounded like the equivalent of wearing sackcloth and ashes' (1983: 106).

Fourth, as we have seen the emphasis on health rather than on animal sentiments gave rise to the demi-vegetarian. According to a Safeway survey of 1991, for example, only 63 per cent of vegetarians ate no meat or fish (Richardson et al. 1994: 57). The Vegetarian Society's own survey of 1991 found that 'half of the adults who classified themselves as vegetarian ate some kind of meat, although younger vegetarians were more rigorous (Richardson et al. 1994: 58). Demi-vegetarians do not deny themselves meat and fish, particularly those that have health advantages such as fish and white meat, but eat them only occasionally. In doing this they avoid total complicity in the intensive meat trade and can be highly selective in encouraging new forms of meat, egg and fish production. Thus, since the 1980s markets for free-range eggs and chickens have expanded dramatically. Consumers have influenced the tuna industry and organic, wild and stress-free meats have an established market share.

While 'concerns about animals suffering are cited by up to 81 per cent of vegetarians, as well as by those considering becoming vegetarian or reducing their meat consumption, health benefits or risks are probably the most commonly acknowledged reasons for reducing meat consumption' (Richardson et al. 1994: 58). In other words, irreducible principles such as animal rights do not dominate contemporary vegetarian attitudes. Rather, views and practices appear to be quite fluid and change according to wider social and economic conditions and issues. Recently the most influential issue has been risk from meat-borne infections. This is addressed in a final section on risk and meat.

RISK AND MEAT

Up until the 1980s, risks associated with meat eating were largely confined to heart disease and even then the risk was principally associated with high levels of animal fats in the diet. However, since the 1980s new risks have been discovered that centre on a range of infectious diseases that can enter the human food chain via diseased or contaminated meat (Figure 8.3). While the modernization of the meat industry gave rise to ethical and health concerns in the past, the worst fears were perhaps confirmed in March 1996 when it was concluded that the eating of beef affected by bovine spongiform encephalopathy (BSE) was directly connected to cases of the fatal human Creutzfeldt-Jacob Disease (CJD) of the brain (Collinge 1996b).

Modern meat eating, particularly since 1945, has been shaped by the Fordization of every process in the animal industry, from birth to burger. Indeed,

FIGURE 8.3   *Intensive factory methods, heart disease and meat scares such as mad cow disease have made beef a target for avoidance. This sign woos them back with the local family farm image, chemical-free growing environment and a safety reassurance (Adrian Franklin)*

Ritzer even offers us 'McDonaldization' as a metonym for service production in late modernity (Ritzer 1983, 1993). It is no surprise therefore that television commentators such as Jonathon Ross and sociologists such as Barry Smart understand McDonald's as embodying the American Dream, the active celebration of modernity, or 'the seductive consumer lifestyle associated with capitalism and liberal democracy in the West as a whole' (Jonathon Ross 1995; Smart 1994: 174). Furthermore, the McDonald's burger bar becomes a nostalgic site of order and safety:

> In addition to product standardisation, the decor, layout services and exchanges with staff are intended to be predictable, are designed to appear familiar. One of the objectives being to promote an informal and safe atmosphere in which food can be ordered, presented and consumed quickly . . . McDonald's offers a simulation of order, security and reassurance in a wider social context increasingly marked by the realities of uncertainty, insecurity and risk. In short, what is provided is programmed pleasure and no surprises . . . Fast food is now so pervasive, its virtues promoted by American presidents, that much of the disapproval has disappeared.
>
> (Smart 1994: 172–3)

The cultural centrality of McDonald's was a fully intended outcome envisaged by its chief procreator, Ray Kroc. In order to enhance the interior and interactional effect, Kroc placed each new McDonald's in a key position within a suburban development, near the churches, 'believing that the pure, wholesome image of his restaurant and the neighbouring church would shine as a beacon of light on each other . . . Even his golden arches, say some commentators, bore a striking resemblance to pictorial images of the gates of heaven' (Rifkin 1992: 268).

This cosy image of McDonald's and of meat eating in general as a central and guaranteed component of the modern diet was dealt a major blow in the 1990s by a series of major food scares centring on meat. The new food scares did something which put into reverse one of the key characteristics of meat eating in modernity. They emphasized to the consumer, the connections between animals and meat, and underlined the processes of animal-into-meat. These rationalized, intensive processes, so studiously hidden from the public gaze, were revealed to be the source of the new risk. In short, the new methods of meat production rendered all meat a potential health risk and it lost its innocence as a marker of modern progress.

To judge by the reaction of the British public to these meat scares, there was a sense of disbelief in the idea that modern meats might be unwholesome, let alone dangerous. After all, as far back as 1862 the British parliament embarked upon a series of investigations and reforms that sought to safeguard the public from dangerous meat. Precisely because modern sensibility insisted upon distancing itself from the business of slaughter, urban consumers simply had no idea about the provenance and safety of the meat they ate. Prior to the development of better epidemiological knowledge and public health measures, it seems a certainty that many people were made sick and died of meat-related illnesses.

Reform might have taken much longer had it not been for the veterinary work of Joseph Gamgee in the 1850s which claimed that 20 per cent of meat eaten came from animals that were considerably diseased:

He [John Gamgee] saw carcases of sick animals cleaned, and the signs of disease cut away, and then sold to butchers who could not kill enough cattle themselves each week for their own trade. In this way, steaks and joints of meat that were at best decidedly unwholesome, and even dangerous to eat, found their way to the tables of the middle and upper classes in London. Also, he found that the sale of meat from diseased animals pervaded the whole of the meat business right from the farmer up to the retail butcher.

(Perren 1978: 51)

Since the nineteenth century a meat inspectorate and a Ministry of Agriculture were formed to safeguard the public from such diseases, which in the latter half of the twentieth century were notable by their rarity. However, this establishment was only trained to deal with a narrow range of animal disease outbreaks that occur naturally among pre-intensive, free-range animal populations. By strictly controlling the possibility of infection, most have been spatially confined or eradicated. In this way, infected animals have been prevented from entering slaughterhouses. In addition, meat inspectorates examined animal carcasses in abattoirs for signs of disease not apparent in the live animal. The recent meat scares pose a serious challenge to such methodical screening. What is new about these scares is that they are specifically related to changes in animal husbandry and meat processing, including changes in inspection regimes. In particular, it appears that new diseases such as BSE can develop under these conditions and food-poisoning bacterias such as salmonella and *E. coli*, which were not a major health risk before, have become difficult if not impossible to control.

In Britain the first of the animal food scares occurred on 4 December 1989 when Junior Health Minister, Edwina Currie, revealed that salmonella had been found inside eggs and that the source of infection was from within an infected hen. This put a question mark over the safety of the battery egg system and not merely its ethical status. Up until then the large number of salmonella poisonings attributed to eggs were assumed to have been caused by unclean shells or from infection in kitchens. Currie's announcement, with its emphasis on public safety, appeared to be justified by the sudden increase in infections during the 1980s. In 1980 there were approximately 7,500 cases of salmonella infection in England and Wales, but these grew to 14,000 cases by 1982, 21,000 cases by 1987 and close to 25,000 cases in 1988 (Johnson 1991: 85). Even the 1980 figure was high relative to rates of infection in the post-World War II period. In 1945, for example, there were less than 1,000 cases, but there was a rising trend: in 1955 there were around 5,000 cases, in 1975 there were 7,000 cases. These increases were not related to changes in the detection or recording of disease.

By 1989 the public in the West had already become familiar with salmonella poisonings through two very prominent large-scale cases. In 1984, between 150,000 and 200,000 people in the USA were infected from a single source of milk. In 1985 sixty-three British infants were infected by dried milk powder from a common factory source. Such was the public concern that the factory owners fell into liquidation shortly afterwards. Although such public reactions are normally described, particularly by sociologists, as overreactions or panics, it is ironic perhaps that in this case the purchasing company, Boots the Chemists, spent £900,000 trying to eradicate the bacteria and failed. Eventually it 'decided to build a completely new plant away from the old site' (Johnson 1991: 84).

In Britain the number of deaths from salmonella are low, approximately fifty per year, but it is a serious illness which often results in hospitalization and rising health costs. In the USA there are over 2,000 deaths per year, but as many as 500,000 hospitalizations. The dangerous bacteria, *Listeria monocytogenes*, which was positively identified with meat, the slaughterhouse trade and new animal feeds, also made headlines in the late 1980s as abnormally high numbers of infections were recorded in both farm animals and the human population. The disease listeriosis causes abortions, neonatal mortality and meningitis in adults. In the UK to date, the numbers of infections are small at about one hundred per year, but 35 per cent of listeria infections result in mortality (Johnson 1991: 84). In the USA listeriosis and staphylococcus infections are also increasing as a result of unsanitary slaughterhouse conditions (Rifkin 1992: 140).

Despite the relatively low risk from meat consumption, the public reaction was substantial and rapid. As early as 1989 a British survey found that 23 per cent of respondents had altered their diet because of concerns about listeria and 43 per cent agreed that 'most raw meat contains bacteria which leads to food poisoning' (Wheelock 1990: 131, cited in Lupton 1996b: 78). Another survey found that, as a result of salmonella and BSE, 'the elimination of micro organisms from meat was a safeguard for which the majority were prepared to pay extra (Richardson et al. 1994: 64). They conclude that 'future changes in meat production techniques are likely to affect meat choice if those changes produce meat that is perceived to be healthier and/or represent a lower risk' (Richardson et al. 1994: 64). Why, we might ask, is the public so responsive to these risks? Should we judge the response to be a panic reaction or a justifiable and enduring shift in consumer demand?

Several factors might account for such responsiveness. The first is that since food-poisoning bacterias typically kill babies, small children, the elderly and infirm, it is understandable that such easily avoidable risks should be eliminated, irrespective of the odds and costs. Second, while the only way in which consumers can reduce the risk is to avoid those foods altogether, they may be willing to do this since safer foods are easily available. Third, it may be that the response is as much to do with a rapid decline in trust as it is with an increase in risk. Modern consumers are highly dependent on large numbers of unseen others in the agriculture and food industries and their willingness to consume these products hinges on trust. In this way the consumer's focus is not so much on the relative risks of any one food as much as the general practices of the producers. The manner by which the new food scares are reported always links the contaminated foods to the new modes of intensive husbandry, new handling practices and deregulation. The specificities of modern human food consumption, which are so hedged in with rules of edibility, not least by observations of hygiene, are delicate enough perhaps to be extremely sensitive to even the remotest possibility that food may be contaminated. Indeed, foods from a particular source, for example, egg batteries and broiler units, or for that matter any intensively reared source, may fall prey to a crisis in consumer confidence, irrespective of the real risk.

When information comes from reliable scientific and governmental sources a crisis of confidence can deepen.

In Britain, information of this sort has been a regular item over the past ten years, some of it taking the form of public announcement as in the 'salmonella-in-eggs' revelation by Edwina Curry. Other important information typically originates from relevant regulatory bodies. In 1994, for example, it was revealed that 50 per cent of British slaughterhouses scored less than 50 out of 100 on the government's own Hygiene Assessment System; 80 per cent scored less than 70 per cent. 'Almost half of slaughterhouses failed to meet the bovine offal regulations' (Newsinger 1996: 23). British slaughterhouses were also criticized by EC inspectors 'who have claimed that they show a general lack of awareness of basic hygiene, which allows gross contamination of meat during carcass dressing. Production lines run too fast, and staff move too freely between "clean and dirty areas"' (Johnson 1991: 86). Public confidence was further diminished, presumably, when slaughterhouses were deregulated and the slaughterhouse inspectorate was cut back.

This sort of explanation, that changes in consumer behaviour occur when critical public confidence is diminished by the sorts of institutions which have been relied on historically to maintain consumer confidence, has considerable appeal since it does not require us to think of consumers as being duped by what Berman (1985: 169) calls 'the visionaries of cultural despair'. According to this thesis, much favoured by sociologists, a litany of anti-modern sentiments ranging from environmental pollution to food contamination and the decline of culture, has become a ready guide for modern reflexivity. So duped by the visionaries of despair are consumers that they are unable to evaluate risk sensibly or, as Smart (1994) seems to imply, appreciate the finer points of the Big Mac and other positive outcomes of modernity. Instead, they exist in a more or less permanent state of panic and hysteria.

Lupton's work on food is a good example of this approach. She avoids the political economy of salmonella and listeria and instead concentrates on the media as a source of consumer despair: 'The news media, in conjunction with nutritional science, medicine and public health, have been central in constructing food as a pathogen, acting as mediators between medico-scientific and lay knowledges' (Lupton 1996b: 78).

> Food is now commonly represented as a pathogen, a source of disease and ill-health. Not only are some foods categorised as 'unhealthy', they are understood as harbouring such health-threatening substances as cholesterol, fats, salt, additives and preservatives, inciting allergic reactions and as contaminating in terms of breeding bacteria with the potential to cause food poisoning.
>
> (Lupton 1996b: 77)

Lupton is not merely arguing that the press exaggerate the facts but that the facts themselves are in some way misrepresentations of the truth. They may or may not be true of course. In order to undermine the scientific facts of the case one might expect a critic to muddy the water by offering contradictory scientific evidence, raising at least some reasonable doubt. Lupton prefers the reader to conceive of the construction, if not the issue itself, as a media phenomenon and expresses little interest in its provenance. The balance of scientific opinion, on the other hand, appears unanimous in its belief that food can be pathogenic and, moreover, that for several important reasons many once reliable foods now carry greater risk of serious contamination as a result of structural changes in the industry.

Accounts such as Lupton's have an important and healthy place in the socio-logical literature though: consumers do not have privileged access to scientific truths, but merely their representational forms. Scientists and the media, often in combination, are an important source of representations of research, the content of which is commonly political and/or moral and the object of which is frequently to identify victims, attach blame or secure research funding. However, Lupton's analysis is in danger of missing or dismissing an important line of investigation. Behind the emergence of the recent food scares there lies an important history of industrial transformations whose significance is economic and political rather than merely biological or epidemiological. Larger agribusinesses involving more intensified production and utilizing cheaper high protein animal by-product feeds, in combination with deregulated, centralized and continuous production-line slaughtering and processing plants, have measurably raised the risk of meat contamination. This has resulted in significant increases in cases of food poison-ing and reduced consumer confidence. There is no clearer example of this than the BSE scare of the 1990s. Again, this largely focused on the highly deregulated British industries, but the worry and concern about BSE had global ramifications. After all, the worst-case scenario is that it threatened to wreck global investments in beef.

BOVINE SPONGIFORM ENCEPHALOPATHY (BSE)

BSE is a cattle disease first identified by the British Central Veterinary Laboratory in November 1986. Somewhat mysteriously, perfectly healthy young cows became first uncoordinated, then unable to move or walk easily and soon after they died. The newly discovered prion disease causes microscopic holes in the brain and progressive brain dysfunction. The cause of the new disease in cattle became known just over one year later, in December 1987. An official study concluded that the only viable source of BSE was from new cattle feeds which included meat and bonemeal from the carcasses of diseased sheep. It was strongly suspected that BSE was contracted from sheep slaughtered originally because they had a disease called 'scrapie', which causes the same brain breakdown and behaviour. Although it had never been known to cross into other species, neither had the bodies of ruminants ever been fed to cattle prior to this. Early in 1988 a special analysis of the feed compounders and feed histories confirmed the hypothesis and the British government commenced action. In mid-1988, it announced a slaughter policy for all suspected cases of BSE in cattle and a ban on the use of ruminant derived feeds. In October 1988 BSE was successfully transmitted to mice via injections of infected brain tissue, thus confirming the worst fear that BSE was transmittable to most mammals, including perhaps humans. In November 1988, the government commenced further actions to prevent transmission into human consumption, beginning with a ban on the use of milk from suspect animals. In June 1989 it announced a ban on the use of bovine offals (the most contaminated organs) which came into effect only in November 1989, four months after the EC placed a ban on the export of British cattle born before 18 July 1988 and offspring of affected or suspect animals.

In the early 1990s BSE became a prominent national concern and began to trigger fears and anxieties about the risks from eating beef. When BSE was successfully transmitted to a pig in laboratory conditions, public alarm was strengthened, starting with a Humberside County Council ban on the inclusion of beef products in school meals. In 1991 a calf born after the ban on ruminant feeds became a confirmed BSE case. The source of contamination was feared to be from fertilizers made from bovine offals. These were promptly banned in 1991 since they were a common all-garden product and spread directly onto pastures and domestic gardens.

Part of the problem and cause of such concern was the extent of the epidemic in cattle themselves. In 1993 the government announced the 100,000th confirmed case of BSE, and British slaughterhouses were so inundated with the killing of infected cattle that alternative plans to destroy and burn cattle on farms were investigated. Since the risk of transmission to humans had not been disproved, the government working party continued to tighten up all possible pathways for infection. They ordered bovine offals to be stained; they set up new safety checks and tighter controls were implemented on the use of bovine vertebral columns for human consumption. On 20 March 1996 the Chief Medical Officer, together with the Ministers for Health and Agriculture, announced that there was a possible link between BSE and a newly appeared fatal human condition which they called new variant Creutzfeldt-Jacob disease (nvCJD).

This announcement, together with a series of subsequent revelations about the failure to maintain safety regulations and inspection processes and conflicting advice from scientists, the livestock industry and the government, finally led to a substantial public reaction. Within a week of the announcement most schools had banned beef from its meals. British beef was taken of the menu at McDonald's. Sales of beef dropped by around 40 per cent causing a price reduction of about £2.00 a kilo. British Airways took British beefburgers off their menu, as did the Granada chains Little Chef and Happy Eater. Many shops closed beef sections and replaced them with other meats (*Electronic Telegraph*, 27 March 1996; *Western Daily Press*, 28 March 1996: 1). In a final attempt to safeguard the European Community against BSE, Commission Decision 96/239 issued on the 27 March prohibited: 'the export from the United Kingdom of live bovine animals, their semen and embryos; meat of bovine animals slaughtered in the UK; products obtained from bovine animals slaughtered in the United Kingdom which are liable to enter the animal feed or human food chain, and materials destined for use in medicinal products, cosmetics or pharmaceutical products; and mammalian derived meat and bone meal' (Ministry of Agriculture, Fisheries and Food, *BSE, A Chronology of Events*, 23 May 1996). In other words, a worldwide ban came into force. This was followed by EC demands for a massive selective slaughter of animals (up to 5 million) in return for an EC compensation scheme for British farmers.

After the dust settled on the possible link between BSE and nvCJD, British consumers remained cautious. More than half of the respondents in a Gallup survey were either 'very worried' (22 per cent) or 'quite worried' (30 per cent). Seventeen per cent were eating less beef; 10 per cent had stopped eating beef altogether. Nearly one-third were eating fewer sausages and beefburgers. Women were more concerned with BSE (61 per cent) than men (42 per cent) and the young (18–34) were more worried than the elderly (over 65) (*Electronic Telegraph*, 5 April 1996). Such fears were not allayed by subsequent revelations that banned parts of cattle had been found in substantial quantities in beef being prepared for beefburgers in Birmingham – after they had been declared fit for human consumption by the Meat Hygiene Service. Although *The Spectator* (30 March 1996) and other commentators could see nothing but madness and irrationality in the panic, citing the small statistical risk involved in eating beef, what was clearly behind the anxiety was a crisis of confidence in the ordering of the meat industry rather than a misjudgement of precise risk factors.

The crisis of confidence has become generalized throughout the meat industry, including regulatory bodies, the overseeing ministries, the chief scientists (who had advised the public on the complete safety and then potential risk of eating beef), the politicians, as well as the farmers and private companies involved. At the centre of the BSE epidemic was the company Prosper de Mulder that introduced for the first time new animal feed production techniques to Britain. According to the *Electronic Telegraph* (1 April 1996): 'In 1990 the company admitted that it was still – perfectly legally – cooking animal food at one of its five factories at "between 115C and 120C", at least 10C below the European safety threshold. Government scientists said that BSE survived and was propagated during the 1980s because renderers began to treat offal at lower temperatures'.

Medical research conflicts with *The Spectator* view, that the British public were overreacting and irrational as a result of mischievous panic mongering. According to a survey carried out by a team of London doctors, the public was well informed and acted sensibly on the basis of its knowledge:

> Overall knowledge of bovine spongiform encephalopathy was good, with 147 of the members of the general public being aware of the disease. Their assessment of the risk of Creutzfeldt-Jakob disease was accurate, with 129 saying that it was either rare or extremely rare and 120 correctly estimating the number of deaths in Britain each year as 50 or fewer. Altogether 134 reported that the media were their source of information, with only five having consulted their general practitioner.
>
> (Gunasekera et al. 1996)

Gunasekera et al. argue that public reflexivity was not only sophisticated (their public sample was compared with a sample of general practitioners), but that the public were able to weigh up the available evidence themselves and use this as a means of judging the advice given to them through the media:

Thus, before the recent statements, the general public seemed to have picked up on the uncertainty about the scientific evidence portrayed in the media, made up their own minds, and acted accordingly. The public are more sophisticated than we give them credit for; public health messages should take this into account. If people are given absolute answers to questions for which the evidence is uncertain they seem not to believe the message.

(Gunasekera et al. 1996)

The 'message' referred to was not, predominantly, that meat was unsafe. The media coverage was dominated, if anything, by the Conservative Party's spin doctors pronouncing the safety of meat and the spectacle of the Minister of Health and the Prime Minister assuring the nation of the safety of British beef. In a somewhat desperate measure to save the situation, Minister of Agriculture, Mr Selwyn Gummer, was photographed feeding British beefburgers to his own children.

While the British government had implemented almost every safeguard imaginable to protect further contaminations of BSE into human foodways, an all-important question remained as to whether, during those years from the commencement of feeding ruminant-based feeds to the termination of such practices, BSE had infected humans. It was known that CJD had a very long incubation period, of ten years or over. Potentially, if infection had occurred through such common foods as beefburgers and sausages, then an epidemic was a possibility. In April 1996, Will et al. (1996) published a *Lancet* paper in which they suggested a strong connection between the new variant CJD and BSE based on the uniqueness and sudden appearance of nvCJD. In June 1996 the Ministry of Agriculture, Fisheries and Food issued a web page called 'BSE and your Health' in which it announced that there were eleven cases of nvCJD in the UK and that 'the Government's scientific advisers have said that the most likely cause was exposure to BSE before controls on the use of specified bovine offals were put in place in 1989' (Ministry of Agriculture, Fisheries and Food 1996: 235). In August 1996 one of the eleven cases of nvCJD, a 20-year-old man who had been a vegetarian for the previous four years, died. The coroner established a legal precedent by recording a verdict of death by misadventure, blaming BSE-contaminated meat products as the most likely cause. He told the Durham inquest:

Investigations have been carried out by the surveillance unit in Edinburgh to see if there is a link between this type of CJD and BSE. The conclusions are that it cannot be proved to the extent required for scientific proof. This is a court of law and the level of proof required is on the balance of probabilities. I am satisfied that it is more likely than not that he contracted this disease prior to 1990 by eating some form of contaminated beef product, probably a product such as a beef burger.

(*Electronic Telegraph*, 20 August 1996)

On 24 October Collinge published a paper in *Nature* which claimed to have direct evidence of the transmission of BSE from cattle to humans. Protein prions in the brain tissue of those who died of nvCJD were discovered to be identical with those In BSE infected cattle, an occurrence that could best be explained by transmission (Collinge et al. 1996: 685–90). This was well received by the scientific community at the time (Bradbury 1996) and became firmly accepted by the end of 1997, following further experiments and developments in prion theory (Wise 1996: 317). This focused attention on the nature and extent of the human epidemic. Subsequent to this, further cases of nvCJD emerged throughout Britain (21 cases by 31 July 1997), though their highly clustered pattern suggested that they may have been linked to contaminations from particular slaughter-houses and rendering plants (Warden 1996). It is still too early to know the precise extent of human contamination from BSE. In December 1997 the new Blair Labour government announced that it was considering a public inquiry into the entire BSE issue. 'The inquiry, by a judge rather than a scientist, would examine the degree of complacency or concealment about the risk of human infection of Creutzfeldt-Jacob disease, first admitted by the previous Conservative government 21 months ago' (Warden 1997: 1). Although there is a clear political advantage in this, the Labour Party is responding to many complaints about the handling of the affair. In particular, the Conservative government may be blamed for failing to act swiftly enough in banning BSE-infected meat and placing the interests of the beef industry before those of the consumer. In addition, as the government of deregulation it may be partly blamed for failure to maintain adequate safeguards on the animal feeds industry and on meat inspection. By contrast, under the new Labour government, the management of risk from meat appears to have returned to former mid-twentieth-century norms. As a result of the recent discovery of BSE in cuts of meat containing spinal nerve materials, the English T-bone steak has now been banned along with all other beef sold 'on the bone'.

CONCLUSION

Far from being simply a matter of taste, the consumption of meat in modern societies is related to a wide variety of social processes and has changed dramatically throughout modernity. Beginning in the nineteenth century, meat was still an elite food, with some wealthier fractions eating large quantities with almost every meal while others ate almost no meat at all. As a result of the takeover and development of the Americas and Australia, modernizing societies of the West began to produce and consume more and more meat. Through Fordist innovations, former extensive production on ranges and pastures gave way to intensive factory plants, linked to advantageous grain-producing areas. Protein consumption from meat sources became a singular register of social and democratic progress. As the meat industries became a significant and influential economic formation in Western economies, this taste culture was rapidly globalized, even to those countries where meat was historically a very minor part of the diet.

Meat consumption was therefore linked not only to powerful commercial formations, but also to a number of agricultural, health and welfarist concerns of the modern Western state. Meat eating is fraught with potential dangers to human consumers and as part of the earliest health reforms of the nineteenth century meat production and processing were subject to the tightest of legislations, controls and inspections. This organized, modern ordering of risk management focused on the formal institution of the state and was predicated on the availability of fiscal surplus. Consumers of meat were increasingly removed from any spatial contiguities with the animals they ate, or from any kind of decision-making as to its goodness and healthiness. The state ensured a good supply of healthy meat and sponsored information on its nutritional superiority and how to cook it safely. What remained of the former proximity to and knowledge of farm animals was a highly sanitized version of rural idyll and contentment.

This social ordering broke down in the postmodern West and, as we have seen, suddenly the consumer was faced with ethical and risk concerns that had hitherto been 'taken care of' by the state. The treatment and consumption of animals are good examples of what Bauman (1995) describes as the required increase in reflexive morality. But individuals are not alone; they are beset now by state-driven advice and information:

Organised risk management retreats, but does not disappear, as states explore ways of shifting costs and responsibilities. That the most attractive way of doing this involves a neo-liberal emphasis on the freedoms and responsibilities of the individual has been noted by many commentators . . . The development of neo-liberal risk management involves a transformation of state activity rather than its elimination. To exaggerate, state agencies become information and advice bureaux rather than agencies of regulation and control.

(Crook 1997: 14)

According to Crook (1997) and others, the neo-liberal regime of risk management produces more risks because the state is cut back from its safe-guarding functions and more information and advice are provided for the individual, resulting in a generalized, heightened if not overloaded sense of risk and anxiety: Beck's (1992) risk society. Crook puts it very well:

The regime tends to the over-production and under-control of risks. The provision of advice and information means, precisely, the 'production' and communication of risks in ever greater numbers. To put it crudely, if you establish an apparatus for the identification of risks, it will identify as many risks as it can. However the only mechanisms available for the control of these newly-identified risks are the risk-calculations and lifestyle modifications open to the individual or the increasingly strained and under-resourced controls associated with the organised regime.

(Crook 1997: 14)

In linking new risks and the rise of risk anxieties with changes in the nature of the state, Crook avoids the need to identify the media and others as the creators of moral and risk panics and the need to view contemporary risk anxiety as mythical, hysterical or wrong-headed. The BSE episode illustrates well how these processes lie in. When the modern organized regime of risk management collapses, not only do we see old problems re-emerge (e.g. inadequately inspected meat), but also the possibility of entirely new ones. Rendering infected ruminant carcasses at below regulation temperatures produced for the first time the transmission of these prion diseases between farm animals. However, the BSE episode also illustrates not only the need for individual reflexive monitoring and assessment of risk, but also the sophistication of the consumers. Despite the government's sanguine information and advice during the panic, consumers refused to believe in the total safety of beef. They were right. The British government and the EC had to take extraordinary and expensive actions ultimately to avert the collapse of the European beef herd and to safeguard consumers. As Gunasekera et al. (1996) found, consumers were well informed, took appropriate action based on that information and did not feel the need to consult their GPs in the process.

Recent changes in the ordering and ethics of meat have, of course, altered irreversibly the way in which it is consumed. The centrality of meat to the Western meal, the superiority of meat as a nutritional protein and the need to concentrate and rationalize the livestock industries were all artefacts of a food and ordering regime that has now passed. Increasingly, meat has become an optional part of an expanded diet. More and more people are vegetarians, demi-vegetarians or occasional vegetarians. Meat is not considered a superior protein, if anything the reverse. Meat has in a sense reverted to the status of an indulgence food, similar though not exactly to the way it was conceived in medieval Europe. Meat is relished in its fatty junk variety or in 'traditional cuts' because it is delicious. Like cream, it is 'naughty but nice'. In moderation consumers can occasionally indulge themselves with meat. Indeed, it is now marketed for its taste, flavours and versatility rather than its essential health and strength giving properties. There are also new avenues for marketing. The Australian Meat and Livestock Corporation (AMLC) successfully increased the consumption of beef by women in its *Iron Campaign* (AMLC 1995). Also, meat is cut, displayed and sold differently to a highly reflexive market. There are now growing premium submarkets for meats produced in non-intensive environments or using low-risk regimes. However, as with other domains of risk management in contemporary society, the place of meat and its future are fundamentally unstable.

9 ANIMAL RITES

In most of the literature on human–animal relations, animal rights represents the apotheosis of change in the twentieth century. So much so that other processes and sites of change have remained obscure and poorly understood. It is only fitting therefore that so much emphasis has been given to these sites and issues in this book, but in the concluding chapter we must now turn to animal rights and to establish how it relates to them. In many ways animal rights is a curious and anomalous development because it prescribes a dramatically different model for human thought and action. In each of the sites considered in this book (zoos, pet keeping, etc.) we have seen how the postmodernization of human–animal relations resulted in a shift from anthropocentric instrumentality to zoocentric empathy. The decentred sensibilities of postmodernity are nowhere better demonstrated than in human–animal relations; in the recent willingness to 'build bridges' between ourselves and other species (Midgely 1994). One sees a clear pattern of de-differentiation of humans and animals throughout contemporary Western society, especially in the last quarter of the twentieth century. Most trends and trajectories suggest a continuation of interaction with animals: contact and interaction with animals is seen as good, beneficial and intensely desirable. In addition, this book has made the claim, in many places, that change has been quantitative as well as qualitative. There has been a net increase in the number and intensity of interactions between humans and animals in the twentieth century.

The number of pets kept have increased, the number of animal-focused leisure activities have increased, the number of memberships of animal-focused organization have increased and new types of interaction with animals and new sites have emerged. In 1993 over 100 million Americans visited 154 accredited zoos and aquariums throughout the USA, which exceeded the combined attendance of all major league baseball, football and basketball games (Anderson 1995: 276). The data suggest that this is more than simply a reflection of increased leisure or affluence. For some reason people have sought new and more intense forms of contact with animals. Later we shall reflect on why this occurred. However, the demands of animal rights are the reverse of these trends. It seeks to disestablish zoos, ban pet keeping, illegalize hunting and angling and encourage vegetarianism (Singer 1990). On the face of it, its puritanical, separatist orthodoxy seems out of kilter with the general direction of change in recent years. It seeks to put an end to all contact and relationships with animals.

In this chapter the origins and development of the idea and practice of animal rights will be outlined. Tester's social constructivist analysis of animals rights will be used to suggest why this strict separation between humans and animals is prescribed and how we can understand the particular form in which animal rights was expressed from the mid-1970s onwards. The animal rights movement will then be described in terms of its changing social content, organizational diversity, strategies and aims. It will be argued that although it is hard to imagine how the pattern of change in late twentieth-century human–animal relations could have occurred without animal rights interventions, particularly in its extension of principles of democratization, we have to understand that it was just one of a number of other trends in Western society that influenced our thinking about animals. As we have seen, others include ecologism and environmentalism, misanthropy and conservationism, ontological insecurity and risk. The strength of conviction with which such alternative, if not opposed, values and anxieties are held suggests that animal rights is strictly limited in terms of its potential to influence and expand. It is likely to win further success in those areas where some demonstrable pain or cruelty is evident, but it is unlikely to be able to stop humans taking a close interest in animals, wanting to see touch and relate to them and even eat them.

ORIGINS AND DEVELOPMENT OF ANIMAL RIGHTS

We have to decide not whether the practice of fox-hunting, for example, is more, or less, cruel than vivisection, but whether *all* practices which inflict unnecessary pain on sentient beings are not incompatible with the higher instincts of humanity.

I am aware that many of my contentions will appear very ridiculous to those who view the subject from a contrary standpoint, and regard the lower animals as created solely for the pleasure and advantage of man; on the other hand, I have myself derived an unfailing fund of amusement from a rather extensive study of our adversaries' reasoning. It is a conflict of opinion, wherein time alone can adjudicate; but already there are not a few signs that the laugh will rest ultimately with the humanitarians.

(Henry Stephens Salt 1892: xi–xii)

Time has indeed vindicated Salt's prediction, the last laugh belongs, posthumously, to him. In 1996 a majority of British members of parliament indicated their support for a bill to ban fox hunting, and in 1997 the incoming Blair Labour government indicated its intention to pass such a bill into law at the earliest opportunity. In 1992 a survey conducted by the European Community found that a majority of Britons (56 per cent) disagreed with the statement: 'Scientists should be allowed to do research that causes pain or injury to animals like dogs and chimpanzees if it produces new information about human health problems'. Majority opposition was found in all European countries except for Portugal (35 per cent) and Greece (36 per cent), with France the most opposed (68 per cent). Similar surveys were conducted outside Europe, but in every case less than a majority agreed with this statement: Canada (49 per cent), USA (42 per cent), Japan (42 per cent). Such views are now politically significant everywhere in the West: other leaders may follow Blair in order to gain political mileage as champions for animal causes.

Salt was an untiring humanitarian thinker and writer. His book on animal rights, *Animal Rights Considered in Relation to Social Progress*, was published in

1892 and contains almost all of the essential arguments that Singer was to make popular in the 1970s; but his were not the first views on the subject. Salt was preceded in England by a number of writers and activists who can be organized into two types of argument or demand, the Demand for Difference and the Demand for Similitude (Tester 1992: 94–169). As Tester argues, Salt revolutionised Western conceptualisation of human–animal relations by combining or reconciling the two demands.

> Contemporary attitudes towards animals share a modernity with the two Demands. Everything that is done to animals, and everything it is said should or should not be done, is prefigured in their debates – everything, that is, except for one very important relationship with animals: the idea of animal rights, which did not appear until the late nineteenth century.
>
> (Tester 1992: 148)

The Demands were introduced in Chapter 1, but let us remind ourselves of them. Tester's analytic dualism is based on 'two demands for a moral treatment of animals which play on the paradox of the human as a different kind of animal' (Tester 1992: 88). One emphasizes the difference side of the paradox, the other the animalness or similarity. We have met those who made the Demand for Difference in Chapter 1, the bourgeois reformers who argued the case for kindliness towards animals and who created a series of anti-cruelty legislations, almost explicitly directed at the urban working classes of the early to mid-nineteenth century. They were men such as Lord Erskine who in 1809 opened the debate in parliament to prevent cruelty to animals and Richard Martin who in 1824 attempted to set up a parliamentary select committee to investigate whether cruel sports such as bear-baiting had 'a mischievous effect on the morals of the people' (Tester 1992: 104). Tester sees the Demand for Difference as an essentially social project in the unique possession of educated nineteenth-century urbanites who, through their consumption of Enlightenment literatures and rejection of anthropocentricism and theological mythologies, were keen to change unruly and violent working-class attitudes and behaviour through a somewhat different path of Enlightenment to their own:

> The Demand for Difference was the first to appear by the space of a few years and, as the label implies, it was an attempt to enhance the privilege of being human through a project of the social extirpation of animality. During the eighteenth and nineteenth centuries, the term animal became a pejorative label which could be applied to humans who seemed to be little more than objects ruled by their natural passions and urges. The Demand for Difference played on an attempt to make humans more subjective and responsive to things which *only humans could know*, primarily the abstract principle of life. Animals were useful they were a stick with which to beat social unruliness and 'beastliness'. Without the ordering of social life, humans would be mere beasts. The Demand involved attempts to create orderly and regulated social relationships through discipline and policing. This involved animal welfare laws and the formation of surveillance organisations such as the RSPCA.
>
> (Tester 1992: 88–9)

Those activists and followers of the Demand for Difference demonstrated their humanity therefore through their regard for and self-restraint with animals. They demonstrated their difference through animals, for only humans could act in this self-conscious, reflexive, and decentred way. However, such a view would not inhibit a healthy and robust appetite for meat and 'civilized' animal sports such as fox hunting and horseracing, or prevent the keeping of domestic pets. Such activities became widely questioned by those who constituted the Demand for Similitude.

Rousseau made the opposite argument, that man was made weaker, more brutish by society; and that 'he' was naturally gentle, noble. Rousseau argued that society and reason were responsible for those behaviours which the Demand for Difference railed against. Only through a return to a state of nature or a relation with nature can men regain their true selves. But Rousseau also emphasized the similarities between humans and animals and found the similarity attractive and beautiful. The devices that man had erected to separate and render hierarchical were arrogant and morally repugnant. Rousseau used modern scientific knowledge and anthropology to support his views: human anatomy and dentistry suggested a frugivorous species, a fact confirmed by our single or twin births as opposed to the large litters of carnivores. To be natural then required that we stop eating meat. It also followed that since humans were naturally gentle and kind, human moral progress rested on modelling more behaviour on the natural and animals, rather than less. Since humans are naturally compassionate, that compassion ought to be extended through natural law to animals; simply because animals cannot understand or recognize law is no argument for not applying it equally to them. Rather, because they too are sentient beings, we should extend humanity to them.

Because this discourse was at the same time one of revolutionary equality, it was influential in British socialist circles and influenced further demands for similitude. Tester runs through some key British protagonists. He singles out such people as Joseph Ritson, the poet Shelley, Thoreau and Wagner to illustrate how these views developed through the eighteenth into the nineteenth century. He shows how Plutarch's notion of the universal spirit which links humans and animals in the possession of a soul, together with the likelihood of transmigration of form – between human and animal – influenced these writers and underpinned their obsessive avoidance of meat. Ritson and Shelley found meat eating to be the cause of both poor health and poor society and provide Tester with a 'fascinating semiotics of food which bestrides the ambiguities of man' (Tester 1992: 143). Ritson and Shelley were both Romantics who saw nature as inspiring and beautiful, so much so that natural living in natural areas became preferred to centres of high culture and the city. As Tester observes, the followers of the Demand for Similitude were reclusive, 'they were all intellectuals who had turned their backs on urban life and became social outsiders. Although they were tapping a rich vein in modern classification when they tried to prove a deep congruity between "Man" and animals, they tended to operate at some remove from the individuals and society they were trying to change' (Tester 1992: 145–6).

In Salt's *Animal Rights*, the two Demands are reconciled and in doing so he effected an epistemological break in modern knowledges of humans and animals: 'The people who said that humans are similar to animals were a loose group of intellectuals who had tried to cut themselves off from the falsities and corruptions of urban life. Meanwhile the argument that humanity must be imposed was the concern of the bourgeoisie, which established urbanised social life as the true domain of the social' (Tester 1992: 147). The former used their writing to persuade by reason, the latter used their organizations to legislate and police, if necessary, by force. Animal rights combines not only their views but their methods:

> Animal rights presents itself as the ultimate way of knowing humanity in relation to animals. Like the Demand for Similitude animal rights is invariably upheld by individuals who are highly concerned with selfhood and therefore critical of society, and, in the specific case of understanding animals, socially interstitial. The morality has immense strength . Because it is held up as an ideal independent of social relationships, it can overcome charges of bias. It resembles the Demand for Difference to the extent that this certainty of moral correctness is a measure of who is or is not properly human. It allows campaigns to discipline and police those who behave in ways which real humans . . . should not.

> (Tester 1992: 149)

Not surprisingly perhaps, Salt's biography lent itself to such a combination. Like Shelley and Ritson, he was middle class, educated and intellectual. He was the son of an army colonel, educated at Eton and Cambridge University and a teacher at Eton prior to a career as a writer. However, he was also a highly conventional Victorian man and, although strongly committed to socialism, his was an active, engaging commitment, closer to the hustle and bustle of the bourgeois reformers than the retiring romantics. His influence has been considerable, if little known: George Bernard Shaw acknowledged Salt to be the source of many of his ideas; he was a friend of Gandhi who recognized Salt's writings as the source of his views on civil disobedience and non-co-operation, which in turn influenced Martin Luther King (Singer 1980: vi).

Although Salt did eventually retire to a cottage in Surrey, this was scarcely Thoreau's retreat to the hills and from this base near London he wrote a steady stream of socialist articles, books and papers. Importantly, his socialist commitment was about societal change and not simply the attainment of individual perfection. Salt engaged in debates of the time and his *Animal Rights* was indeed framed by the trends and issues of his day, notably the debates on race and evolution and a growing awareness among left-wing circles in Europe that indigenous peoples were being inhumanely treated by the colonists. Salt opposed the view, derived from Darwin, that although 'Man' was no longer a singular and special creation, 'he' was nonetheless special if not superior. Salt countered this zoological anthropocentricism with a similar argument that had been applied convincingly and widely to indigenous peoples before: although they were inferior by some selected measure, they were nonetheless fully individual, reasoning and autonomous and as deserving of moral consideration and rights as anyone else.

As with Bentham before him, Salt could not see where a morally significant line could be drawn between humans and animals; animals possessed the same qualities that allowed all humans to be morally enfranchised. Animals were therefore conceived as 'lower races' of life 'in a universe of individuals' (Tester 1992: 152). As with indigenous peoples who, in the view of late nineteenth-century English socialists, were not to be mistreated, dispossessed of their lands and livelihood and were to be accorded rights, it was the moral responsibility of proper humanity to recognize this and to enforce it:

> Animality is a difference of degree not kind. Salt has pulled the two faces of 'Man' together. He simultaneously upheld the position of the Demand for Similitude that 'Man' is naturally one animal among many, and the view of the Demand for Difference that 'Man' is separate from all other creatures. 'Man' is also different because 'he' is able to be more perfect than any other living thing.
>
> (Tester 1992: 153–4)

> Animal rights pushes humans into the order of the beast, whilst simultaneously pulling us into the starry heaven of perfection and virtuous civilisation.
>
> (Tester 1992: 170)

Animal Rights argues that animals possess the right not to have their freedom restricted by humans. The language of rights insists that humans are free to do what they want providing they do not restrict the freedom of others. Salt who spent much of his writing career promoting the idea of rights was simply extending it to animals. Salt was a vegetarian and his notion of animal rights demanded that people stop farming for and eating meat. Hunting was to stop, the fur and feather trade should cease, vivisection should be made illegal. There were to be no exceptions: animal rights was entirely clear as 'a comprehensive principle'. Curiously, however, he was ambiguous with regard to wild animals: the English rural fox is a wild animal and should be left alone by hunters, but wild animals in wild places were not covered by the same rights. Salt was most likely thinking of hunters and gatherers or those travelling through wild country when he argued that killing in self-defence or for necessity (e.g. for food) is permissible and wild animals might also be killed in the protection of crops.

But animal rights, as the full title of his book acknowledges, is about human progress. It is one of a number of ways in which modern human society was to progress towards a more perfect future. Salt felt very strongly about animal rights, but this was only one of many just causes for the extension of rights or human progress. Late nineteenth-century Britain was awash with issues that needed progressing and Salt's readership were too preoccupied with those affecting humans to do much about rights for animals. In particular human life and death issues such as poverty and health were political priorities of the left at the turn of the century and made all the more difficult and intractable by long-term economic instability. The recognition of a case for rights may be easily won but that is never simultaneously the case for priority. Salt's book fell into obscurity soon after publication.

By the mid-1970s when Singer's *Animal Liberation* was published, animals remained an outstanding category of 'otherness'. Their time had come and a newly expanded and radical intelligentsia was accomplished at championing new issues and social movement organization. Wherever humans had been subject to such a range of oppressions as those affecting animals, they had become the subject for liberational movements. Animals were imprisoned in zoos and egg batteries, they were tortured by dastardly animal experimenters and careless farmers, they were kept in appalling accommodation on intensive farms and they were eaten in increasing quantities by uncaring consumers. Most of Singer's book is a catalogue of horrors. Indeed, his opening paragraph likens the condition of animals to those previously affecting black humans:

> This tyranny has caused and today is still causing an amount of pain and suffering that can only be compared with that which resulted from the centuries of tyranny by white humans over black humans. The struggle against this tyranny is a struggle as important as any of the moral and social issues that have been fought over in recent years.

> (Singer 1990: vii)

As Tester observes, Singer created the possibility that animal rights would become an item on the political agenda. Unlike Salt, moreover, Singer's publication was a call to action rather than merely a case for rights. He used the language of social movements and liberation in the book, even including a vegetarian recipe chapter which emphasized an action approach and personal responsibility as well as its moral worth, as its title implies: 'Becoming a Vegetarian . . . or how to reduce animal suffering and human starvation at the same time'. The content of Singer's argument for animal rights was essentially the same as Salt's, as he himself acknowledges (1980: viii); only the manner of active application was different. Singer also coined a slogan term which not only wrapped together the various and sometimes conflicting strands of animal rights, but also identified the precise offence which non-supporters commit: speciesism. This new publication was an instant hit and the speed with which his ideas were taken up by would-be activists surprised him.

In Tester's analysis of animal rights he gives considerable attention to the activism which followed the publication of *Animal Liberation*. To the activists, animal rights appeared as a natural truth, something that exists 'out there' which they have realized and to which they have dedicated themselves. To Tester they fail to see animal rights for what it really is, a social construct, an issue about what it is to be properly human, how to behave in the world. When socially constructed things appear to people as natural, existing independently in their own right, with a life and agenda of their own, sociologists from Marx on have called them fetishes. Cultures produce images of themselves and fall down in worship before them. Marx talked about the fetishism of commodities, notably the commodity money. Money in fact expresses the social relationships of exchange, of the exchange value of human effort or labour power. But money appears before us seemingly expressing the relationship between things. It seems to have an independent magic property and is worshipped. Tester argues that animal rights is also a fetish and that activists behave in a manner which confirms it. He describes conversion scenes; how in seeking to liberate animals and to live apart from animals on a vegetarian/vegan diet the activist senses the achievement of perfection. He argues that like the supporters of the Demand for Similitude they distance themselves from society:

> Today, and in the name of a natural, ahistorical truth, some individuals radically change their lives. They certainly distance themselves from any relationship with animals and thereby begin to know themselves all the better. They also move out of kilter with relationships which the rest of society has with animals, and in this respect at least, can be defined as interstitial; they are the individuals who treat animals perfectly in an imperfect world.
>
> (Tester 1992: 178)

Tester's assumptions here are based on fragments of quotes and press releases from British organizations. Were these views formed from his focus on a particularly eccentric British form of animal rights, or were they more universal? More systematic studies of animal rights activists in the USA support his contention. Summarizing the work of Sperling's (1988) interviews with American animal rights activists, Elizabeth Lawrence notes, 'she found that animal rights proponents believe in human perfectibility':

> They embrace a tradition of hope for the redemption of human nature and foresee a future in which humanity will live in peace with other species. Animal rights activists tend to be deep thinkers who are critical of many aspects of modern society. Typically, they are dissatisfied with technological manipulation of both people and animals, and are opposed to patriarchal power in Western culture which they believe fosters war, oppression of the poor, racism and sexism, as well as speciesism. They assert that science and technology, as agents of pollution and environmental destruction, need to be controlled and they view animal experimentation as symbolic of the human subjugation of nature . . . activists feel they are in contact with the very roots of existence, of cosmic, social and cultural order.
>
> (Lawrence 1994: 1)

Clearly, animal rights shares at least some transatlantic coherence. Animals rights involves such certainty, moral conviction and urgency (animals are suffering out there) that the fetish easily mutated into a fundamentalist cult whose purificatory rituals were not merely personal avoidances (living the pure life of non-contact with animals) and the consumption of clean uncontaminated foods, but the purification of others: the destruction of sites of speciesism. Hunt saboteurs were in existence in Britain since 1964, and on the whole they were simply trying to spoil the hunt by non-violent means. The Band of Mercy was a group, presumably impatient with the lack of progress on animal rights, that decided to use violence against violence. They damaged hunters' cars initially and moved on to burning property. Singer's book was published shortly after some members were caught and imprisoned. Shortly after that in 1976, the Animal Liberation Front (ALF) was formed. It continued the work of the Band of Mercy on a larger scale and the violence escalated towards animal experimenters, battery farmers, furriers and hunts. The Animal Liberation Militia was formed in the early 1980s and went a step further with letter bombs – including one to the Prime Minister, Margaret Thatcher. Tester does not explore the social composition of animal rights. He argues that it is: 'quite impossible to know how many people practically respect the rights of animals. The membership numbers of the different societies can provide no clue. None of the societies, whether they exist to stop hunting, look after welfare, oppose vivisection, or promote vegetarianism, is fully included within the orbit of animal rights' (Tester 1992:178–9).

Elsewhere he suggests that it is 'quite impossible to suggest what the social background and number of the militants will be; just as impossible as it is to predict the constituency of any other cult which appeals to individuals *as* individuals rather than any definite social groups' (Tester 1992: 190). Rather, 'animal rights is not important on the grounds of who upholds it, but because of the very fact that it is upheld at all'. Tester is interested mainly in the fanatical fundamentalism in animal rights and the sociology of it as cult rather than its actual manifestation as a series of different organizations, with different emphases, different interpretations of the ethical arguments and different means of supporting and promoting them. One simply cannot discuss animal rights by bracketing off all but self-defined pure versions and purists, even if they are extremely interesting, newsworthy and worrisome. Just as significant are the others, a majority that has been swayed by the arguments in one form or another and whose behaviour has been changed by them. Of interest are the different organizations and trends in organization formation, memberships, trends in memberships, support bases and trends in support, their financial status, their mobilizations and campaigns.

SOCIAL COMPOSITION AND ORGANIZATION OF ANIMAL RIGHTS

Although Tester is correct not to take all pro-animal organizations as evidence for the scale of support for animal rights, it is nonetheless useful to consider the social bases of animal welfare and rights even if they do not amount to coherent and exact data. It is precisely that the content of animal rights can be so widely interpreted and acted on that this is important. In Britain, the pro-animal groups are a mix of nineteenth-century organizations originating from debates focused around Tester's two Demands and those of more recent origin in the twentieth century. Following the national protests and disturbances sparked by live animal export in 1995, the conservative British newspaper, *The Daily Telegraph*, ran a series of articles on the animal rights issue. It was struck by the social diversity of the protesters and their growing strength:

Since October, when the current demonstrations against live animal exports began, a tiny political movement has burgeoned. The sight of cattle lorries trundling through towns and villages has provided a focus for a bizarre mix of protesters – from middle-class ladies in sensible shoes to ranting, dreadlocked anarchists ... Though a few belong to well-established organisations, none of those can claim total credit for turning mainstream public disquiet into direct and occasionally violent protest. Indeed most of those who have taken to the streets have done so for the first time. The demonstrations have captured the public mood, and the imagination of the animal welfare movement, which hopes a new contingent of middle-class supporters can help to secure wider objectives such as the Wild Mammals (Protection) Bill, which gets its second reading in the Commons on Friday and would effectively outlaw hunting.

(*Electronic Telegraph*, 28 February 1995)

Who were the organizations involved in this extraordinary efflorescence of British pro-animal protest in the mid-1990s? First, there were the old organizations established in the nineteenth century. The RSPCA was founded in 1824 and currently has 22,000 members and 500,000 supporters. Although it was founded 'for the purpose of preventing cruelty to animals', it has been changed by the animal rights debates in recent times:

Mrs Angela Walder, 50, a vegetarian and RSPCA council member, said changing perceptions of animal welfare had affected the society. 'From 28 people on the RSPCA's council, about 17 are vegetarians. I suspect that 10 years ago the figure would have been two.

'Sixteen years ago a woman was asked to leave an RSPCA platform for talking about vegetarianism and candidates used to keep quiet about it for fear of putting people off. Now they include it on their CVs,' she said.

(*Electronic Telegraph*, 28 February 1995, Home News)

The British Union for the Abolition of Vivisection was established in 1898 by Frances Power-Cobb, welfarist and reformer, who also founded the National Anti-Vivisection Society. It has a significant membership of 10,000 who seek the abolition of animal experimentation and support non-violent exposés of cruelty in scientific experimentation. The League Against Cruel Sports was established in 1824 by Henry Amos and Ernest Bell, former RSPCA members who objected to the society's pro-hunting stance at the time. It is opposed to all hunting, gives free legal advice to farmers who do not want hunting on their land and funds research into the impact of wild animals on human interests. It has 40,000 members and supporters. The Vegetarian Society was established in 1847, ostensibly to encourage vegetarianism, but in recent years, like the RSPCA, it has broadened its aims and now has a strong focus on animal rights. For many years the Vegetarian Society remained an obscure and insignificant organization, but its numbers have increased dramatically since the 1960s and it claims that there are now 4 million vegetarians in Britain and a further 10 million people who are attempting to cut their meat intake.

Three significant organizations which appeared in the post-war period have a more mixed and international scope; although they have a welfarist rather than a rights stance, their concerns also span both. The World Society for the Protection of Animals was established in 1955 and aimed to end the exploitation of animals. This society does not oppose meat eating or animal farming but has an interest in endangered and war-torn animals which, as we have seen, can lead to a misanthropic view similar to that of animal rights. Its membership consists of a network of 340 societies in more than 70 countries and it has consultative status with the UN. Compassion in World Farming was founded in 1967 by Peter Roberts, a dairy farmer dismayed that the only way to increase profitability was to use more intensive methods. It currently has a membership of 10,000 and aims to highlight what it sees as the secret cruelties of factory farming and the use of animals as 'production machines'. Here again, this organization is not opposed to farming or even eating animals, but, like the more radical rights organizations, it is fiercely opposed to intensive, factory methods. The International Fund for Animal Welfare was established in 1969 and campaigns against hunting, cosmetic tests on animals, bullfighting and trade in endangered species. It claims a worldwide membership of 1.5 million.

Since 1970 more rights-orientated organizations have emerged. Tester's analysis focuses on the ALF because it fits his model of a cult, but ignores the more peaceable Animal Aid which was modelled on Singer's book, or the international organization People for the Ethical Treatment of Animals (PETA). The ALF was the first major organization to be explicitly dedicated to animal rights. Established in 1976 by Ronnie Lee, a trainee solicitor, anarchist and hunt saboteur, it is a direct action organization dedicated to the economic sabotage of animal exploiters. But as we have seen it moved from acts of pure animal liberation (e.g. freeing battery hens and mink) to car bombings and arson. According to the *Daily Telegraph* it has 'a local cellular structure in which activists band together to attack targets nearby'. The structure is so disparate and disorganized that, 'unbeknown to each other, two cells once turned up to attack the same site at the same time'. Respect for Animals was established in 1993 and continues the work of the former anti-fur group Lynx. This is a direct action group dedicated to 'speak up for and help millions of cruelly treated animals who cannot defend themselves'. It does not disclose its membership.

Arguably, the radical violent organizations have been eclipsed by the large and more respectable. Animal Aid is a pressure group founded on the principles of Peter Singer which opposes those who use violent means to achieve animal rights. It was established in 1977 by Jean Pink and has high-profile patrons such as Spike Milligan. Although it is peaceful, its message is hard line: a recent campaign declared that 'food, household goods, medicines and to some extent clothing and entertainment are all dependent upon causing pain and misery to other living creatures'. It has 100 local voluntary groups in Britain. More significant still is PETA, the largest animal rights organization in the world, which has half a million members worldwide (but concentrated in the USA and Europe). 'Founded in 1980, PETA is dedicated to establishing and defending the rights of all animals. PETA operates under the simple principle that animals are not ours to eat, wear, experiment on or use for entertainment' (PETA 1997a: 1). While the ALF is secretive, low profile and unpopular, PETA aims to be the opposite and has succeeded rather well. London's *Time Out* dubbed 'animal rights the number one "hip cause," thanks largely . . . to the high profile campaigns of "super-trendy" PETA' (PETA 1997b:4). It has enlisted the help of musicians such as Pearl Jam, k.d. Lang, the B-52s and Paul and Linda McCartney, and supermodels Cindy Crawford, Naomi Campbell and Christy Turlington to stage a wide range of protests against fur and anti-vivisection and to make the ethics of animal rights appealing to young people. For example, in 1995 every private and public elementary school in the USA received a free PETA teacher pack, reaching what it hoped would be an estimated 9 million young Americans. Schools, colleges and universities are very willing to have PETA staff members to visit and give talks. However, their strategies are very mixed and apart from public education they fund cruelty investigations, rescues, legislation work, special events, celebrity involvement and direct action. While PETA is outspoken, radical and trendy, the Humane Society of the US (HSUS) and its international body (HSI) presents a more respectable establishment face to animal rights and has more appeal among older and corporate Americans (Simonds 1995: 24–5).

Although the *Daily Telegraph* underlined the diversity of people engaged in the live animal export affair in Britain, all anecdotal evidence suggests that those involved in animal rights organizations tend to be young rather than middle aged or old, and middle class or at least college educated. It is also likely that universities and colleges are significant sites of animal rights 'enlightenment' and recruitment. *Animal Liberation* and associated literatures are not difficult texts, but then again they are not easy either. They originate from ethical philosophy and are not written in a popular style. Consider Singer's opening page:

> 'Animal Liberation' may sound more like a parody of other liberation movements than a serious objective. The idea of 'The Rights of Animals' actually was once used to parody the case for women's rights. When Mary Wollstonecraft, a forerunner of today's feminists published her *Vindication of the Rights of Women*, her views were widely considered absurd, and before long an anonymous publication appeared entitled *A Vindication of the Rights of Brutes*. The author of this satirical work (now known to have been Thomas Taylor, a distinguished Cambridge philosopher) tried to refute Mary Wollstonecraft's argument by showing that they could be carried one stage further.

> (Singer 1980: 1)

This is scarcely the sort of material to hook a middle-aged, working-class reader who picks it up. Rather, it is precisely the heroic language of the undergraduate bestseller and presupposes the reader to be widely read in liberational history and interested in the irrelevant gossip of the academy. These were the people whom Singer, an experienced academic, knew only too well and he understood what fired their imagination. By comparison, PETA starts work with the younger children of a more diverse social background and reaches them via their teachers, who also know how to arouse their curiosities and passions. Singer's book was a rally cry to an intellectual vanguard while PETA's information packs are building electoral support. Although Singer himself was appalled that some activists chose the path of violence in their pursuit of animal rights, it is not surprising that so many turned out to be arts graduates. On the 5 March 1995 David Callender, a 38-year-old history graduate from Liverpool University, UK, was found guilty of conspiring to damage property and of plotting a firebombing campaign across Britain. It was reckoned that Callender had been at the forefront of ALF campaigns for more than ten years. He was found to be organizing a bomb factory with sufficient detonators and timers to make more than 100 petrol bombs and he had a list of targets ranging from the Milk Marketing Board and British Association of Shooting to the Cambridge Hunt (*Electronic Telegraph*, 6 March 1996). It is not likely that the ALF will give up its struggle but it may find that organizations such as PETA will eclipse it in time. In Britain the Blair government has made it clear that it wishes to see an end to fox hunting and other hunting with hounds, but here at the cutting edge of contemporary politics they are still talking animal welfare rather than rights. According to Tony Banks, Labour MP for West Ham:

> Animal welfare is not some nerdy preserve, nor is it a conflict between town and country. The Labour Party is simply accurately reflecting public concern. It is true that the greatest concentration of that concern is among white, middle-class females with conservative leanings. But perhaps this is hardly surprising, since those struggling to survive from day to day can be excused for worrying more about what animal they can eat rather than save. But even then, when asked, the overwhelming majority of people in this country express compassion for animals . . . I am totally confident that early in the new Parliament a vote will be taken on the principle of hunting with hounds. When that is won, banning legislation will closely follow. The days of fox-hunting, deer-hunting, hare-coursing and mink-hunting are numbered. When gone, we will look back on them with the same distaste and disbelief with which we now regard badger-baiting, cock-fighting, dog-fighting and bear-baiting – all seen in their days as traditional British sports.

> (*Electronic Telegraph*, Saturday 19 April 1997)

Survey evidence for Germany and the USA shows that it is far from being a 'nerdy preserve' elsewhere. The two most highly ranked 'basic attitudes' to animals in Germany and the USA were described as 'moralistic' ('primary concern for the right and wrong treatment of animals, with strong opposition to the perceived overexploitation of and/or cruelty to animals') and 'humanistic' ('primary interest and strong affection for individual animals such as pets or large mammals with strong anthropomorphic associations'), while the utilitarian ('primary interest in the practical value of animals, or in the subordination of animals for the practical benefit of people') and dominionistic ('primary interest in the mastery and control of animals') attitudes were ranked very low. However, there is significant variation in the rankings and in the standardized mean scores in Germany and the USA. Moralistic attitudes were ranked first in Germany (0.63) and humanistic attitudes second (0.31), while these were the reverse in the USA: humanistic first (0.38), moralistic second (0.275) (Serpell 1994: 167–73). Equally, Americans demonstrated significantly higher utilitarian and dominionistic scores than Germans, reflecting perhaps the more secular and urban nature of modern Germany. Although the humanistic attitude is also ranked first in Japan,

It is distinctive from Western societies in its ranking 'negativistic' ('primary orientation an active avoidance of animals due to dislike or fear') second and 'dominionistic' third.

Here is the crux of the matter. The popular base of such animal welfare support in the West are the pet keepers, birdwatchers and other animal lovers of the twentieth century. Their bottom line is not that we should live apart but that we should work out a moral and ethical way of living together. The point is not that people want less contact with animals but, if anything, more. To acknowledge that we need to do more than understand the origin of animal rights. To PETA perhaps, their growing support and 'hip' status may be seen as a victory in ethical education and extension of the rights principal, that people have begun to support the notion of rights for animals. But support for these organizations does not necessarily demonstrate this. It may simply display that people care for animals a great deal and like them so well that they will gladly go out of their way to assist those who appear to be fighting on their behalf. Moreover, their involvement may be interpreted as gratifying personal desires to maintain links with animals rather than terminate them. Although PETA's web page clearly indicates that it is an animal rights organization and promotes vegetarianism, it steers clear of any hard-line messages about meat, the need to avoid pet keeping and their aim to separate humans from animals. On the other hand, it does emphasize its activity on an impressive range of fronts and its successes. Paradoxically, support for such an organization gives the animal lover the feeling of a closer, more meaningful and political relationship with animals rather than a righteous, respectful backing off. Supporters of these organizations are motivated less by ethical argumentation and idealism than by sentiments and emotions. The story cannot end with the claim of ethical victory; rather it has to begin with an account of the emergence of such transformed sentiments and emotions. This book has tried to make such a beginning: let us now rehearse the main findings and arguments.

FINDINGS

This book has sampled key sites of human–animal relations in the twentieth century, from pet keeping to hunting. More work needs to be done to establish the key routines and variations at these sites, but from the work presented here a clear pattern has emerged.

First, in the twentieth century there have been significant qualitative and quantitative changes in human–animal relations: people now seek more time with animals and do more things involving animals, and the nature of these relationships has changed fundamentally.

Second, we can identify two paradigm states of human–animal relations in the twentieth century, which correspond, approximately, to the social conditions of modernity and late or postmodernity. Relations in modernity were characterized by a relatively fixed and restricted series of interactions, with a relatively narrow range of species. Relations were dominated by the anthropocentric priorities of human progress and animals were largely the subject of human consumption and human entertainment. Sentiments were restricted to a narrow range of highly anthropomorphized and neotenized animals while most others were of interest as objects of use or scientific knowledge (the value of which was also tied to human progress). Neo-Romantic and neo-Darwinian doctrines originating in the nineteenth century continued to define a range of possible popular relations with animals in the twentieth century. While the former placed animals at the pinnacle of a human aesthetic of nature, the latter placed humans alongside animals as creatures of instinct, natural hunters and killers. Both doctrines, however, preached the conservation of animals and their habitats, which resulted in an uneasy alliance with respect to the preservation and use of 'wild' areas. They were essentially urban ideas and practised by urbanites with new powers to visit natural areas and to commune with or consume animals – or both.

Postmodern relations with animals are the reverse, more or less. Postmodernity can be described as the fragmentation of the idea of progress and of the priority of humanity. The decentred sensibilities of postmodernity were caught up in acts of reflexive remodelling in relation to a range of 'Others' (including people of different race, gender, age and sexual orientation) and, in turn, this reflexivity dissolved the former certainty of anthropocentricism in relation to animals. We found relations with animals to be expressive of new values: empathy, understanding, support, closeness. Sentiments expanded to include all or most forms of animals (how can we chose between them?); understanding and empathy extended to animals other than those with superficially human-like characteristics; our relations were dominated by a wish to know more about them but not merely for our advantage, and by our uncertainty as to the lines which separate humans and other animals. New explorations into the possibilities and potencies of human–animal relationships were made: play with killer whales and Siberian tigers; the discovery that pet relationships melt away human stress; learning about the cultures of birds; creating suburban environments for humans and animals. The Western desire for contact with and information about animals increased enormously and encounters with animals were preceded by 'a circulation of [their] possible meanings in the mass media' (Clarke 1997: 84). In this way, views that were changing rapidly among intellectual and educated circles were quickly reflected in books, film, documentary and other media, in addition to those institutions which framed the institutionalized zoological gaze. Pets became companions rather than entertaining playthings or fashion accessories and the seriousness of that companionship was reflected in growing demands for better (i.e. human) quality services for companion animals (e.g. dental care, clothing, gourmet foods, etc.) and concerns with relationship dynamics (e.g. pet selection agencies, psychological counselling, bereavement counselling) and the introduction of rites of passage (e.g. funeral rituals and animal burial). New social movements based on the extension of animal rights came into being and forced debate and legislation beyond the confines of anti-cruelty.

However, we have also seen how these changing attitudes and practices are unevenly distributed – as were their impacts – and particular attention has been paid in the previous chapters to their content and pattern. One can detect, for example, class variations along a variety of dimensions: in the social organization of hunting, in the pattern of pet keeping, in the consumption of meat, and so on However, new patterns of consumption are organized culturally and simple taxonomic variables such as class are less useful than the social composites specified by Bourdieu (1984) or Savage et al. (1992) who adapted lifestyle group categories from market research classifications. Savage et al.'s study of UK middle-class consumption found interesting correlations between lifestyle groups and the consumption of nature. Their groups were defined through a combination of sectoral and occupational locations in conjunction with income and cultural capital. Hence the trend-setting ascetic aesthetes were relatively low-paid, well-educated, public-sector workers (in government, health and education, in particular) whose consumption in recent years has been very sensitive to changing issues relating to justice, environment, nature, health and risk. Indeed, one of their common experiences is an involvement in the development of institutional and organizational social change. As consumers they pioneered the consumption of health foods, whole foods, organic foods, alternative medicine and eco-tourism, for example (Savage et al. 1992: 106–12). Further research may find that this group has had the most profound impact on human–animal relations in the West. According to Savage et al., the ascetic aesthetes directly influence a second lifestyle group which they call 'postmoderns'. These are characterized as more affluent professionals working particularly in media, design and creative areas who are also well educated. While they follow new patterns and modes of consumption pioneered by the former group, they do so with more luxury, in more exclusive settings and with less puritanical zeal. Thus, we might find that the ascetics dominate the ranks of birdwatchers, wildlife photography, vegetarian organizations and hunt sabotage, while the postmoderns dominate the more exclusive domains of whale watching, Antarctic wildlife tours and venues such as SeaWorld in Florida or San Diego, and swell the ranks of mainstream voluntary-charitable conservation organizations. Together these two groups inherited, maintained and elaborated Western traditions of romanticism with respect to animals. They differ from the Romantics of the nineteenth century, however, because of their central and influential positions in mainstream social and cultural life and their numerical strength.

Nineteenth-century Romantics, by contrast, occupied largely eccentric and marginal positions in society and although their writers were enormously influential, their influence was largely confined to a small educated elite. Byron and his followers were unremitting in their condemnation of fox hunting in the 1820s but even their most eloquent objections failed to achieve change. Since the 1960s, by contrast, the ascetic and postmodern middle-class lifestyle groups have been far more effective in shifting opinion in the West. Utilizing their organizational and lobbying skills they have produced a popular will to ban hunting with hounds in the UK and have seen it securely placed on the parliamentary business of Blair's first year of office.

In the USA an equally significant bundle of similar hunting law reforms are under way in Michigan, Washington, Idaho, Alaska, Massachusetts, Oregon and Colorado (Washington State 1996: 6). In Australia duck and quail shooting were recently banned in the state of New South Wales on the basis of cruelty. Shooters are banned from hunting on public lands in Queensland and Western Australia and a similar change is proposed for Victoria (Jackson 1996: 4; McDougall 1997: 14–15). In all three nations the debate has been framed as an urban–rural polarization, with middle-class lifestyle groups making their presence felt in the country. While the protagonists for change tend to be middle-class urbanites, it is not at all clear, as we have seen in Chapter 6, that the hunters are exclusively rural.

From recent surveys of hunting in the USA and Australia it is clear that a substantial section of hunters are affluent urbanites, particularly from among business and private sector management backgrounds. It is perhaps significant that Savage et al. (1992) found that traditional field sports, including hunting, were strongly associated with a middle-class lifestyle group dominated by private sector managers. These were not the most affluent group among the British middle class, nor the most highly educated, but they had achieved a degree of social mobility within mainstream private sector organizations such as banking, trading and finance and they clearly aspired to the culture and lifestyle of their bosses. Their consumption pattern shows a keenness to consume those goods, services and leisure associated with the traditional upper classes: thus they are distinguishable by their consumption of malt whiskies and red meat, and by their interest in golf, fly fishing and shooting. The marketing of safari-style hunting tourism to such groups is very evident in the hunting trade, as is the associated demand for ostentatious displays of trophy 'heads' and other taxidermy (Hummel 1994). An interest in pitting themselves against wild animals, particularly the potentially dangerous such as bears in the USA, rhinos, hippos and elephants in Africa and wild boar and water buffalo in outback Australia, together with an interest in associated hunting skills such as survival techniques and food gathering from wild sources, corresponds closely to what Cartmill (1993) calls neo-Darwinism. This was tied closely to a critique of modernity and its unhealthy demand for restraint and self-regulation of the body, and the sedentary, desk-bound lifestyles of the city business class. It advocates a need to express our animality, our ties with nature and above all our desire and instinct to hunt and kill.

Working-class lifestyle groups tend towards two types of relation with regard to animals. The first might be called instrumental, an essentially premodern view that animals are a food resource. Much marine recreational fishing in the West is expressed in these terms, as is bass fishing in the USA and barramundi fishing in Australia, and rural working-class people everywhere shoot or trap small game locally, predominantly for the pot. Working dogs are highly valued among such groups. This is clearly different from neo-Darwinism: it is more routinized in traditional utilitarian cultures, less tied to status and health and contiguous with other self-provisioning interests such as gardening, pigeon keeping, beer making and so on. A second working-class group can perhaps be identified by their more moral stance with regard to animals, through their association with animal protection societies or pet fancies, their consumption of the literatures and ideas of the ascetic middle class and their long-standing involvement in conservation. Although British coarse fishers appear to be more aligned with the first group, in fact their records show a long association with conservation, a growing reluctance to eat or harm their quarry and a keen interest in the natural history of their waterways.

Human–animal relations in the modern West are marked by significant gender differences. In a simple gender comparison, historically women are less enthusiastic consumers of meat and are more likely to be vegetarian or cutting down meat consumption. Hunting and fishing are literally fraternities among whom women barely register a presence. Further, several surveys have shown distinct gender differences with respect to attitudes to animal rights. Hills (1993) found that women held less instrumental and more empathetic attitudes towards animals than men and that this difference occurred within subgroups of farmers, the general public and animal rights supporters. Similarly, Pifer et al. (1994) found that women were considerably less supportive of animal experimentation for medical purposes than men in every one of the fifteen countries surveyed. In the USA, for example, 65 per cent of men thought that scientists should be allowed to do medical research which causes pain or injury to animals such as dogs and chimpanzees compared with only 43 per cent of women. In a recent Australian study, McFarling found that 52 per cent of women tend towards a neo-Romantic orientation as compared with only 15 per cent of men; and that 26 per cent of men held neo-Darwinian views as compared with only 9 per cent of women. 'Significantly more women (57 per cent) disagreed with any hunting compared with men (17 per cent)' (McFarling 1995: 34).

We have also seen how attitudes to animals vary by race, ethnicity and nationality. Afro-Americans appear considerably less interested in animal-related leisures than American whites; over 50 per cent of Japanese people are supportive of painful and injurious animal experimentation for human medical knowledge as compared with only 27 per cent of the French, 29 per cent of West Germans and 32 per cent of Italians. Within Europe, however, there are some nations such as Portugal and Spain where instrumental attitudes are more evident (Kellert 1994).

Although hunting and fishing have a very significant urban following, it is nonetheless true that attitudes to animals also vary along an urban–rural dimension. Hence, Hills (1993) found farmers to be less empathetic and more instrumental than her urban sample. McFarling (1995) found that 35 per cent of her urban sample expressed neo-Romantic views as compared with only 19 per cent of her rural sample.

ARGUMENTS

Keith Tester's *Animals and Society* (1992) is arguably the most fully developed sociological thesis on human–animal relations, providing a useful point of departure for our concluding discussion, not least because of its focus on animal rights. According to Tester, the expansion of animal rights emerged because 'rights' discourses were as dominant an expression of humanity in the 1970s as anti-cruelty had been in the early nineteenth century. The objection to this argument is not that it is wrong, but that it is incomplete. It does not explain why in the 1970s animals were considered fitting objects for the extension of human rights. In other words, although Tester is surely correct in seeing the extension of rights to animals as part of a wider pattern in which most categories of 'others' made demands for and received rights, he does not explain how animals had become sufficiently close to humans for that to be conceivable or thinkable. Tester's analysis of human–animal relations, which encompasses the approaches of a full range of opinion and theory, from Thomas, through structural anthropology to Elias and Foucault, has to be understood as a specially created prehistory for animal rights. There are relationships and theorizations of those relationships that are not simply not there (hunting and other leisure relations and leisure theory; the consumption of animals in the twentieth century and consumption theory; animals and gender, and so forth). Tester is, of course, explicitly constructing the narrative development of animal rights, but one perhaps unintended consequence is that animal rights appears to have become elevated as an endpoint in human–animal relations in the twentieth century, or at least such a significant endpoint that other relations need not be referred to.

Consider, for example, the huge hole in Tester's narrative, between the publication and subsequent obscurity of Salt's *Animal Rights* in 1892 and the publication of Singer's *Animal Liberation* in 1975 (Singer 1990) and the efflorescence of an animal rights movement from there on. One of the principal aims of this book has been to fill this gap and to argue that an equally significant series of changes in the twentieth century has led to a relatively stable and broad consensus of human–animal relations quite opposed to animal rights. This finding of course is the result of a different methodology and theory of change. Tester attempts to show the somewhat extreme nature of some animal rights activism, but the reader is left in no doubt that this is merely an extreme form of what has become widely accepted. The lack of empirical depth, however, leaves the reader with no hard evidence for this. Tester's approach is highly ideational: the words and writings of a select band of major and minor intellectuals, reformers, visionaries and artists are used to construct a putative causal backcloth to social change. Change is indicated by new arguments and debates at this level which, of course, is confined mainly to the educated middle classes. There is a disturbing lack of political economy and social history in Tester. We have little sense of the ways in which alterations in production and consumption and the modernization of popular culture might have influenced change. Tester admits to this at the end of the book (pp. 195–6). Only urbanization is singled out for special consideration (p. 197 especially) as a change which changed everything. That is, urbanization dissolved the compulsive, necessary relations with animals such as the need to kill to eat, the need to protect crops and defend against predators. For urbanites there is complete freedom and, as he argues, 'perhaps all moral codes can be usefully understood as attempts to make the relationships between animals and society more aesthetic . . . Animals are turned into poor, suffering cuddly creatures precisely because they present no threat at all, precisely to the extent that we are free from any compulsion in the treatment of them' (1992: 197). The trouble with this view is that while urbanization might be necessary for the development of animal rights and other discourses of the late twentieth century, it is not a sufficient explanation in itself. It cannot explain why changes occurred when they did – quite the opposite in fact. Since the West become a largely urban culture much earlier it begs the question as to what, in addition to urbanization, could be associated with such dramatic change.

The central argument we are making here is that something in the twentieth century did change the sentiments expressed towards animals, namely that a number of social processes associated with postmodernity further eroded the social distance between humans and an increasing number of animal categories. There are three processes particularly associated with this outcome: the decline of ontological security, misanthropy and the rise of ecologism, and the development of risk-reflexivity.

ANIMALS AND ONTOLOGICAL INSECURITY

The decline in ontological security is an endemic and chronic tendency in postmodern societies, the result of a breakdown or fragmentation of key sources of social and cultural order, regulation and identity. We have identified changes in domestic and familial relations, local community, regional and national identity as particularly relevant to changing human–animal relations. The nature and role of pets as replacement siblings, partners, parents, children, friends, companions and protectors is particularly clear, but it has also been suggested that widespread attachments to local and national wildlife, protection and feeding activities and postmodern totemic attachments to particular animal species (e.g. the love of particular dog breeds, the attachment of anglers to particular fish species, social identities built around birdwatching or animal photography) can all be understood in this way. As regional and national identity are dissolved by globalization, the specific and concrete relation of local culture to local nature is frequently underlined and heightened as one of several means to prevent its loss. Such a process is particularly poignant where local wildlife is also under threat of some sort. Hence the English have always rallied to the cause of the native red squirrel threatened by the invasive American grey squirrel.

Australians have become increasingly identified with their wildlife in recent years, a development with clear connections to rapidly changing ethnic compositions and political and trading futures. But the idea that Australian wildlife is under serious threat from a set of acclimatized European animals such as the cat and fox makes for a powerful metaphoric narrative of social identity. Although anthropologists and sociologists have pointed to the paradoxical nature of the human understanding of animals, that they are both like us but not us, it is also true that different sides of the paradox can and have been emphasized, depending upon the precise historical and cultural circumstances. What makes animals special, socially unique in late modernity is their potential to be like us and for the categorical boundary between humans and animals to be blurred. Of particular importance is their potential to be available, reliable, stable and predictable in their relations with humans at a time when human social relations are the opposite. In addition, animals are embodied, like us. The physicality and embodiment of important human social relationships is often what is missing, even where a relation is intact – the absentee parent, the grown child moved far away, relationships which are frequently maintained by telephone. Friendship and family networks are more spatially scattered and we belong to abstract and increasingly virtual communities of interest. There appears to be something deeply distressing about the disembodied nature of contemporary social life and pet animals provide a range of ordinary but significant embodied benefits – touch, someone to come home to, someone to doze with, cuddle, groom, feed, even clothe.

As we have seen, some of the more recent developments in relations with companion animals are simply extensions of domestic human activities. In the 1960s such substitutions were seen as social pathologies because social progress was linked to shoring up the family and re-establishing community. At the turn of the twenty-first century, however, we are resigned to inescapable social fragmentations and quite open about the social significance of companion animals. Following Baudrillard, we can say that the extensive range of social displacements in human–animal relations in late modernity are simulations of 'real' social relations – or hyperrealities. So-called real human relations such as husband–wife, father–son, brother–sister, 'best friends' and neighbours became increasingly problematic in late modernity, not simply because they proved more difficult to maintain under tighter labour market conditions, greater mobility, stressed home life and social and sexual freedoms, but also because they became increasingly questioned as ideals and began to lose their grip on patterns of social practice and reproduction. As the need to conform to a clear sense of normal social reality and relationships dissolved, people became free to play around with more individualized representations. 'The historical condition of the present is one of hyperreality, in which identity, practice and association are organised around the process of simulation' (Rojek 1993: 133).

Moreover, human–animal relations often take on a spectacular form, as with leisure and tourism activities in postmodernity:

> Since authenticity is no longer an issue under postmodernism, it is reasonable to expect that these forms would be preoccupied with spectacle and sensation. The consumption experience is accompanied with a sense of irony. One realises that what one is consuming is not real, but nonetheless the experience can be pleasurable and exciting, even if one recognises that it is also 'useless'.
>
> (Rojek 1993: 134)

The fervour and energy which characterize many human–animal relations in late modernity – the zeal and eccentricity of pet keeping cultures, toad watching, twitching, the homemaking simulations of the Penguin Experience or Jungle World – can be understood as simulated enactments of displaced human needs to care, love, receive and give affection, to have friendship. Of course relations with animals were only one form of simulation of these human relationships, but animals are particularly good signifiers and receptacles of human emotions. One knows with sufficient irony that one's cat or dog is not a human loved one; one knows that wrapping a small dog in a warm, fashionable coat or helping toads to cross roads is a touch eccentric or sensational, but the fact is it that it does not matter. Dog owners experience delight when their dogs are pleased to see them; it is pleasurable to return that love (e.g. through the gift of a coat); and one feels responsible and neighbourly in assisting a fellow victim of increased traffic. There is a confident razzamatazz about the ironic eccentricities of the animal lover that is now so widespread as to be commonplace and endearing. Pet keeping and other caring human relationships with animals no longer attract the deep scepticism and bursts of social outrage of the 1960s, when human progress and humanitarian realism dominated social and political agendas; when a rationally planned and organized system could deliver social order; and when a close relationship with a pet animal was regarded as an unhealthy deviation from the path of progress. In the late twentieth century we do not believe in those old certainties or the attainability of those aspirations for secure social relations. Instead we create versions of them in colourful and spectacular displays of individualism and episodes of neo-tribalism using, among other things, animals as identity props and emotional mirrors. That bit of animals that is 'like us' is sufficiently flexible in postmodernity to replace that bit of ourselves we have lost.

Human–animal intimacies are overlaid by relations of dependency similar to those characterizing traditional familial and community relations. The dependencies are interlaced; we depend on our dog for companionship but we are also aware of how dependent wild animals have become on our care and protection. The essentially moral nature of this relationship with animals has both a local and a global presence in our lives, making it difficult if not impossible to see ourselves as a different sort of community. In a recent article the geographer Philo (1995) proposes that animals constitute a 'social' group in the modern city:

> An alternative perspective is proposed in which animals are regarded as a marginal 'social' group discursively constituted and practically affected by human communities, and a group which is thereby subjected to all manner of sociospatial inclusions and exclusions.

> (Philo 1995: 655)

Moreover the extent and significance of the moral claims made upon us by animals cannot be overemphasized. This view has been distilled and championed by animal rights but it is much more widely distributed elsewhere, albeit in a more dilute form. The moral claim made by animals is not simply for the irreducible ethical reason that they can feel pain (like us), as the animal rights argument would have it, but that in their vulnerability and undeserved oppression in the face of so-called human progress, they remind us of our own moral standing. In our reflections about animals in late modernity we reflect on ourselves; the issue is not the ethical consideration of the 'other' but the moral consideration of 'ourselves'. That reflection is increasingly couched in misanthropic terms: humans have become a sick and deranged species, destructive, out of control and a danger to themselves and others.

ANIMALS, MORALITY AND MISANTHROPY

We have seen how misanthropy has emerged in recent years alongside ecologistic concerns and a range of animal-focused anxieties. Misanthropy is explicitly tied to a perceived crisis of morality and disorder in late modernity. While modernism was predicated on human progress, postmodern economy and society put such a project into reverse: individualism was privileged over collectivism; consumerism was privileged over welfarism; decentralization was privileged over centralized bureaucracy; privatization was privileged over national ownerships; deregulation over systems of standards, inspection, regulation and management. 'Society' can no longer be identified as a focus and organizer of moral certainty or, as Bauman puts it, a 'National Ethics Service' (1995: 5). Indeed, Western society is increasingly seen as morally bankrupt and moribund, even if paradoxically, in postmodern times individuals are forced (after a very long period of not having to do so) to make moral decisions for themselves (Bauman 1995: 6–9). Of significance here is the extent to which the former compromise between development and modern human progress broke down and exposed humanity as an evil destructive force. Destruction of the environment and the endangerment of animals was always acceptable, though regrettable, if a human imperative such as the avoidance of starvation, the need for housing or livelihood could be identified. When that greater good was no longer in evidence or the prime mover of development, and serial rounds of development and environmental destruction could be linked to the free and unbounded operation of an indifferent market, the conditions for a misanthropic discourse were created.

The misanthropic discourse was a popular polemic championed often by those admired for their commitment to the care of animals – John Aspinall is a good example. The more humanity became the evil destroyer of animals, the more simple demonstrations of care and protection of animals attained a clear moral certainty. For the activist, expressive political and practical acts on the behalf of animals became, in a sense, a means of restoring a feeling of moral worth. As Bauman argued in *Postmodern Ethics* (1993), postmodernity is 'the moral person's bane and chance at the same time'. In late modernity we are forced to make moral choices in conditions of great social complexity and uncertainty. If postmodernity precludes the possibility of a clear moral order in the human world, it creates at the same time a nostalgic longing for its return. The new pattern of animal sentiments may therefore be related to misanthropy and moral disorder. First, animals provide an outlet for 'good works' and morally unambiguous projects, where humans form a cast of saviours, champions and heroes. This provides welcome relief from the misanthropic gloom of contemporary society. Heightened sentiments towards animals may be the result of displaced moral anxiety and a means of challenging the ascendancy and hegemony of 'new right' sensibilities in the wake of the fragmented project of modernity. Heightened animal sentiments may offer the nostalgic, softer face of social paternalism that sections of the educated middle class and organized working class are loath to let go. Once again, we show what it is to be properly human through our dealings with animals.

Following Giddens, however, we can say that the form which human–animal relations takes recognizes the impossibility of modernist reorderings. Such displacements are like therapy; they are attempts to fix up the symptoms, to attack the problematic manifestations of disorder rather than tackle the lack of order itself. Animals are visible victims of development but, rather than tackle the impossibility of stopping development, producing a rational and planned ordering of the natural world, it is easier to pick off and deal with (in a morally and ethically correct manner) such issues as endangered species as they arise. Similarly, relations with pet animals can be very easily tailored to individual circumstances of need; they are practical and efficient, flexible and convenient and, unlike the human relations they replace, they are mostly ideal and enduring.

The future of Western relations with animals seems almost certainly to be one of great diversity. The animal rights lobby is very likely to be able to win legislations to ban the more extreme forms of activity in which animals are made to suffer for no apparent (human) good, but quite what counts as 'animal' and 'suffering' will be the subject of hot debates. Singer thinks it is permissible to eat oysters but not prawns, fish or higher animals. This is based on putative similarities to the human nervous system which make pain possible. However, the outcome of public debates is likely to hinge on a more complex set of considerations than how creatures are wired for the experience of pain. Most evidence would support the idea that the cut-off for significant animal sentiments is somewhere above fish. Although sentiments can be extended to fish and all manner of lower animals, it is nonetheless true that the popular cultures of the West privileged and continue to privilege the warmer blooded animals over the cold blooded. Fish are also prized foods all over the world and deemed especially healthy in modern diets. They are the object of a popular form of self-provisioning that is robustly attractive in the modern world and they have proved to be capable of a secure and guaranteed future under conditions of managed exploitation. For these reasons, it is most unlikely that the animal rights lobby will secure anything other than a sprinkling of cosmetic prohibitions on fishing.

Hunting, however, is likely to be less secure in the future, although again it is not entirely clear that the animal rights organizations will secure a complete ban. It is hard to imagine the Australians banning the hunting of the rabbit for instance; and the European deer hunter is likely to be allowed controlled access to deer culls on environmental and herd management grounds. There are many more mitigating circumstances and contingencies.

It is also likely that the West will continue to eat meat, particularly if it can be persuaded that the animals are kept in acceptable conditions, that they do not suffer unduly in being killed for the table and that the meat is safe to eat. In Chapter 8 all these considerations were identified as the cause of considerable anxiety and changed consumption, but the point is that, once addressed, there seems every reason to suppose that people will return to a confident if not more diverse diet of meats. This is not to say that vegetarianism will dwindle, quite the opposite. It must be imagined that an increasing number of people will find the lack of necessity to eat meat grounds enough for some variant of a vegetarian diet.

The animal rights position will be most opposed in the demand for animal company and contact. This has emerged as a major trend in Western cultures in late modernity and is likely to continue, particularly because it chimes well with a wider optimism that the categorical and interactional distinctions and differences between animals and humans can be challenged or broken down. The de-differentiations of postmodern human–animal relations seem, at the turn of the twenty-first century, more attractive than the apartheid advocated by animals rights. Whereas the 1970s were about the extension of rights and the autonomous space in which to build strength, the mood at the turn of the century is one of reconciliation, community building and empathy.

REFERENCES

Adams, C.J. (1990) *The Sexual Politics of Meat*, Cambridge: Polity.

Akiyama, H., Holtzman, J. M. and Britz, W.E. (1986–7) 'Pet ownership and health status during bereavement', *Omega*, 17: 187–93.

Albert, A. and Bulcroft, K. (1988) 'Pets and urban life', *Anthrozoos*, 1 (1): 9–23.

American Animal Hospital Association (1996) 'Top dog and cat names are human', *AAHA Pets News Release*, 8 November.

Anderson, K. (1995) 'Culture and nature at the Adelaide zoo: at the frontiers of "human" geography', *Transactions of the Institute of British Geographers*, 20: 275–94.

Anderson, W.P., Reid, C.M. and Jennings, G.L. (1992) 'Pet ownership and risk factors for cardiovascular disease', *The Medical Journal of Australia*, 157: 298–301.

Ash, R. (1996) *The Top Ten of Everything 1996*, London: Dorling Kindersley.

Aspinall, J. (1976) *The Best of Friends*, London: Macmillan.

Australian Bureau of Statistics (1992) *Apparent Consumption of Foodstuffs and Nutrients, Australia 1988–89*, Canberra: AGPS.

Australian Bureau of Statistics (1995) *Social Trends*, Canberra: AGPS.

Australian Meat and Livestock Corporation (1995) *The AMLC Iron Campaign*, Sydney: Australian Meat and Livestock Corporation.

Australian Meat and Livestock Corporation (1996) *Statistical Review – July 94–June 95*, Sydney: Australian Meat and Livestock Corporation.

Bartrip, P. (1988) 'Food for the body and food for the mind: the regulation of freshwater fisheries in the 1870s', *Victorian Studies*, 28 (2): 285–304.

Bauman, Z. (1993) *Postmodern Ethics*, Oxford: Blackwell.

Bauman, Z. (1995) *Life in Fragments*, Oxford: Blackwell.

Beardsworth, A. and Keil, T. (1992) 'The vegetarian option: varieties, conversions, motives and careers', *Sociological Review*, 40(2): 252–93.

Beck, U. (1992) *Risk Society*, London: Sage.

Benton, T. (1993) *Natural Relations: Ecology, Animal Rights and Social Justice*, London: Verso.

Berger, J. (1971) 'Animal world', *New Society*, 25 November: 1043–5.

Berger, J. (1980) *About Looking*, London: Writers and Readers.

Berman, M. (1985) *All that is Solid Melts into Air: The Experience of Modernity*, London: Verso.

Bostock, Stephen St C. (1993) *Zoos and Animal Rights*, London: Routledge.

Bourdieu, P. (1984) *Distinction*, London: Routledge and Kegan Paul.

Bradbury, J. (1996) 'Molecular marker for CJD may facilitate diagnosis', *Lancet*, 348 (9036): 1230.

British Medical Journal (1997) 'The prion hypothesis is finally accepted by the establishment', 315 (7114): 2.

Burnett, J. (1966) *Plenty and Want*, London: Nelson.

Cain, A. O. (1983) 'A study of pets in the family system', in A. H. Katcher and A.M. Beck (eds) *New Perspectives in Our Lives with Companion Animals*, Philadelphia: University of Pennsylvania Press.

Canadian High Commission (1996) 'Trends in petfood consumption in Britain', London: Canadian High Commission.

Cartmill, M. (1993) *View To A Death in the Morning*, Cambridge, MA: Harvard University Press.

Cashel, K. and English, R. (1987) 'Meat and poultry consumption and composition', *Food Technology in Australia*, 39 (5):185–6.

Charles, N. and Kerr, M. (1988) *Women, Food and Families*, Manchester: Manchester University Press.

Cherfas, J. (1984) *Zoo 2000*, London: BBC Publications.

Clark, S. (1977) *The Moral Status of Animals*, New York: Scribner.

Clarke, N. (1997) 'Panic ecology – nature in the age of superconductivity', *Theory, Culture and Society*, 14 (1): 77–96.

Clutton-Brock, J. (1995) 'Aristotle, the scale of nature, and modern attitudes to animals', *Social Research*, 62 (3): 421–39.

Cockburn, A. (1996) 'A short meat-orientated history of the world: from Eden to Mattole', *New Left Review*, 215: 21–5.

Collinge, J. (1996a) 'Creutzfeldt-Jakob disease in a young woman: report of a meeting of physicians and scientists, St Thomas' Hospital, London', *The Lancet*, 347: 945–8.

Collinge, J. (1996b) 'Prion protein gene analysis in new variant cases of Creutzfeldt-Jakob disease', *The Lancet*, 348: 56.

Collinge, J. (1996c) 'New diagnostic tests for prion diseases', *New England Journal of Medicine*, 335 (13): Editorial.

Collinge J., Sidle, K.C.L., Meads, J., Ironside, J. and Hill, A. E. (1995) 'Unaltered susceptibility to BSE in transgenic mice expressing human prion protein', *Nature*, 378: 21–8.

Collinge J., Sidle, K. C. L., Meads, J., Ironside, J. and Hill, A. F. (1996) 'Molecular analysis of prion strain variation and the aetiology of "new variant" CJD', *Nature*, 383: 685–90.

Conway, W. (1985) 'Report of the General Director', *New York Zoological Society Annual Report 1984–85*: 4–15.

Corson, S. A. and O'Leary Corson, E. (1980) 'Pet animals as nonverbal communication mediators in psychotherapy in institutional setings', in S.A. Corson and E. O'Leary Corson (eds) *Ethology and Nonverbal Communication in Mental Health*, Oxford: Pergamon Press.

Council for Science and Society (1988) *Companion Animals in Society*, Oxford: Oxford University Press.

Crook, S. (1997) 'Ordering risks', paper presented to 'Risk and Socio-Cultural Theory Conference', Centre for Cultural Risk Research, State Library of New South Wales, 4 April.

Crook, S., Pakulski, J. and Waters, M. (1992) *Postmodernization*, London: Sage.

Curruthers, P. (1992) *The Animal Issue*, Cambridge: Cambridge University Press.

Dahles, H. (1993) 'Game killing and killing games: an anthropologist looking at hunting in a modern society', *Society and Animals*, 1 (2): 2–8.

Darnton, R. (1985) *The Great Cat Massacre and Other Episodes in French Cultural History*, Harmondsworth: Penguin.

Darvill, T. (1987) *Prehistoric Britain*, London: Batsford.

Daunton, M.J. (1983) *House and Home in the Victorian City*, London: Edward Arnold.

Dempsey, K. (1990) *Smalltown*, Melbourne: Oxford University Press.

Descola, P. and Palsson, G. (eds) (1996) *Nature and Society*, London: Routledge.

de Worde, W. (1496) *Boke of St. Albans*, St Albans.

Dickenson, R. (1996) 'Why true love is like puppy chow', *American Demographics*, January.

Douglas, M. (1966) *Purity and Danger*, London: Routledge and Kegan Paul.

Douglas, M. (1975) *Implicit Meanings*, London: Routledge and Kegan Paul.

Douglas, M. (1984) *Food in the Social Order: Studies of Food and Festivities in Three American Communities*, New York: Russell Sage Foundation.

Driver, C. (1983) *The British at Table – 1940–1980*, London: Chatto & Windus.

Durant, H. (1938) *The Problem of Leisure*, London: Routledge.

Dyer, C. (1988) 'Changes in diet in the late middle ages: the case of harvest workers', *Agricultural History Review*, 36 (1): 21–37.

Elias, N. (1986) 'An essay on sport and violence', in N. Elias and E. Dunning (eds) *Quest for Excitement*, Oxford: Blackwell.

Elias, N. (1994) *The Civilising Process*, Oxford: Blackwell.

Elias, N. and Dunning, E. (1986) *Quest for Excitement*, Oxford: Blackwell.

Electronic Telegraph (electronic version of the UK Daily Telegraph) http://www.telegraph.co.uk

Environmental and Planning D: Society and Space (1995) *Bringing the Animals Back in – the World of Animals*, 13 (6).

Fairbrother, J.G. (1988) 'The poultry industry – technology's child two decades on', *Food Australia*, November: 456–62.

Farm Animal Welfare Network (1995) *Today's Poultry Industry*, Huddersfield: FAWN.

Farson, N. (1983) *Going Fishing*, London: Hamlyn.

Fiddes, N. (1991) *Meat: A Natural Symbol*, London: Routledge.

Fiedler, L.A. (1967) *Love and Death in the American Novel*, London: Cape.

Finch, J. (1989) *Family Obligations and Social Change*, Cambridge: Polity.

Fish and Wildlife Service/Bureau of the Census (1991) *1991 National Survey of Fishing, Hunting and Wildlife-associated Recreation*, Washington, DC: US Department of the Interior.

Fletcher, D. (1995) 'Young women are giving up meat to stay healthy', *Electronic Telegraph*, 12 April.

FAO (Food and Agriculture Organisation) (1967) *World Protein Hunger*, Rahway, NJ: FAO.

Food Australia (1991) 'Consumer attitudes towards meat', 43 (1): 479.

Foucault, M. (1970) *The Order of Things: An Archaeology of the Human Sciences*, London: Tavistock.

Fox, M.W. (1974) 'Pet–owner relations', paper given to the British Small Animals Veterinary Association 'Symposium on Pet Animals and Society', London.

Fox, M.W. (1984) *Farm Animals – Husbandry, Behaviour and Veterinary Practice*, Baltimore: University Park Press.

Franklin, A. S. (1996a) 'On fox hunting and angling: Norbert Elias and the sportisation process', *Journal of Historical Sociology*, 9 (4): 432–56.

Franklin, A.S. (1996b) 'Australian hunting and angling sports and the changing nature of human–animal relations in Australia', *Australian and New Zealand Journal of Sociology*, 32 (3): 39–56.

Franklin, A. S. (1997) 'An unpopular food: the decline of fish consumption in Britain', *Food and Foodways*, 7 (3): 55–94.

Friedmann, E., Katcher, A. H., Lynch, J.J. and Thomas, S.A. (1984) 'Animal companions and one-year survival of patients after discharge from a coronary care unit', *Public Health Reports*, 95: 307–12.

Gaard, N.H.H. (ed.) (1993) *Ecofeminism – Women, Animals, Nature*, Philadelphia: Temple University Press.

Garrity, T.F., Stallones, L., Marx, M.B. and Johnson, T.P. (1988) 'Pet ownership and attachment as supportive factors in the health of the elderly', *Anthrozoos*, 3 (1): 35–44.

Geertz, C. (1973) *The Interpretation of Cultures*, New York: Basic Books.

Gerrard, F. and Mallion, F.J. (1980) *The Complete Book of Meat*, 2nd edn, London: Virtue.

Giddens, A. (1990) *The Consequences of Modernity*, Cambridge: Polity.

Giddens, A. (1991) *Modernity and Self Identity*, Cambridge: Polity.

Gierach, J. (1986) *Trout Bum – Fly-Fishing as a Way of Life*, New York: Simon and Schuster.

Gierach, J. (1990) *Sex, Death and Fly-Fishing*, New York: Simon and Schuster.

Goodman, D. and Redclift, M. (1991) *Refashioning Nature – Food, Ecology and Nature*, London: Routledge.

Grigg, D. (1993) 'The role of livestock products in world food production', *Scottish Geographical Magazine*, 19 (2): 66–74.

Grigson, J. (1994) *Jane Grigson's Fish Book*, Harmondsworth: Penguin.

Gunasekera, K.D., Hapgood, A.I., Harvey, E.L., Hayfron Benjamin, T.R.M., Jachuck, M.S.J., Jackson, A., Kronfeld, N.P.A., Manikon, A.L., Mearns, C.J., Mushtaq, N. and Adshead, F. (1996) 'CJD and BSE: Members of the public make up their own minds about risk' [Letter], *British Medical Journal*, 312 (7037):1038.

Hannigan, J.A. (1995) *Environmental Sociology – A Social Constructionist Perspective*, London: Routledge.

Harris, M. (1965) 'The cultural ecology of India's sacred cattle', *Current Anthropology*, 7: 51–66.

Harris, M. (1990) *Our Kind*, New York: Harper Perennial.

Harvey, B. (1993) *Living and Dying in England 1100–1540 – the Monastic Experience*, Oxford: Clarendon Press.

Harvey, D. (1989) *The Condition of Postmodernity*, Oxford: Blackwell.

Headey, B. and Anderson, W. (1995) *Health Cost Savings: The Impact of Pets on the Australian Health Budget*, Melbourne: Petcare Information and Advisory Service.

Hills, A.M. (1993) 'The motivational bases of attitudes toward animals', *Society and Animals*, 1 (2):1–11.

Hummel, R. (1994) *Hunting and Fishing for Sport: Commerce, Controversy, Popular Culture*, Bowling Green, OH: Bowling Green State University Popular Press.

Hummel, R.L. and Foster, G.S. (1986) 'A sporting chance: relationships between technological change and concepts of fair play in fishing', *Journal of Leisure Research*, 18 (1): 40–52.

Huxley, J. (1970) *Memories*, London: George Allen & Unwin.

Ingold, T. (1988) *What Is An Animal?*, London: Unwin Hyman.

Ingold, T. (1994) 'From trust to dominion: an alternative history of human–animal relations', in A. Manning and J. Serpell (eds) *Animals and Human Society*, London: Routledge.

Itzkowitz, D.C. (1977) *Peculiar Privilige – A Social History of English Fox-hunting*, Hassock: Harvester.

Jackson, B. (1996) 'Editorial', *Guns and Game*, 9: 4.

James, P. (1996) *Nation Formation*, London: Sage.

Japan Statistical Association (1993) *Japan Statistical Yearbook*, Tokyo: Japan Statistical Association.

Johnson, A. (1991) *Factory Farming*, Oxford: Blackwell.

Jones and Jones (1985) *Kansas City Master Plan*, Seattle: Jones and Jones.

Jordan, T. (1993) *North American Cattle Ranching Frontiers*, Albuquerque, NM: University of New Mexico Press.

Katcher, A.H. and Beck, A.M. (eds) (1983) *New Perspectives in Our Lives with Companion Animals*, Philadelphia: University of Pennsylvania Press.

Katzen, M. (ed.) (1977) *Moosewood Cookbook*, Berkeley, CA: Ten Speed Press.

Kellert, S.R. (1994) 'Attitudes, knowledge and behaviour toward wildlife among the industrial superpowers', in A. Manning and J. Serpell (eds) *Animals and Human Society*, London: Routledge.

Kellert, S.R. and Wilson, E.O. (eds) (1993) *The Biophilia Hypothesis*, Washington, DC: Island Press

Lash, S. and Urry, J. (1987) *The End of Organised Capitalism*, Cambridge: Polity.

Lash, S. and Urry, J. (1994) *Economies of Signs and Space*, London: Sage.

Lawrence, E.A. (1994) 'Conflicting ideologies: views of animal rights advocates and their opponents', *Society and Animals*, 2 (2): 1–5.

Leach, E. (1964) 'Anthropological aspects of language: animal categories and verbal abuse', in E.H. Lenneberg (ed.) *New Directions in the Study of Language*, Cambridge, MA: MIT Press.

Leach, E. (1974) *Lévi-Strauss*, London: Fontana/Collins.

Le Heron, R. and Roche, M. (1995) 'A "fresh" place in food's space', *Area*, 27 (1): 23–33.

Leopold, A. (1949) *A Sand County Almanac*, New York: Oxford University Press.

Lévi-Strauss, C. (1962) *Totemism*, London: Merlin Press.

Lévi-Strauss, C. (1964) *Mythologiques: Le Cru et le Cuit*, Paris: Plon.
Lévi-Strauss, C. (1966) *The Savage Mind*, London: Weidenfeld and Nicolson.
Levinson, B.M. (1969) *Pet-Oriented Psychotherapy*, Springfield, IL: Charles C. Thomas.
Levinson, B.M. (1980) 'The child and his pet: a world of nonverbal communication', in S.A. Corson and E. O'Leary Corson (eds) *Ethology and Nonverbal Communication in Mental Health*, Oxford: Pergamon Press.
Lienhardt, G. (1961) *Divinity and Experience*, Oxford: Oxford University Press.
Lowerson, J.R. (1980) 'Battles for the countryside', in F. Gloversmith (ed.) *Class, Culture and Social Change – A New View of the 1930s*, Brighton: Harvester.
Lowerson, J.R. (1988) 'Brothers of the angle: coarse fishing and English working-class culture, 1850–1914', in J.A. Mangan (ed.) *Pleasure, Profit and Proselytism*, London: Cass.
Lupton, D. (1996a) 'Sugar and snails: the gendering of food and food preferences', in J. Germov and L. Williams (eds) *The Sociology of Food and Nutrition: Australian Perspectives*, Newcastle, NSW: Laurijon.
Lupton, D. (1996b) *Food, the Body and the Self*, London: Sage.
Lyons, N. (1977) *Bright Rivers*, Philadelphia: Lippincott.
McDougall, J. (1997) 'Out for a duck in '97', *Guns and Game*, 13: 14–17.
McFarling, C.J. (1995) 'Tasmanians and nature tourism: an analysis of variations in taste for nature based tourism', Honours thesis, Department of Sociology, University of Tasmania.
✱ Mack, A. (ed) (1995) 'In the company of animals', *Social Research*, 62 (3).
MacKenzie, J.M. (1988) *The Empire of Nature*, Manchester: Manchester University Press.
Maclean, N. (1976) *A River Runs Through It*, Chicago: University of Chicago Press.
Macnaghten, P. and Urry, J. (1995) 'Towards a sociology of nature', *Sociology*, 29 (2): 124–37.
McNamee, B. (1966) 'Trends in meat consumption', in T.C. Barker, J.C. McKenzie and J. Yudkin (eds) *Our Changing Fare*, London: Macgibbon and Kee.
Maffesoli, M. (1996) *The Time of the Tribes: The Decline of Individualism in Mass Society*, London: Sage.
Manning, A. and Serpell, J. (1994) *Animals and Human Society – Changing Perspectives*, London: Routledge.
Marshall, G., Rose, D.,Vogler, C. and Newby, H. (1985) 'Class, citizenship and distributional conflict in modern Britain', *British Journal of Sociology*, 36 (2): 259–84.
Marshall, G., Vogler, C., Rose, D. and Newby, H. (1987) 'Distributional struggle and moral order in a market society', *Sociology*, 21 (1): 55–73.
Marx, M.B., Stallones, L. and Garrity, T.F. (1988) 'Demographics of pet ownership among U.S. elderly', *Anthrozoos*, 1 (1): 36–41.
Marx, M.B., Stallones, L., Garrity, T.F. and Johnson, T.P. (1988) 'Demographics of pet ownership among U.S. adults 21 to 64 years of age', *Anthrozoos*, 2 (1): 33–37.
Masters, B. (1988) *The Passion of John Aspinall*, London: Jonathon Cape.
Mayrhofer, D. (1991) 'Fututech to revolutionise meat industry', *Food Australia*, 43 (2): 44–5.
Mennell, S. (1992) *Norbert Elias: An Introduction*, Oxford: Blackwell.
Mennell, S. (1993) *All Manners of Food*, Oxford: Blackwell.
Mennell, S., Murcott, A. and van Otterloo, A.H. (1992) 'The sociology of food: eating, diet and culture', *Current Sociology*, 40 (2).
Mertens, C. (1991) 'Human–cat interactions in the home setting', *Anthrozoos*, 4 (4): 214–31.
Midgely, M. (1979) *Beast and Man*, Ithaca, NY: Cornell University Press.
Midgely, M. (1994) 'Bridge-building at last', in A. Manning and J. Serpell (eds) *Animals and Human Society*, London: Routledge.
Ministry of Agriculture, Fisheries and Food (1992) *Household Food Consumption and*

Expenditure, Annual Reports of The National Food Survey Committee, London: HMSO.

Ministry of Agriculture, Fisheries and Food (1996) *BSE, A Chronology of Events*, MAFF website.

Mitchell, B.R. (1995) *International Historical Statistics*, New York: Stockton Press.

Moneymaker, J.M. and Strimpel, E.O. (1991) 'Animals and inmates: a sharing companionship behind bars', *Journal of Offender Rehabilitation*, 16 (3–4): 133–52.

Morris, H. (ed.) (1991) *Uncommon Waters – Women Write About Fishing*, Seattle: Seal Press.

Morris, D. and Morris, R. (1968) *Men and Apes*, London: Sphere.

Mullan, B. and Marvin, G. (1987) *Zoo Culture*, London: Weidenfeld and Nicolson.

Murphy, R. (1995) 'Sociology as if nature did not matter: an ecological critique', *British Journal of Sociology*, 46 (4): 688–707.

Nash, R. (1967) *Wilderness and the American Mind*, New Haven and London: Yale University Press.

National Rivers Authority (1994) *National Angling Survey 1994*, London: HMSO.

Newby, H., Vogler, C., Rose, D. and Marshall, G. (1985) 'Class, citizenship and distributional conflict in modern Britain', *British Journal of Sociology*, 36 (2): 259–84.

Newby, J. (1997) *The Pact for Survival*, Sydney: ABC Books.

Newsinger, J. (1996) 'The roast beef of Old England', *Monthly Review*, 48 (4): 21–25.

Nielson, J.A. and Delude, L.A. (1994) 'Pets as adjunct therapists in a residence for former psychiatric patients', *Anthrozoos*, 7 (3): 166–71.

Norwood, V. (1993) *Made From this Earth – American Women and Nature*, Chapel Hill and London: University of North Carolina Press.

O'Brien, M. (1996) 'Fishing – is it an endangered sport?', *Mid-Atlantic FlyFishing Guide*, September: 25–8.

Ovid (1986) *Metamorphoses*, Oxford: Oxford University Press.

Paxman, J. (1995) *Fish, Fishing and the Meaning of Life*, Harmondsworth: Penguin.

Pearce, C. (1991) *Twentieth Century Design Classics*, London: H.C. Blossum.

Pelto, G (1976) *The Human Adventure: An Introduction to Anthropology*, New York: Prentice-Hall.

People for the Ethical Treatment of Animals (1997a) 'PETA's mission', PETA website

People for the Ethical Treatment of Animals (1997b) 'PETA history: compassion in action', PETA website

Perl, L. (1980) *Junk Food, Fast Food, Health Food – What America Eats and Why*, New York: Clarion Books.

Perren, R. (1978) *The Meat Trade in Britain 1840–1914*, London: Routledge and Kegan Paul.

Petcare Information and Advisory Service (1977) *Pets as a Social Phenomenon*, Melbourne: Petcare Information and Advisory Service.

Philo, C. (1995) 'Animals, geography, and the city: notes on inclusions and exclusions', *Environment and Planning D: Society and Space*, 13 (6): 655–81.

Pifer, L., Shimizu, K. and Pifer, R. (1994) 'Public attitudes towards animal research: some international comparisons', *Society and Animals*, 2 (2): 95–113.

Plutarch (1957) *Moralia*, vol. 12, London: Heinemann.

Podberscek, A.L. (1994) 'Dog on a tightrope: the position of the dog in British society as influenced by reports on dog attacks (1988 to 1992)', *Anthrozoos*, 7 (4): 232–41.

Raines, H. (1993) *Fly Fishing Through the Midlife Crisis*, New York: Anchor Books.

Ray, A.G. (1995) 'Calling the dog: the sources of AKC [American Kennel Club] breed names', *Names*, 43 (1): 3–28.

Regan T. (1983) *The Case for Animal Rights*, Berkeley and Los Angeles: University of California Press.

Regan, T. and Singer, P. (1976) *Animal Rights and Human Obligations*, Englewood Cliffs, NJ: Prentice-Hall.

Richardson, N.J., MacFie, H.J.H. and Shepherd, R. (1994) 'Consumer attitudes to meat eating', *Meat Science*, 36 (1): 57–65.

Rifkin, J. (1992) *Beyond Beef: the Rise and Fall of the Cattle Culture*, New York: Dutton.

Ritson, J. (1802) *An Essay on Abstinence from Animal Food, as a Moral Duty*, London: Richard Phillips.

Ritvo, H. (1987) *The Animal Estate: The English and Other Creatures in the Victorian Age*, Cambridge, MA: Harvard University Press.

Ritvo, H. (1994) 'Animals in nineteenth-century Britain', in A. Manning and J. Serpell (eds) *Animals and Human Society*, London: Routledge.

Ritzer, G. (1983) 'The "McDonaldization" of society', *Journal of American Culture*, 6 (1): 100–7.

Ritzer, G. (1993) *The McDonaldization of Society*, Thousand Oaks, CA: Pine Forge Press.

Rival, L. (1993) 'The growth of family trees: understanding Huaorani perceptions of the forest', *Man*, 28 (4): 635–52.

Rival, L. (1996) 'Blowpipes and spears – the social significance of Huaorani technological choices', in P. Descola and G. Palsson (eds) *Nature and Society*, London: Routledge. pp. 145–64.

Robb, S.S. (1983) 'Health status correlates of pet–human association in a health-impaired population', in A. H. Katcher and A.M. Beck (eds) *New Perspectives in Our Lives with Companion Animals*, Philadelphia: University of Pennsylvania Press.

Rocco, F. (1996) 'A growing menace', *Electronic Telegraph*, 570, 14 December.

Rojek, C. (1993) *Ways of Escape*, London: Macmillan.

Rojek, C. (1995) *Decentring Leisure*, London: Sage.

Ross, Jonathon (1995) 'Rich, Fat and Stupid'. TV documentary for Channel 4.

Russell, J. (1941) *Britain's Food in Wartime*, Oxford, Oxford University Press.

Sahlins, M. (1974) *Stone Age Economics*, London: Tavistock Publications.

Salmon, P.W. and Salmon, I. M. (1983) 'Who owns who? Psychological research into the human pet bond in Australia', in A. H. Katcher and A.M. Beck (eds) *New Perspectives in Our Lives with Companion Animals*, Philadelphia: University of Pennsylvania Press.

Salt, H.S. (1892) *Animal Rights Considered in Relation to Social Progress*, London: George Bell and Son.

Sartre, J. P. (1967) *Words*, London: Hamilton.

Saunders, P. (1984) 'Beyond housing classes: the sociological significance of private property rights and means of consumption', *International Journal of Urban and Regional Research*, 8 (2): 202–27.

Savage, M., Barlow, J., Dickens, P. and Fielding, T. (1992) *Property, Bureaucracy and Culture*, London: Routledge.

Senate Select Committee on Animal Welfare (1990) 'Report by the Senate Select Committee on animal welfare', Washington, DC.

Serpell, J. (1986) *In the Company of Animals*, Oxford: Blackwell.

Serpell, J. (1994) 'Attitudes, knowledge and behaviour towards wildlife among the industrial superpowers: the United States, Japan and Germany', in A. Manning and J. Serpell (eds) *Animals and Human Society*, London: Routledge.

Serpell, J. (ed.) (1995) *The Domestic Dog: Its Evolution Behaviour and Interactions with People*, Cambridge: Cambridge University Press.

Serpell, J. and Paul, E. (1994) 'Pets and positive attitudes to animals', in A. Manning and J. Serpell (eds) *Animals and Human Society – Changing Perspectives*, London: Routledge.

Shelley, P.B. (1954) *Shelley's Prose*, D.L. Clark (ed.), Albequerque, NM: University of New Mexico Press.

Shoard, M. (1987) *This Land Is Our Land*, London: Paladin.

Siegel, J.M. (1990) 'Stressful life events and use of physician services among the elderly: the moderating role of pet ownership', *Journal of Personality and Social Psychology*, 58: 1081–6.

Siegel, J. M. (1993) 'Companion animals: in sickness and in health', *Journal of Social Issues*, 49 (1): 157–67.

Simonds, C. (1995) 'Wildlife conservation', *Sporting Shooter*, November: 24–5.

Simmons, I.G. (1993) *Environmental History*, Oxford: Blackwell.

Singer, P. (1980) 'Preface' to H.S. Salt's *Animal Rights Considered in Relation to Social Progress*, Clark Summit, PA: Society for Animal Rights.

Singer, P. (1990 [1970]) *Animal Liberation*, New York: New York Review Books.

Smart, B. (1994) 'Digesting the modern diet – gastro-porn, fast food, and panic eating', in K. Tester (ed.) *The Flaneur*, London: Routledge.

Soares, C.J. (1985) 'The companion animal in the context of the family system', *Marriage and Family Review*, 8 (1): 49–62.

Soper, K. (1995) *What is Nature? Culture, Politics and the Non-Human*, Oxford: Blackwell.

Spencer, C. (1980) *Gourmet Cooking for Vegetarians*, London: Robin Clark.

Sperling, S. (1988) *Animal Liberators: Research and Morality*, Berkeley: University of California Press.

Stratton, J. (1986) 'Australia – this sporting life', in G. Lawrence and D. Rowe (eds) *Power Play: Essays in the Sociology of Australian Sport*, Sydney: Hale and Iremonger. pp 85–114.

Tester, K. (1989) 'The pleasure of the rich is the labour of the poor: some comments on Norbert Elias's "An Essay on Sport and Violence"', *Journal of Historical Sociology*, 2 (2): 161–72.

Tester, K. (1992) *Animals and Society: The Humanity of Animal Rights*, London: Routledge.

Texas Cattle Feeders Association (1996) *Cattle Feeders Annual* (http://www.worldmeat.com.au/world/consump.html).

Thomas, K. (1983) *Man and the Natural World: Changing Attitudes in England 1500–1800*, London: Allen Lane.

Thomas, R.H. (1983) *The Politics of Hunting*, Aldershot: Gower.

Thoreau, H.D. (1981) *Walden and Other Writings*, New York: Bantam.

Thorogood, M., Mann, J., Appleby, P. and Mcpherson, K. (1994) 'Risk of death from cancer and iscaemic heart disease in meat and non-meat eaters', *British Medical Journal*, 308 (4): 1667–70.

Traver, R. (1960) *Trout Magic*, New York: St. Martin's Press.

Tuckwell, C. (1993) 'Farming of emus and processing of emu meat', *Food Australia*, 45 (12): 574.

Twigg, J. (1983) 'Vegetarianism and the meanings of meat', in A. Murcott (ed.) *The Sociology of Food and Eating*, Aldershot: Gower. pp. 18–30.

United States of America (1967) *The World Food Problem – A Report of the President's Science Advisory Committee, Vol. II*, Washington, DC: US Government Printing Office.

Urry, J. (1990) *The Tourist Gaze*, London: Sage.

Urry, J. (1996) *Consumption, Place and Identity*, London: Sage.

US Agricultural Trade Office (1993) *Japan Market Brief: Pet Food*, Tokyo: US Agricultural Trade Office.

Verderber, S. (1991) 'Elderly persons' appraisal of animals in the residential environment', *Anthrozoos*, 4 (3): 164–73.

Vialles, N. (1994) *Animal to Edible*, Cambridge: Cambridge University Press.

Vidal, J. (1997) *McLibel – Burger Culture on Trial*, London: Pan Books.

Voith, V.L. (1985) 'Attachment of people to companion animals', *The Veterinary Clinics of North America (Small Animal Practice)*, 15 (2): 289–96.

Walsh, J.P. (1989) 'Technological change and division of labour – the case of retail meat-cutters', *Work and Occupations*, 16 (2): 165–83.

Walsh, P.G. and Mertin, P.G. (1994) 'The training of pets as therapy dogs in a women's prison – a pilot study', *Anthrozoos*, 7 (2): 124–8.

Walton, I. (1971, 1653) *The Compleat Angler*, London: Hamlyn.

Warden, J (1996) 'Call for inquiry into CJD cluster', *British Medical Journal*, 315 (7104): 1.

Warden, J. (1997) 'UK government bans sale of beef on the bone', *British Medical Journal*, 315 (7112): 1.

Washington State (1996) *Washington State Voters Pamphlet – Edition 17*, Seattle: Washington State Government.

Wheelock, J. (1990) 'Consumer attitudes towards processed foods', in J. Somogyi and E. Koskinen (eds) *Nutritional Adaptations to New Life-Styles*, Basel: Kruger. pp 125–32.

Will, R.G., Ironside J. W., Zeidler, M., Cousens, S.N., Estibeiro, K. and Alperovitch, A. (1996) 'A new variant of Creutzfeldt-Jakob disease in the UK', *Lancet*, 347: 921–5.

Willis, R. (1974) *Man and Beast*, London: Hart-Davis, MacGibbon.

Willis, R. (ed.) (1990) *Signifying Animals*, London: Routledge.

Wilson, C. A. (1976) *Food and Drink in Britain, from the Stone Age to Recent Times*, Harmondsworth: Penguin.

Wilson, E.O. (1993) 'Biophilia and the conservation ethic', in S.R. Kellert and E.O. Wilson (eds) *The Biophilia Hypothesis*, Washington, DC: Island Press.

Wise, J. (1996) 'Scientists find low level transmission of BSE', *British Medical Journal*, 313 (7053): 317.

Wise, J. (1997) 'Agents of new variant CJD and BSE are identical', *British Medical Journal*, 315 (7112).

Woodbury, R. (1996) 'Hunting's bad sports', *Time Magazine*, 148 (20): 1–2.

INDEX